Mining and Materiality

Neolithic Chalk Artefacts and their Depositional Contexts in Southern Britain

Anne M. Teather

Archaeopress Archaeology

Archaeopress Publishing Ltd
Gordon House
276 Banbury Road
Oxford OX2 7ED

www.archaeopress.com

ISBN 978 1 78491 265 9
ISBN 978 1 78491 266 6 (e-Pdf)

© Archaeopress and A M Teather 2016

All rights reserved. No part of this book may be reproduced, or transmitted, in any form or by any means, electronic, mechanical, photocopying or otherwise, without the prior written permission of the copyright owners.

Printed and bound in Great Britain by
Marston Book Services Ltd, Oxfordshire

This book is available direct from Archaeopress or from our website www.archaeopress.com

Contents

List of Figures	iii
Foreword	v
Acknowledgements	vii

Chapter 1: Mining and Materiality — 1
  1.1 Introduction — 1
  1.2 Aims of this Study — 2
  1.3 Outline of the Argument — 2
  1.4 Flint Mines and Materiality — 2

Chapter 2: Situating Flint Mines in Neolithic Studies — 3
  2.1 Introduction — 3
  2.2 Mining on Different Geology — 4
  2.3 Tracing Functional Interpretations — 5
  2.4 Axes: Product and Purpose? — 7
  2.5 An Overview of Sites Studied — 11
  2.6 The Context and Location of Mines — 15
  2.7 Chronology — 18
  2.8 Deposition and Art at Flint Mines — 20
  2.9 Conclusion — 23

Chapter 3: Addressing Functionality with Materiality and Phenomenology — 25
  3.1 Introduction — 25
  3.2 A History of Artefact Studies — 25
  3.3 Defining Archaeological Artefacts and their Ambiguity — 28
  3.4 Theoretical Basis of this Study: Integrating Materiality and Personhood — 30
  3.5 Applying Structured Deposition — 34
  3.6 Methodology — 36
  3.7 Conclusion — 39

Chapter 4: Non-Portable Chalk: Art and Artefacts — 41
  4.1 Introduction — 41
  4.2 Chalk Art as Functional and Non-Functional Evidence — 41
  4.3 Considering Chalk Art and Deposits as Artefacts — 42
  4.4 Chalk Art in the Flint Mines — 43
  4.5 Comparisons with Contemporary Monuments — 54
  4.6 Understanding Chalk Art and Non-Portable Artefacts in the Neolithic — 57
  4.7 Conclusion — 63

Chapter 5: Portable Chalk Artefacts — 65
  5.1 Introduction — 65
  5.2 Emerging Understandings: A History of Portable Chalk Artefacts — 65
  5.3 Structuring Typology: Adding Categorisation — 66
  5.4. Chalk Artefact Typology and Categorisation — 67
  5.5 Including Portable Chalk Artefacts from Mines with Comparable Forms — 71
  5.6 Chalk Artefact Forms in Regional Context — 76
  5.7 Understanding Portable Chalk Artefacts — 79
  5.8 Conclusion — 81

Chapter 6: Natural Objects to Cultural Artefacts — 83
  6.1 Introduction — 83

6.2. Reconsidering Animal and Human Remains ... 84
6.3 Expanding Contexts: Creating Artefacts ... 84
6.4 Excavated Artefacts ... 85
6.5 Transformed Artefacts ... 90
6.6 Aesthetic Deposits: Two Examples ... 94
6.7 A Special Case: Human Genital Forms and Mutable Substances ... 96
6.8 Conclusion ... 98

Chapter 7: Beyond Extraction ... **101**
7.1 Introduction ... 101
7.2 This Study ... 101
7.3 Expanding Interpretations ... 102
7.4 Negotiating Presence ... 103

Bibliography ... **105**

Index ... **113**

List of Figures

Figure 2.1 Map of southern England showing the location of Neolithic flint mines	4
Figure 2.2 Recalibrated radiocarbon dates from Neolithic Langdale axe quarries	8
Figure 2.3 Plan of Easton Down	11
Figure 2.4 Plan of Long Down	11
Figure 2.5 Plan of Harrow Hill	11
Figure 2.6 Plan of Grimes Graves	12
Figure 2.7 Plan of Stoke Down	13
Figure 2.8 Plan of Martin's Clump	13
Figure 2.9 Plan of Cissbury	13
Figure 2.10 Plan of Blackpatch	14
Figure 2.11 Plan of Church Hill	14
Figure 2.12 Table of possible number of shafts or pits at each site	14
Figure 2.13 Table of approximate depth of shafts at each site	15
Figure 2.14 Recalibrated radiocarbon dates from Neolithic flint mines	19
Figure 2.15 Table of suggested chronological activity at mine sites	20
Figure 2.16 Table of proposed dating of Blackpatch 'barrows' including chalk artefacts present	23
Figure 4.1 No 2 Escarpment Shaft, Cissbury	44
Figure 4.2 Shaft 27, Cissbury	45
Figure 4.3 The Cissbury cave pit complex art	47
Figure 4.4 The Cissbury cave pit complex, architectural features	48
Figure 4.5 Harrow Hill Shaft 21/13 complex	50
Figure 4.6 Photograph of chalk block from Harrow Hill	52
Figure 4.7 Table of flint mine shafts with art	53
Figure 4.8 Photograph of The Trundle chalk ammonite	55
Figure 4.9 Photograph of The Trundle incised block	55
Figure 4.10 Table of art and decorated blocks within Neolithic monuments contemporary with the flint mines	57
Figure 4.11 Table of the types of decoration on deposited chalk blocks	57
Figure 4.12 Photograph of the Fyfield Down polissoir	62
Figure 4.13 Photographs of polissoirs at Lewes Museum	62
Figure 4.14 West Kennet long barrow	63
Figure 5.1 Table summarising Varndell's suggested typology for chalk objects	68
Figure 5.2 Table summarising the revised chalk typology	69
Figure 5.3 Table summarising Varndell's categories of chalk artefacts	70
Figure 5.4 Table of recategorised artefacts following Figure 5.2	70
Figure 5.5 Table summarising the numbers of chalk artefacts in the mines	71
Figure 5.6 Photograph of Blackpatch chalk axe	72
Figure 5.7 Photograph of Cissbury Shaft 27 burial charms	72
Figure 5.8 Photographs of chalk cylinders from Blackpatch	73
Figure 5.9 Photograph of Church Hill chalk disc	73
Figure 5.10 Photograph of The Lavant Drum	74
Figure 5.11 Photographs of Church Hill plaque surfaces	76
Figure 5.12 Photographs of Church Hill plaque sides where ochre slip can be seen	76
Figure 5.13 Table of mining sites with early-mid Neolithic chalk artefacts	77
Figure 5.14 Table of mining sites with mid-late Neolithic chalk artefacts	77
Figure 5.15 Table of chalk artefacts in contemporary early-mid Neolithic monuments	77
Figure 5.16 Table of chalk artefacts in contemporary early Neolithic long barrows	77
Figure 5.17 Table of chalk artefacts in contemporary late Neolithic to early Bronze Age monuments	78
Figure 5.18 Table illustrating a chronology of chalk artefacts in Neolithic Britain	78

Figure 5.19 Chart comparing chalk artefact types at different early Neolithic monuments	79
Figure 5.20 Chart comparing chalk artefact types between later Neolithic monuments	79
Figure 6.1 Photograph of flint nodule resembling a cat skull, Blackpatch	86
Figure 6.2 Photograph of Cissbury Shaft 27 flint/fossil phallus	87
Figure 6.3 Photograph of phallic grouping from Durrington Walls	87
Figure 6.4 Photograph of assorted fossils from Pull's excavations	88
Figure 6.5 Photograph of fossils from Pull's excavations	89
Figure 6.6 Table of the deposits of fossil, antler and animal bone from the flint mine shafts	96
Figure 6.7 Table of Neolithic and Bronze Age phalli	96

Foreword

This book was initially submitted as a doctoral thesis in archaeology at the University of Sheffield in 2008. The research reported here concerns the British Neolithic flint mines and their deposits. It is argued that the interpretation of flint mines has suffered through an overly-narrow emphasis on the mechanics of flint extraction and, in comparison to other contemporaneous sites, they have been seen as peripheral to the wider societal and monumental changes that occurred in the British Neolithic. This book is presented with little alteration and some trepidation. I have read the theses of many and found they often hold a charm in being both bold and naïve; I hope the reader finds this of mine. The only changes are the omission of some poor quality photographs; recalibration of some radiocarbon dates; some of the figures have been redrawn to improve their quality and a few sections of rather rambling text have been tightened, though I fear many remain. Needless to say while the text remains largely unchanged my understanding of some of the topics here have changed, for example I no longer agree with the version of the Mesolithic-Neolithic transition in Britain I present here.

A history of the study of mines and an overview of their general morphology is undertaken in Chapter 2. Much of this review is still current as there have been no new excavations in Britain. However analyses and descriptions of new European mine sites, with radiocarbon dates, have been published. The best sources for this material are three publications - Allard *et al.* (2008); Capote *et al.* (2011) and Edmonds and Davis (2011). Baczkowski (2014) has recently argued for a northern European origin of mining technology though the paucity of radiocarbon dates for the early Neolithic flint mines of southern Britain do not necessarily provide a viable platform for comparison. Furthermore, the 20 radiocarbon dates for seven of the flint mine sites now sit very uncomfortably next to projects that have comprehensively dated the causewayed enclosures and other early Neolithic sites in Britain (Whittle *et al.* 2011) and the re-dating at Grimes Graves (Healy *et al.* 2014). As this book goes to press I have applied for funding for more dates, and a project is about to commence led by Stephen Shennan which will result in more comprehensive radiocarbon dating of flint mines.

For Chapter 3, Conneller's (2011) theoretical work discussing materiality in the Mesolithic resonates with some of the discussions I made particularly on the deposition and use of fossils. Jones *et al.* (2015) have recently published results of their new analysis of the Folkton Drums and in passing referred to the Lavant Drum, incorrectly claiming that I misidentified a pottery sherd from the same deposit as Grooved Ware. During my primary research in 2005 I only examined the Drum itself and any information I had with regard to its context I learned orally from museum staff and the excavator. This is clarified and re-emphasised in Chapter 5 to prevent any future confusion. The original wording can be accessed in my thesis (Teather 2008: 207).

In the last seven years I have published part of Chapter 4 (Teather 2011) and completed analyses on the chalk artefacts found as a result of the Stonehenge Riverside Project excavations (2003-9) that are due for publication within the site monographs (Teather in press a, in press b, in press c). I also have publications in review that expand on elements of Chapters 3, 5 and 6. I completed new research in 2015 and found examples of incredible incised art from the 1870s excavations at Cissbury at the Ashmolean Museum, Oxford (Teather 2015). I think this perfectly illustrates how we can still learn a great deal about these monuments: the flint mines have much more to tell us.

Anne Teather
November 2015

Allard, P., Bostyn, F., Giligny, F. and Lech, J. (eds.) 2008. *Flint Mining in Prehistoric Europe: Interpreting the Archaeological Records: European Association of Archaeologists, 12th Annual Meeting, Cracow, Poland 19th–24th September 2006*. Oxford: Archaeopress (British Archaeological Reports International Series 1891).

Baczkowski, J. 2014. Learning by experience: the flint mines of southern England and their continental origins. *Oxford Journal of Archaeology* 33:2: 135-53.

Capote, M., Congsuegra, S., Diaz-Del-Rio, P. and Terrados, X. (ed.) 2011. *Proceedings of the UISPP Commission on Flint Mining in Pre- and Proto-historic Times (Madrid, 14–17 October 2009)*. Oxford: British Archaeological Reports International Series 2260.

Conneller, C. 2011. *An Archaeology of Materials: Substantial Transformation in Early Prehistoric Europe*. London: Routledge.

Edmonds, M. and Davis, R. V. (ed.) 2011. *Stone Axe Studies, Vol. 3*. Oxford: Oxbow.

Healy, F., Marshall, P., Bayliss, A., Cook, G., Bronk Ramsey, C., van der Plicht, J. and Dunbar, E. 2014. *Grime's Graves, Weeting-with-Broomhill, Norfolk. Radiocarbon Dating and Chronological Modelling Scientific Dating Report*. English Heritage Research Report Series, no. 27-2014.

Jones, A. M., Cochrane, A., Carter, C., Dawson, I., Diaz-Guardamino, M., Kotoula, E. and Minkin, L. 2015. Digital imaging and prehistoric imagery: a new analysis of the Folkton Drums. *Antiquity* 89: 1083-95.

Teather, A. M. 2008. *Mining and Materiality in the British Neolithic*. Unpublished PhD Thesis. Department of Archaeology, University of Sheffield.

Teather, A. M. 2011. Interpreting hidden chalk art in southern British Neolithic flint mines. *World Archaeology* 43:2: 230-51.

Teather, A. M. 2015. The first British Neolithic representational art? The chalk engravings at Cissbury flint mine. *Antiquity Project Gallery* http://www.antiquity.ac.uk/projgall/teather347

Teather, A. M. (in press a). The chalk artefacts. In Parker Pearson, M., Pollard, J., Richards, C., Thomas J. and Welham, K. *Stonehenge for the Ancestors. The Stonehenge Riverside Project Volume 1*.

Teather, A. M. (in press b). The chalk artefacts. In Parker Pearson, M., Pollard, J., Richards, C., Thomas J. and Welham, K. *Durrington Walls and Woodhenge: A Place for the Living. The Stonehenge Riverside Project Volume 2*.

Teather, A. M. (in press c). The later chalk and chalk pig from the palisade. In Parker Pearson, M., Pollard, J., Richards, C., Thomas J. and Welham, K. *After Stonehenge: Later Prehistory and the Historical Period in the Stonehenge Landscape. The Stonehenge Riverside Project Volume 3*.

Whittle, A. W. R., Healy, F. and Bayliss, A. 2011. *Gathering Time: Dating the Early Neolithic Enclosures of Southern Britain and Ireland*. Vols. 1 and 2. Oxford: Oxbow.

Acknowledgements

I was fortunate enough to have direction and information regarding flint mines, axes and chalk from Martyn Barber, Dave Field and Pete Topping, Miles Russell (Bournemouth University), Mark Edmonds (University of York), Gill Varndell (British Museum), Martin Green, Mike Pitts and Robin Holgate. The staff at the following institutions were very accommodating to my requests to view chalk artefacts, records and any 'odd objects': Salisbury Museum, Norfolk City Museum, The Novium, The Alexander Keiller Museum at Avebury, the British Museum, Worthing Museum and Art Gallery, and Lewes Museum many of whom also kindly gave permission for me to reproduce my photographs. Martin Green generously allowed me time at his private museum on Down Farm and provided both a lovely lunch and continued correspondence which has been very helpful. Staff at the British Geological Survey assisted in various ways, particularly in discerning details on the Durrington Walls fossil phallus and describing animal-gnawed chalk from humanly-altered chalk; my thanks for clarifying a difficult area and another nice lunch. The Arts and Humanities Research Board (now Arts and Humanities Research Council) sponsored this study and my MA. Due to family commitments I could not have done this without their support and as a consequence of my family commitments, I submitted far more forms and requests than usual.

Support from the Universities of Sheffield and Manchester was much appreciated and I would like to thank the staff and postgraduate students I had the pleasure to work alongside at both institutions. Umberto Albarella deserves specific thanks for suggesting I keep thinking about form - a clarification which helped me more in primary recording than I think he could have imagined. It is only recently I have fully understood how the two years I spent at the University of Southampton as an undergraduate gave me an appreciation for social anthropology which framed this study. The courses I took with Clive Gamble and Yvonne Marshall are particularly memorable even fifteen years later. Mike Parker Pearson, Julian Thomas, Ian Heath and Steve Matthews read parts or all of the text and provided encouragement and help, tempering some of my more outlandish interpretations. I am particularly grateful to Bob Johnston and Julian Thomas for their patience with me. Bob spent an enormous amount of his time both reading drafts and discussing theoretical and practical issues face to face, and this study is considerably improved as a result. Julian was generous following some extremely long and confusing queries of mine. I am grateful to my examiners Josh Pollard and Roger Doonan for their insightful comments at my viva. Thanks to Freddie August for his technical support in producing my original thesis. My dear friend Rebecca Pullen has wielded her magic with InDesign to wrestle this to publication with an expert eye. Any remaining errors or omissions are my responsibility.

As a single parent I had a veritable army of people, mostly women, who supported me through seemingly endless ad hoc childcare. There are too many to name and I know I thanked you in person numerous times. To my friends, who watched and wondered why I needed to do this but still supported me; you reminded me that some people don't mind how much I know about archaeology. There are also my friends in archaeology who don't mind how much I know about archaeology either: they have made this journey much more fun. The staff and students of the Stonehenge Riverside Project 2004-2007 in particular ensured I took at least two weeks of my holiday allowance not thinking about flint mines. Becca Pullen, Karen Godden, Catherine Parker, Meggen Gondek, Dave Shaw, Steve Matthews, Louise Revell, Freddie August, Julie Edwards, and Mike and Amy Teather all provided oases of calm away from the frenetic writing up stages in 2007/8 whether they realised it or not. Andrew Chamberlain and Becca Pullen have done the same service for this 2015 stint. My family cannot be thanked enough for their understanding and support in all sorts of ways. Sophie Scott, Molly Teather †, Christine Teather †, Carole and John Pangbourne and David Teather all provided practical support with my children while I excavated or conducted research. I'm not sure I'd recommend pursuing a PhD as a single parent, but it is achievable. Amongst all this madness two very patient children grew up and learnt about the world (including how to order take-out and mix screwdrivers). This book is for Jack and Ella.

Chapter 1

Mining and Materiality

1.1 Introduction

Stone tools were a necessary part of life in prehistoric communities before the advent of metals. During the Mesolithic in Britain the raw material to produce them – usually flint and chert – was either collected from the surface or, rarely, extracted by shallow quarrying. By the very earliest Neolithic there was a fundamental change in the technology of extracting flint, alongside the production of new types of tools – most notably polished axes and large arrowheads and blades. This was arguably part of broader programme of economic and social change from the hunting, fishing and gathering lifestyle of the Mesolithic and preceding millennia, to a focus on monumentality, new forms of material culture, domesticated animals and crop cultivation.

The new method of extracting flint involved digging deep shafts into bedrock to extract sub-surface flint nodules laid down in layers within the chalk. Galleries extended from the base of these shafts, in some cases up to 13 metres (m) from the surface, creating a subterranean network of tunnels. They are now visible on the surface as depressions alongside corresponding mounds of extraction spoil which often resemble later Bronze Age barrows in size and shape. The monumental character of these mine workings is interpreted as an indication of an organisational shift within early Neolithic communities involving the mobilisation of large numbers of people to focus their labours on particular places in the landscape, as in the construction of other monuments such as causewayed enclosures and long barrows.

The new forms of material culture contribute to our understanding of the Mesolithic-Neolithic transition in different ways. Pottery, both as a clay-based substance and finished vessel, brought new cultural practices and skills to Neolithic communities. In a similar way, chalk artefacts such as cups and phalli were a cultural reinvention of an existing substance: both clay and chalk are encountered as geological deposits. This creation of new artefact forms, and their use and deposition, are key evidence in proposing the move of Neolithic communities to adapt and alter their world to them, rather than finding different ways to adapt themselves to their environment (Whittle 1996, Thomas 1999a). This change is therefore argued as also having been prompted by an alteration in ideological and perhaps cosmological understandings which manifested in different practices.

Yet, despite these broader arguments, interpretively flint mines have often been seen as peripheral to this transition in both their monumental form and deposits. While they began to attract the attention of early Victorian archaeologists from the 1860s, their interpretation has almost always concentrated on their function as extraction sites. Changes in theoretical archaeology in the last twenty-five years encouraged interpretations which referenced ethnographic data, focussing on practices and symbolism at other Neolithic sites, particularly monuments, that was in turn applied to flint mines. For example, Miles Russell (2000: 146) discusses how the extraction of flint may have fitted within these wider Neolithic cultural beliefs:

> they were places of initiation and ceremony, places where one could descend into a subterranean world of darkness totally removed from the natural and familiar; places of ancestral significance, where one could tame the land; places from which deeply bedded flint could be won at a cost and prestige items could be manufactured.

Evocatively rendered, flint mines therefore became Neolithic monuments, viewed as separate spaces that produced different experiences to those usually encountered during a Neolithic person's life. Flint, as the product of mining, was perceived as a goal to win; the aim being to produce 'prestige items' implicated in relations of social dominance and control either through their ownership and display or through exchange. However, other deposits within flint mines remain unexamined. Is this peripheral view correct and how has it been constructed? We cannot assess if flint mines should be viewed as outside any Neolithic 'norm' without further consideration of their morphology and deposits; in effect they need to be assessed on a comparable basis to other Neolithic monuments before that judgement can be made. This book attempts to start this process.

1.2 Aims of this Study

The aims of this research are to:

- Critique prevailing interpretations of flint mines as economic and ritual resources in the Neolithic by examining how theories of 'otherness' have influenced the understandings of the mines.

- Formulate theoretical frameworks that overcome the function-ritual divide, particularly with reference to concepts of materiality, the inter-relatedness of substances and depositional practice.

- Use the theoretical framework to examine the architectural morphology and depositional histories of flint mines, with special reference to chalk artefacts and art.

- Draw conclusions as to how flint mines and their deposits contribute to understanding substances, artefacts and deposits within the existing cultural repertoire of the southern British Neolithic.

1.3 Outline of the Argument

The flint mines in Britain occur on chalk deposits where flint was laid down in seams within the chalk. They have been recognised as archaeological by a distinctive topography of circular depressions and mounds, and have been the subject of excavations for nearly a hundred and fifty years. The mines were built within existing social landscapes, and many sites were subject to later prehistoric activity rendering greater complexity to their surface morphology and depositional histories. Chapter 2 discusses these factors in more detail, giving an overview of flint mine locations and their history of excavation and interpretation.

The concept of materiality has been an important element in both the British Neolithic and wider archaeological discourses, its motivation being to tease interpretation from artefacts and architecture in a more integrated way. In this research I have approached materiality through phenomenology; a method that I think is both the most straightforward and, with the lack of historical records, almost singularly the most effective way of examining the evidence. Materiality is a human engagement, phenomenology a human embodied approach. A fuller discussion of materiality follows (Chapter 3), yet the premise is that artefacts and their context actively structure meaning. Hence, from the perspective of materiality, all aspects of the artefacts and their deposition, substance and indications of use wear, contribute to meaning, and any variations in this have an influence upon interpretation.

While many artefact categories are well studied in the Neolithic, chalk artefacts and art are not among them. Therefore, it has been necessary to interpretively review them as they form a considerable part of flint mine deposits (in terms of importance if not number). With regard to the artefacts themselves, it was felt that size and portability have a significant role in interpreting artefacts and what their likely socio-cultural roles had been in the past (Root 1983). Therefore, chalk artefacts are divided this way: non-portable chalk artefacts and art are examined in Chapter 4, and portable chalk artefacts in Chapter 5, where a new typology of portable chalk artefacts is offered. This has been achieved through an approach of materiality: that artefacts, their construction, substance and form are meaningful. Therefore chalk artefacts have been recognised and placed within a typology through phenomenological means. The analyses in Chapters 4 and 5 are situated within a regional context (where available) of similar artefacts from contemporary monuments.

It is also argued that new artefact categories come into being in the Neolithic, constructed from natural substances or materials such as faunal remains, fossils and iron pyrites and materiality is used to deconstruct functional interpretations. Phenomenological interpretations of materiality cannot focus on one artefact type as materiality is a relational activity, so all deposits are considered. Chapter 6 concentrates on those artefacts previously ignored as deposits in the mines, while also re-considering human and animal remains as artefacts. These arguments are summarised and the study concludes in Chapter 7.

1.4 Flint Mines and Materiality

The flint mines studied here occur across the chalklands of southern and eastern Britain and understanding their place within Neolithic Britain is of equal importance to considering any other monument of the period. Their archaeological deposits contribute to Neolithic interpretations in a similar way to that of contemporary momuments. The study of them and examination of chalk artefacts and art is a long overdue enterprise that begins here.

Chapter 2

Situating Flint Mines in Neolithic Studies

2.1 Introduction

This study attempts to challenge the view that Neolithic flint mines were different from other classes of monument in the British Neolithic through an analysis of their deposits (especially chalk art and artefacts) and a critique of functional and non-functional perceptions of material culture. This chapter provides a background to flint mining sites in Britain, their morphology, excavation history and previous interpretations in order to illustrate how these concepts of 'otherness' and functionality have been continually reinforced, in different ways, over decades of study.

It is only through appreciating the historical depth of these opinions that we can begin to challenge the theoretical assumptions which have underpinned and reinforced them - the subject of the following chapter. This chapter outlines the parameters of the study (2.2) before reviewing the history of flint mining and functional interpretations (2.3). The primary product of both Neolithic mining and quarrying extraction sites appears to have been axes and a consideration of functional interpretations of axes as artefacts contributing to this debate follows in 2.4. In 2.5 I review more recent research on mines which draws on quarrying as an extraction activity, and ethnographic parallels, to bring a review of flint mine interpretation up to date.

In 2.6 I begin a more archaeological review of the sites to be studied in this research, concentrating on issues such as site size, morphology and location, turning to chronology in 2.7, before examining the nature of deposition in mining contexts (2.8). During this I discuss how chronology and deposition need consideration before we can examine chalk artefacts, art and other deposits at the mines with a degree of chronological sensitivity. Simply recognising this material as artefactual has often caused problems. Some pieces of carved chalk were thought to either be the result of animal activity or weathering and therefore little or no accurate recording of their placement was taken during excavation (Worthing Museum Acc No 1961/1584). Antler picks and caches of knapped flint were often placed at the level of the galleries (Worthing Museum Acc No 1961/1585). At the Sussex mines, a fossil deposit occurred at Shaft 1 at Blackpatch (Chapter 6). Most of the animal bone appears to be disarticulated and degraded, indicating midden material though no middens have been interpreted by excavators to date. The purpose of this research is to give voice to all the Neolithic archaeological material recorded from these sites. The chapter concludes with a summary in 2.9.

The early history of flint mine discovery is filled with amusing tales of the experiences and personalities of late Victorian excavators and the topic has been ably covered in Russell's general book on the mines (2000). I would urge readers to indulge themselves by reading the early chapters of his book as due to limits of space this detail cannot be repeated here. Uncovering underground chambers and deposits are among the more astonishing and rare fieldwork encounters one usually experiences as an archaeologist. The suspected and often real dangers of the collapse of galleries while excavating, in addition to the 'other worldliness' of these sites, seems to have brought a sense of privilege to archaeologists who have been involved with them.

However, despite many excavations there is a lack of detailed twentieth century published excavation accounts of many sites, though it is appreciated that producing excavation reports of these complex sites must be challenging and time consuming. This complexity has also often resulted in a delay in their publication; for example with recent excavations at Harrow Hill conducted in 1982, it was fourteen years before the publication of the report (McNabb *et al.* 1996) and the majority of the 1970s excavations at Grimes Graves remained unpublished until the 1990s (Clutton-Brock 1984; Legge 1992; Longworth and Varndell 1996; Longworth *et al.* 1988, 1991). Furthermore a considerable number of the Sussex mine excavations were completed by John Pull, a local amateur who worked at weekends, and hence many excavations took months to complete. Regrettably, his publications are of an inconsistent standard with only one monograph on Blackpatch (Pull 1932) and notes being published in the local press during the early twentieth century. Pull's murder while working as a security guard in 1960 prevented him collating his life's work in archaeology. A publication by Russell (2001) has amassed much information for the academic audience but a considerable amount of detail is simply lacking from the original accounts (Worthing Museum AQ No 61/1684). The unpublished MA thesis completed by Elizabeth Pye in 1968, a student of Stuart Piggott, is the only primary data synthesis of Pull's work on the mines and is referred to by the later Royal

Commission of Historical Monuments of England/English Heritage survey published in 1999 (Barber *et al.* 1999) and Russell publications (2000; 2001). As Pye had access to the original manuscripts before they became mixed by decades of researchers and museum curators it is by some margin the most reliable cohesive source material.

The RCHME/EH survey of the 1990s (Barber *et al.* 1999) has allowed some of the more general details of the mines to be published and hence it is now possible to view flint mines as a cohesive Neolithic monument group. Russell's book (2000) provides a more accessible account for the general reader while clarifying some of the morphological similarities of the mines in greater detail than the RCHME/EH account. With the benefit of recent work, this study (the parameters of which are outlined below) should be seen as the next step in incorporating flint mines into current Neolithic dialogues.

2.2 Mining on Different Geology

Prehistoric flint mines occur across northern and eastern Europe, from Britain to France and Poland, and are restricted to flint bearing geology of which there are two types: primary and secondary deposits (Weisgerber 1987). This study concentrates on Neolithic flint mining sites on the geological primary chalk deposits in mainland Britain. In primary deposits such as the chalkland hills of the South Downs in southern Britain and the Anglo Paris chalk basin, the flint is laid down as horizontal seams within the chalk bedrock, in tabular or nodule form (*ibid.*). As a primary geological deposit, the English chalk is the result of sedimentation on the sea bed between 144 and 65 million years ago; however the actual creation of flint within it is still poorly understood (Barber *et al.* 1999: 23; Shepherd 1980: 34). Mining sites present on these primary deposits use vertical shafts and horizontal tunnels to follow and extract the flint layer or layers.

Despite much historical conjecture there are only ten certain Neolithic flint mine sites of this type in the UK (Barber *et al.* 1999). These are traditionally bounded into three geographical areas - Hampshire/Wiltshire, Sussex and Norfolk - with the sites contained within them as follows: in Hampshire and Wiltshire - Martin's Clump, Easton Down and Durrington; in Sussex – Long Down, Stoke Down, Cissbury, Blackpatch, Church Hill and Harrow Hill, and in Norfolk - Grimes Graves (Figure 2.1). These sites form the core of this study. Chalk bearing flint is also present in Dorset, and while no mines are certain, one Neolithic 'shaft' is present and will be discussed further in Chapter 4.

Many more sites could exist from this early period, and there are undoubtedly more sites to be identified in the future, but the lack of formal excavation and finds from secure contexts render these arguments unsubstantiated. For a fuller discussion of those sites not acknowledged please refer to Barber *et al.* (1999: 74-80). Confirmed Neolithic flint mine sites not included in this study are those on secondary deposits of flint occurring in Scotland and Ireland: Den of Boddam, Skelmuir Hill (both Scotland) and Ballygally Hill (Northern Ireland). In morphological terms, flint mining in glacial secondary deposits (such as Scotland and Grand Pressigny, France) is entirely different to that of primary deposit extraction, being more likely to exhibit quarrying or open cast mining due to the instability of the surrounding deposits (Saville 2005).

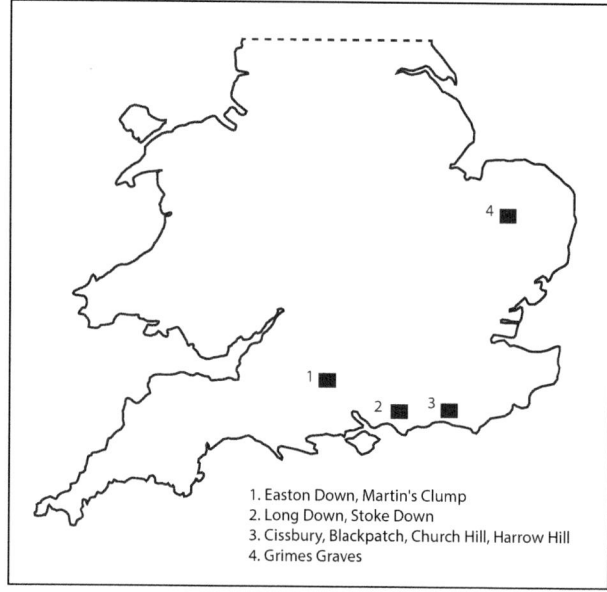

FIGURE 2.1 MAP OF SOUTHERN ENGLAND SHOWING THE LOCATION OF NEOLITHIC FLINT MINES

The two Scottish sites occur on the Buchan Ridge Gravel north of Aberdeen. They are distinct from the southern English mines in that the flint occurs in the gravel as cobbles. As the shafts are dug within glacial gravel deposits they appear to have been relatively unstable; the levels at which the flint occur varies and some pits were unfruitful (Saville 2005). Although these sites produce a large amount of struck flint at the surface, finished artefacts are rare. Saville conjectures that the size of the flint pebbles from the quarries (average *c.*10cm, maximum 25cm) confined the final products to arrowheads or smaller tools; no axe roughouts or pre-forms have been found (*ibid*: 4,7).

It was felt that inclusion of these sites within a study of the southern flint mines would prove unproductive for the following reasons. Firstly, the method of extraction and sub-surface geology is different, producing different extraction practices to that of the chalk bedrock of primary deposits. Additionally, noting recent work on regionality within Neolithic studies (Thomas 1999a; Whittle 2003), these sites are too far removed from the southern flint mines to allow for comparative and regional analyses. Furthermore, the inclusion of the Scottish sites at such a geographical distance from the main body of mines could only serve to confuse and detract from the analysis. Having discounted the Scottish sites on such grounds, it was felt prudent to exclude Ballygally Hill in Northern Ireland for similar reasons. Hence, the following section focuses on the history of flint mining, at primary geological flint sources occurring in southern Britain, their functional interpretations and concerns over the authenticity of some deposits.

2.3 Tracing Functional Interpretations

The two earliest Neolithic flint mines excavated in Britain were Grimes Graves and Cissbury. Excavations at these sites were taking place sequentially and almost simultaneously between the 1860s and early-mid 1870s. Flint mining was initially confirmed at Grimes Graves by Canon William Greenwell in 1870, much to the later consternation of Colonel Augustus Henry Lane Fox who had excavated at Cissbury during 1867/8 but his excavations were not of a great enough depth to uncover the shafts beneath the Iron Age hillfort. Following Greenwell's discoveries at Grimes Graves, in autumn 1873 Ernest Willett fully excavated a shaft Lane Fox had commenced, confirming that these were flint mines similar to Grimes Graves. He published the results of his work together with the account of Plumpton Tindall's (also referred to as Tindale) 1874 excavation in 1875, as Tindall had regrettably died before reporting his findings (Willett 1875). Understanding his error, Lane Fox returned to Cissbury for excavations between 1875 and 1877, working alongside Lord Rosehill, Willett and J. P. Harrison (also known as Park Harrison), when approximately thirteen shafts were excavated either in whole or part (Lane Fox 1876: 360; Harrison 1877a, 1877b, 1878; Rolleston 1877, 1879).

Due to their form, architecture and the historical perspective of industrialisation, flint mines were initially perceived as industrial sites, Cissbury being repeatedly referred to by Lane Fox as a 'flint implement factory' (e.g. Lane Fox 1876: 358). This perception created both a bias and simplicity in their interpretation and study - whereas other archaeological sites were seen as cultural centres, or cattle enclosures, the mines were conceived of solely as 'workplaces'. Furthermore, the bias and promotion of evolutionary perspectives for human behaviour (Darwin's *On the Origin of Species* being published in 1859), and cross-cultural generalisations evoked through encountering non-Western tribes, created a debate concerning the age of the flint mines. Lubbock's 1865 definition of a 'New Stone Age' or Neolithic was still a novelty clear in Lane Fox's first Cissbury report (*ibid.*). Concurrently, the discovery of European mines in the nineteenth century had stimulated a European debate by the 1860s and 1870s when many sites (such as Grimes Graves and Cissbury, Rijkholt, Grand Pressigny, Spiennes and Oburg) were first being described in publications (Smolla 1987).

These factors seem to have created a Europe-wide effort to claim the earliest flint mines in order to gain an advantage on this perceived cultural evolutionary progress scale. It led to a wider discussion concerning the antiquity of the UK mines and in particular if they were Neolithic or Palaeolithic in date, encapsulated in Reginald Smith's 1912 paper. This confusion resulted from the complexities of chipped flint at the sites: some items were finely worked, others very crude. It has now been shown that as at stone quarries such as the Langdales (Bradley and Edmonds 1993; Edmonds 1995), the variety in the flint or stone working can represent different strategies in the production process. However to the late Victorian excavators, it seemed initially as though the axe roughouts were crude Palaeolithic axes rather than an earlier stage of Neolithic axe manufacture.

After this initial flurry of activity at Cissbury, the site was not re-excavated until Pull's work in the 1950s yet other sites in the region were investigated. After approximately twenty years new activity began commencing with Major A. Wade's 1910-13 excavations at Stoke Down (Wade 1922). This was added to a decade later with Pull's excavations at Blackpatch between 1922-32 (Pull 1932) and E.C. Curwen and E. Curwen, Goodman and Lovell's at Harrow Hill in 1924-5, (Curwen and Curwen 1926). Pull and his contemporaries were members of the Worthing Archaeological Society (WAS) and despite their early collaboration on the Blackpatch excavations at Shaft 1, there were differences in opinion with regard to practice and interpretation resulting in separate accounts being published (Goodman *et al.* 1924; Pull 1932). As a consequence Pull rejected the WAS, a situation which was to last many years (Russell 2001: 251-56). Leading up to the commencement of the Second World War, Church Hill was excavated by Pull between 1932 and 1939 (Russell 2001), Harrow Hill was excavated by Holleyman in 1936 (1937) and Easton Down by Stone from 1930 to 1932 (1932a, 1932b, 1933a, 1933b, 1935).

Much of this work in Sussex was perhaps prompted by the intense activity at Grimes Graves, which after an interval of forty-four years was under almost constant excavation between 1914 and 1940. These excavations were well funded and accessible for the Prehistoric Society of East Anglia members (PSEA, which became the Prehistoric Society in 1935) and it was under their sponsorship this fieldwork was undertaken. The excavations took place successively under W.G. Clarke (1915), Dr A.E. Peake (1915, 1917, 1919), E. Lingwood, Rev. H. Kendall (1920), Derek Richardson (1920), Dr A. Favell, and A. Leslie Armstrong (1921, 1922, 1924a, 1924b, 1926, 1932, 1934).

In Sussex, two of these excavations; Major A. Wade's 1910-13 seasons at Stoke Down and J.F.S. Stone's Easton Down interwar work, produced more secure Neolithic dating evidence for both sites (Russell 2000: 22). This detail allowed a greater precision to the argument, and by the time J.G.D. Clark and Stuart Piggott published 'The Age of the British Flint Mines' in 1933, it was largely accepted that flint mines were Neolithic in date. Armstrong, the principal excavator at Grimes Graves, continued to argue for a Palaeolithic date (1932), although it was declining in favour to such a point he was almost a single voice (Barber *et al.* 1999: 10). Armstrong argued that there were two types of shafts at Grimes Graves: primitive pits which were shallower and earlier Palaeolithic mines, with the deeper mines being Neolithic. He was at this time, and had from the early 1920s, promoted items of Palaeolithic-looking art from the mines (mostly flint engravings, discussed below) as proof of this early date, although it was met at the time with some scepticism and recently there is new evidence to suggest it was a hoax (see also Russell 2001: 38-40). Grimes Graves was not the only site to suffer with such focus, as at Cissbury a series of animal depictions were also treated with suspicion (*ibid.*: 47).

The later excavations conducted by Armstrong remain unpublished almost certainly due to the cloud of suspicion hanging over the final days of excavations in 'Pit 15' of Grimes Graves in 1939. Armstrong was responsible for arguably the most famous questionable find of Neolithic archaeology, the Palaeolithic-reminiscent carved chalk 'Goddess' from this shaft. This part of the excavation was not well documented at the time and questions were being asked immediately the Goddess was uncovered. Recent literature still suggests that this was planted as a ruse to query the dating of mines in general, although any reason to do so by either Armstrong himself or his supporters for this action would seem motiveless as Armstrong was arguing Pit 15 was a Neolithic and not Palaeolithic shaft (Hutton 1997; Russell 2000; Varndell 1991). The 'Goddess' was found within a group of seven deposited artefacts, comprising a three flint phallic arrangement of two spherical shaped pieces of flint with one long slender one, a cumbersome carved chalk phallus, an arrangement of seven antler picks and a platform of mined flint. That these all occur at the base of the shaft is consistent with other types of deposition, and it is difficult for it to be suggested all these elements were faked, though parts of it may have been planted with the archaeology as a joke.

However, the history of British flint mines is pitted with discussions of the disputed nature of some of the evidence. Some artefacts have been so entrenched with suspicion (with some justification), that the issue of what can be accepted 'normal' and what needs to be ignored or treated tentatively requires some attention. For example, the flint engravings found by Armstrong and Peake have been subject to further analysis by Varndell (2005). As discussed in Armstrong's paper (1922) many flint engravings were discovered by him and in contrast to the linear scratches present on those found by Peake, Armstrong's are representative of animals and concluded to be fabricated by Varndell. The lack of widespread acceptance of many unusual forms in chalk, or flint and engravings in the mines (or in the Neolithic as a whole) could originate from the notoriety gained through Armstrong's activities at Grimes Graves. However, Armstrong's bias is easily read, as his desire was for artefacts which resemble those recovered at Palaeolithic sites on the continent. Hence we can dismiss his faunal representations and the crude 'Goddess' and phallus from Pit 15 without rancour.

Chalk art (often referred to in reports as 'graffiti' or 'graffito') has been found in many mine contexts, either as non-portable artefacts or in situ art, and appears to be contemporary with mining activity. Of the approximately thirteen shafts excavated at Cissbury between 1875-78, either whole or in part, three shafts exhibited art and marked chalk blocks: the No 2 Escarpment Shaft, 'Cave Pit' (or Shaft I) and Shaft VI (Harrison 1877a; 1877b). Pull's return to Cissbury found additional art in Shaft 27 and its associated galleries (Russell 2001: 112, 170). Moreover, art was noted at Grimes Graves (Clarke 1915), with marks and decorated blocks also being found at Harrow Hill (Curwen and Curwen 1926; McNabb *et al.* 1996) and Church Hill (Russell 2001).

After the war, Pull's excavations continued at Cissbury between 1952 and 1956 (Russell 2001), Salisbury (1961) at Long Down between 1955 and 1958; A. St J. Booth and Marcus Stone excavated at Durrington in 1952 (1952) and B. and J. Watson excavated at Martin's Clump for J.F.S. Stone between 1954 and 1955 (Ride and James 1989). During the 1970s both Roger Mercer and Gale Sieveking (with the British Museum and Dutch Geological Society) excavated sequentially at Grimes Graves (Mercer 1981a, 1981b; Sieveking *et al.* 1973; Sieveking 1979; Saville 1981; Clutton-Brock 1984; Legge 1992; Longworth and Varndell 1996; Longworth *et al.* 1988, 1991). P.J. Felder excavated at Harrow Hill in 1982 (McNabb *et al.* 1996) and Robin Holgate was involved in an amount of excavation and survey work between 1984 and 1986 at Long Down, Church Hill and Stoke Down (1995a, 1995b, 1995c). David Ride excavated with the Porton Down Conservation Group in 1984 at Martin's Clump in response to activity including the placement of a new underground electrical cable (Ride 1998, Ride 2006). Martin's Clump and Easton Down are on Military of Defence land and therefore access to them has been restricted for most of the twentieth century.

The majority of excavation and study on flint mines occurred between the 1860s and 1950s, yet without doubt the later publications provide much more detailed excavation accounts. It is unfortunate that more information was not forthcoming from the 1980s Harrow Hill excavation although rumours suggest the possibility the excavators may have been simply unprepared for the complexity and volume of data the site produced. By the 1970s excavations at Grimes Graves ideas of craft specialisation and mining as a Neolithic industry were being proposed. Mercer's calculations on the human effort required for extraction (15-16 men over 2-3 months), the size of cultivation of cereal required to fuel the effort (one hectare) and the estimate of axes from a single shaft (between 1.12 and 2 tons of axes from 8 tons of flint) are impressive (1981a: 112-3). Yet the picture they draw of Neolithic mining is almost entirely devoid of human behaviour apart from people as work units. This is somewhat acknowledged by Mercer, who comments when discussing the presence of Grooved Ware rather laments; 'little has emerged of a cultural unit (in a Childean sense)' (*ibid.*: 113). This dissatisfaction in not finding evidence of other 'household' activities led to his conclusion that 'the overwhelming impression gained from the site is one implying the work of a highly institutionalised and "professional" mining community' (*ibid.*: 112).

The British Museum excavations of 1972-76 resulted in five fascicules of which the fifth contains the most interpretation (Longworth & Varndell 1996: 79-89). In many respects this is similar in tone to Mercer's work, concentrating on factual data concerning the amount of flint extracted and the labour required. The lack of settlement evidence at mining sites in general had led to the understanding that such activities of daily life did not take place in the immediate vicinity of mine sites. Regional tribal groups initially proposed by Drewett (1978) were evoked, supporting ideas of these tribes being socially categorised as 'miners', in opposition to other categories of person ('farmer' etc) and through this, indicating an industrial approach and a segmented, fairly sedentary society.

The classification of flint mines as industrial led to the focus of academic study on the one artefact consistently interpreted as being produced in mining contexts – axes, although Healy (1998: 230-1) has recently argued that discoidal knives may have been a product of the mines at Grimes Graves in the later Neolithic period. Through the above view of regional groups, interpreting flint mine sites and axes as purely functional began to merge together. As the mines clearly produced tonnes of flint, their purpose was for this flint to be worked into axes. It has long been noted that the quality of flint from mines may be slightly better than surface deposits but not so much as to impact on manufacturing technique. Gardiner (1990: 119) suggests that the size of nodule required to make a flint axe and the quality of it would be critical for axe manufacture: only large good-quality flints would be effective for the production of a sizeable tool. The evidence from 'working floors' at mines sites suggested that although the flint was worked into a basic axe shape, or roughout, at the mine sites there is little evidence of knapped debris from finishing the axes, or polissoirs, which would indicate grinding and polishing. Hence, mining was viewed as simply an extractive process for the purpose of obtaining raw material for axe production, the later finishing taking place elsewhere (Mercer 1981a: 113).

The last large excavation to be conducted at Harrow Hill refrains from any lengthy conclusions but suggests that 'axe production should be seen more as a manufacturing continuum than as a structured activity with distinctly perceived sub-divisions' (McNabb *et al.* 1996: 37). It is even suggested that perhaps even primary flakework was not taking place around the shaft and could have been taking place elsewhere.

Summary

This account of excavation and interpretive history brings to a close the direct influence of academic study and fieldwork on the interpretation of mines. Several problems have been highlighted. Not only have flint mines been perceived as functional sites, but suspicion has been levied at some artefacts recovered from them. The majority of excavation has taken place directly within shafts or the immediate area and little work has been expended in locating indications of activity outside the immediate mining area (with the exception of Stone's work at Easton Down and Pull's at Blackpatch). Yet the study of flint and stone axes, distribution, manufacture and social interpretation have a separate body of history which has been influential in mine studies. It has been usual for any interpretations offered with regard to axes to be part of a dialogue encompassing stone axes and quarrying, in addition to flint axes and mining. However extraction by each method, chronology and artefact distribution are different and these factors will be given a brief overview below.

2.4 Axes: Product and Purpose?

This section seeks to provide additional background to the study of mines by focussing on approaches to axes over the past thirty years. An examination and review of recent approaches to flint or stone axes and implements has not been undertaken due to both limitations of space and lack of immediate relevance to this study. While it would have been informative to see how the developments in social theory have moved these dialogues forward in recent years the primary purpose of reviewing this material is to illustrate how interpretations of axes as an artefact class have supported ideas of the social segregation of mining sites and extraction.

Chronology and Distribution

In the past 30 years three trajectories of study have emerged concerning axes: the distribution of axes from source; the technological aspects of axe production and the social placement of axes within Neolithic society. This focus on axes has resulted in a situation where it is impossible to discuss flint axes in the Neolithic without reference to stone axes. Furthermore, one cannot discuss stone axes without reviewing quarrying sites. While the purpose of this research is to investigate flint mining and its social and depositional implications, I suggest that the existing interpretations of these have grown (through the absence of published data and secure radiocarbon dates) largely from a reflection of the interpretations of stone axe studies and quarrying.

There are two critical differences between Neolithic stone and flint axes: chronology and distribution. Flint axes and mining sites predate the quarrying of stone axes in the

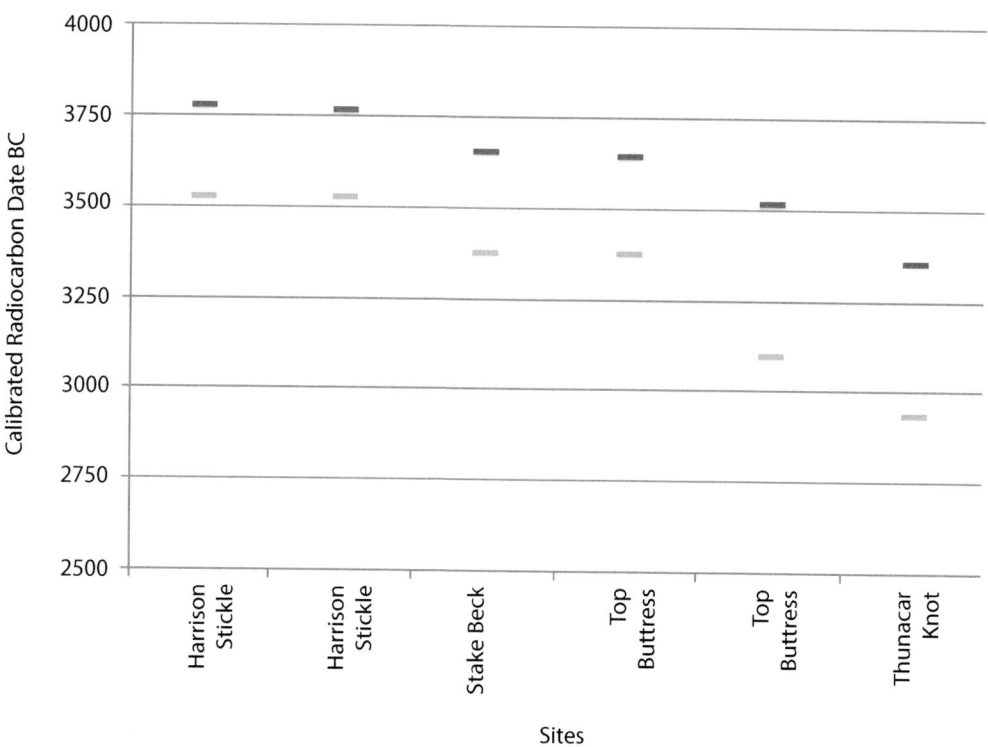

FIGURE 2.2 RECALIBRATED RADIOCARBON DATES FROM NEOLITHIC LANGDALE AXE QUARRIES (AFTER BRADLEY AND EDMONDS 1993: 81 [THUNACAR KNOTT BM 676, 4474 +/- 52], 113 [STAKE BECK OXA-2181, 4790 +/- 50] 116 [HARRISON STICKLE BM 2625, 4870 +/- 50], 117 [HARRISON STICKLE BM 2626, 4880 +/- 50], 128 [TOP BUTTRESS BM 2628, 4760 +/-50; BM 2627, 4590 +/- 50]; CALIBRATED USING OXCAL V.4.2, INTCAL 13, BRONK RAMSEY 2009)

British Isles. Axe quarrying is suggested from radiocarbon dates to occur in its initial phase during the 400 years from c. 3700cal BC to 3300 cal BC (Bradley and Edmonds 1993: 81, 106, 113, 128). By contrast, flint mining appears to commence just prior to c. 4000 cal BC and extends into the 3rd millennium BC (2.6 later). Furthermore as stone axes appear visually distinctive from each other, and from flint, their sources clearly vary considerably. The majority of flint, by comparison, is visually fairly similar. The sourcing of stone axes to quarrying sites received much attention in the twentieth century, implement petrological studies commencing in 1936 with Alexander Keiller and Piggott (Grimes 1979: 1). This resulted in various work mapping quarry sources and major groups of axe finds, aided by the visual distinctions in stone types (Craddock *et al.* 1983).

Some sourcing has also been completed on flint axes through petrological analyses. The mapping of the distribution of flint axes among contemporary and later Neolithic sites demonstrates variation in the distribution of axes from different sources. The axes from Sussex mines are found in East Anglia and in Wessex (Gardiner 1990), though there are a fewer number of axes from East Anglia or Wessex in Sussex. Gardiner investigated both flaked and polished axe distributions in some detail and discusses how the majority of polished stone axes in this area are found in the Weald, and are whole and unbroken in contrast to the numbers found on and around the mine sites. Moreover, there are a large amount (several hundred) polished axes from Sussex in Dorset, especially on Cranborne Chase. Gardiner (*ibid.*) notes that the presence of axes is almost ubiquitous on the chalk, and the absence of large quantities noticeable from the off the chalk, her conclusions suggesting that the chalklands were where the populations were settled. Furthermore, she proposes that axe distribution does not follow previous suggestions of usual fall-off patterns and is therefore unlikely to represent an industrial or specialist production economy (Renfrew 1976). Gardiner's evidence seems to suggest instead localised groups which also correspond with groups of contemporary or later archaeological sites, possibly indicating people travelling to flint sources or participating in exchange networks (of flint and possibly other materials) between, for example, a Sussex group and a group in Dorset. However Pitts (1996) questions the validity of petrological analyses to detect sources of flint. He argues that flint is geologically too similar across many deposits in England, and the possibility of geological flint outcrops of similar petrology too large, to identify flint sources with enough certainty using this method. This does cast doubt on some of Gardiner's analysis. Yet, flint axes are moving from likely sources at mines to other areas in the landscape and while perhaps secure sourcing evidence cannot be achieved it does not negate the probability of groups moving across and between regions. For the later Neolithic mining at Grimes Graves, the distribution of flint tools is discussed by Healy (1998: 227) where the presence of floorstone-like cortex on some examples suggests that the mined flint is predominantly found closer to the mine with flint surface deposits being preferentially exploited even as little as 4.5km from the mining site.

The perceived social importance of axes is further argued through production techniques applied to them. Polishing an axe, in part or whole, takes a great deal of time and effort. Where studies have been completed (e.g. Harding 1987; Bradley and Edmonds 1993) they suggest that polishing axes would require tens of hours labour. The scale and effort has highlighted the apparent social importance of axes; they take a lot of time to produce and therefore they are important and useful social objects as well as useful and long-lived tools (Harding 1987). Therefore, a valuable polished axe would be re-sharpened rather than replaced.

Hayden (1989) has studied the possibilities of why re-sharpening techniques should change in lithic assemblages. He discusses how this had been widely assumed to be evolutionary following common preconceptions of the early twentieth century – that hard hammer (more wasteful) sharpening techniques would occur chronologically earlier than soft hammer (less wasteful) with grinding being the most culturally advanced. While this may be broadly true, his work suggests that most lithic forms are produced through, and as a product of, re-sharpening techniques and that these are dependent on the technological requirements i.e. what the stone tool is required to do. He concludes through the study of indigenous Australians and Native Americans that 'in every major culture area in the world where edge grinding adzes or axes has become important, wood-cutting requirements were unusually high' (*ibid.*: 14). He also suggests that other edge ground tools are useful when there is a large amount of work to be done within a short space of time, when the longevity of the sharpness of the ground tool would be of paramount importance. By way of example he cites the butchering of salmon in the north west of America, where they needed to be butchered, split and dried within a few weeks. He argues it would be impossible during this period of high intensity work for time to be expended on the procurement and knapping of chipped tools which would only last a fraction of the time a ground edge would (*ibid.*: 15). Hence interpretively, axe production could be seen as part of the wider Neolithic dialogue of forest clearing for agricultural purposes, implying that ground polished axes would be more useful at repetitive tree-felling work.

This concept of investing time in tools has been employed in studies of hunter-gatherers and is contained within strategies of 'risk management'. These social strategies are often discussed in processual archaeology to describe the ways different cultures adapt to their environment. Bleed (1986) has constructed two types of technologies that may be seen in hunter-gatherer societies: maintainable and reliable. He does not suggest that these create an either/or situation but rather are present on a spectrum which will depend on the ecological position of the group in question in their adaptation to the environment.

Maintainable technologies he would argue, represent a portable, adaptable toolkit which would enable flexibility; tools would be manufactured, used and repaired between activities. Reliable technologies are almost the opposite: there is an investment in time to produce high quality tools. Torrence (1989: 63) discusses how the 'reliability' of tools is therefore a response to the severity of risk, maintainable technology a response to the timing of risk. To clarify, if tool failure is very important then a reliable strategy to tool manufacture would be prudent, conversely if the unpredictability and timing of risk were variable a maintainable strategy would be more useful. She goes on to argue that during the move to pastoralism from hunting a reliable tool kit would no longer be required (*ibid.*: 64), and axes were produced and exchanged as prestige goods required for social interaction and possibly the gaining of marriage partners (*ibid.*: 65). She therefore implies that this tree-felling may have been chronologically sensitive to local ecological concerns, becoming a prestige artefact when forest clearance has largely been completed for agriculture.

These technological views have given us differing social responses. It appears from all these well researched studies that ground or polished tools are time-consuming to produce yet extremely reliable. The investment of effort in production may be to increase their reliability in use, or their reliability in exchange where they embody value in social interaction as a prestige artefact. Their use may be linked with a great need for woodworking, something we have little surviving evidence for in the British Neolithic. The invisibility of this in the British evidence (except as a negative in terms of forest clearance), perhaps should be countered by some of the continental evidence. At the Danish late Mesolithic site of Tybrind Vig wooden stained and decorated paddles were discovered along with fishing spears, bows and two dug out canoes (Tilley 1996: 30-32). Woodworking may have been an important factor in the production and distribution of axes but the extent of this is never likely to be proven.

This brief overview has intended to illustrate the integrated nature of axes and technological matters and how they influence interpretation. Axes are often placed at the very core of explaining the Mesolithic-Neolithic transition in terms of how it was manifested (e.g. forest clearance, or artefact prestige). More recently new ideas of social processes involved in axe production have evolved through ethnographic studies.

Social Interpretations of Axes and Quarrying Site Locations

It is only since the later 1980s and partly through the discovery of the limitations of petrological analyses (Berridge 1994; Pitts 1996), that the symbolic and cultural importance of flint mines has been argued and the depositions and practices at sites begun to be situated in broader discussions of the Neolithic. As more recent excavation has been completed on quarrying sites in the past twenty years (Bradley and Edmonds 1993; Cooney 2005) there has been a tendency to see flint mines and mining as a reflection of this quarrying activity – the same arguments in reverse topography. I will describe how this has arisen and the concerns it raises.

While outcrops of stone for quarrying do occur at lower levels, it appears that the exploited stone source sites for axe production in Britain at the Langdales and Cumbria deliberately occur at distinctly identifiable and difficult to reach places (Bradley 2000: 85-6). This has suggestions of a wider European tradition as these difficult to access locations are similar to chronologically earlier axe quarrying sites in Norway (e.g. Hespriholmen and Stakaneset, *ibid*.: 83). Some archaeologists have suggested that axe production may be a key element in the puberty rituals of males in the Neolithic following ethnographic analysis, a view promoted by Edmonds (1995, 1999), and Cooney (2005). Both these archaeologists have worked on axe quarrying sites and, having used in part phenomenological approaches to landscape, concluded that the difficulty in gaining access to the chosen extraction sites at the tops of mountains could be part of a rite of passage (Van Gennep 1960). There is also a suggestion following ethnography that flint artefacts are male, or owned and manufactured by men or boys. As Edmonds states with regard to the larger and well worked flint and stone tools "many [ethnographic] accounts talk of a symbolic and practical link with men and, while axes were probably used by women too, there may have been times when these more categoric links were brought into focus" (1999: 41).

Few burials are recorded at the mine sites, and indeed the burials are more often recorded female (Barber *et al.* 1999: 66) leading Topping (2005: 75) to suggest mines may be affiliated with women though noting that due to issues of a lack of physical strength their role may have been 'passive'. At other Neolithic sites such as causewayed enclosures the burial of women and children predominate (Thorpe 1984: 49) and therefore mines could be argued to be fairly consistent with contemporary practices. As to be expected, there is no evidence of rites of passage for either sex in the archaeological record. Regardless of these possible affinities with ethnography, there remains no prevailing evidence for the social construction of only two genders in the Neolithic based on physical and biological appearances or properties and other ethnographies contradict such divides (Fowler 2004).

Rites of passage as an interpretation have been applied to all British Neolithic sites in some form, which does not negate the possibility they may have played a part in their use. However, the implication of the ethnographic argument that axes are produced by and for men and boys in quarrying, has through the artefact type of axes, inferred that these arguments are also valid for mining sites. These arguments have also encapsulated interpretations of deposition at mining sites. For example, a schematic representation of the common depositional position of artefacts within mine shafts and galleries has been produced to argue that this structure represents activity beyond simple flint extraction and implies ritualistic behaviour (Barber *et al.* 1999: 61). Topping (2005) expands this further in a later publication when offering a comparative ethnographic analysis of flint mining with a different types of quarrying; the extraction of stone for pipes at the Red Pipestone Quarry in Minnesota. He argues that the deposition at mine sites could be said to be representative of a similar type of sacred place for raw material, as that of the Native American tribes of Minnesota. In discussing the deposition at Shaft 27 at Cissbury, he relates the types of deposition in the shaft and its infill as possibly having correlations in the cleansing, purification and offering rituals noted by ethnographers. Topping explains that access is allowed to the sacred quarries for the purpose of extracting the stone, and no other reason. Tenure by the tribe in the locality is therefore not absolute, and access cannot be refused for the correct purpose. Using a similar ethnographic analogy of Native American quarry sites, Russell (2000: 142) suggests that access to the mine sites may have been fairly unrestricted.

Therefore two arguments concerning access are offered: that the chosen inaccessibility of stone quarrying at sites may have been socially significant, hence the difficulty in obtaining flint from mines would also have been perceived as a challenge and also, as ethnographically local tribal groups hold control over access to quarrying sites, this may have been similar with mining in the British Neolithic. This rather peculiarly brings an impression of both a type of Neolithic sedentism and land ownership or control to mine sites without any archaeological evidence. The time consuming nature of extraction is what is perceived as difficult, not the actual access to the sites, as with quarrying. Clearly, surface flint outcrops do not produce the same inaccessibility; mines have to be created in order for the flint to become difficult to obtain. Moreover, artefacts have been affiliated with this quarrying ethnographic argument; axes by Edmonds and ritual deposition by Topping. In summary, an interpretation of mining flint is that it is of social and cultural importance in part due to the inaccessibility of it as a source, yet flint mine sites and their deposits have not been rigorously examined to produce these: they are produced simply through ethnographic analogy.

This section has skimmed over an enormous body of work in an attempt to illustrate the integration of interpretations between stone and flint axes, and quarrying and mining as extractive processes. It is an initial stage in one of the arguments threading through this book - that flint mines are more akin to other Neolithic monumental sites in terms of deposition than not. Continually focussing on the differences will only allow this interpretive separation to increase. There is some subtlety in argument to come in this study, to both include mines in wider discourses and yet scrutinise these overarching interpretations. During the Neolithic in Britain, this complete separation of extraction sites and other ritual or domestic site may not be as distinct as this comparison of quarrying and mining suggest. The next section begins a comprehensive overview of mine sites; their morphology, size location and deposition.

2.5 An Overview of Sites Studied

Morphology and Site Size

The identification of flint mines on the primary chalk deposits was conducted in the 1990s using a variety of methods such as field survey and aerial photography (Barber *et al.* 1999). The close network of vertical shafts, in-filled after use, created a dip or depression in the surface overlaying the top of the shaft, and simplified plans of the mines are shown in Figures 2.3 - 2.11. Circular mounds containing the upcast of mine material are also found by the depressions, creating a topography which is densely undulating. The methodology to ascertain site size is to assume each pit or depression is a shaft, and each mound its corresponding spoil, though this is acknowledged as a rather crude approach (Barber *et al.* 1999: 38). We know from completed excavations that some depressions may not be deep, or may represent other forms of activity, or some mounds may represent barrows. At Long Down, Holgate noted that a shaft appeared underneath a mound during excavation (1991). Despite these reservations, using the same methodology can allow for the extent of sites to be assessed at least in relative terms.

Barber *et al.*'s (1999) study suggested that each site may have as many as the following numbers of shafts (Figure

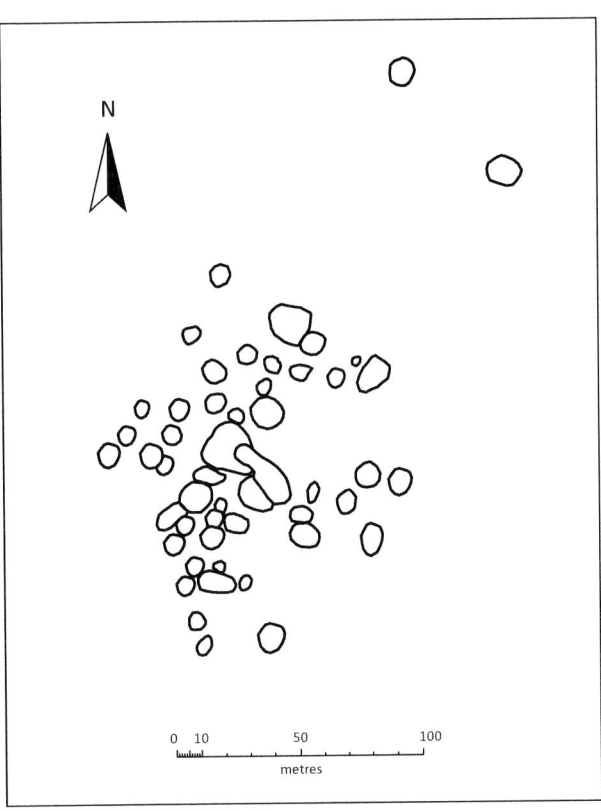

FIGURE 2.4 PLAN OF LONG DOWN (REDRAWN FROM RUSSELL 2000: 82)

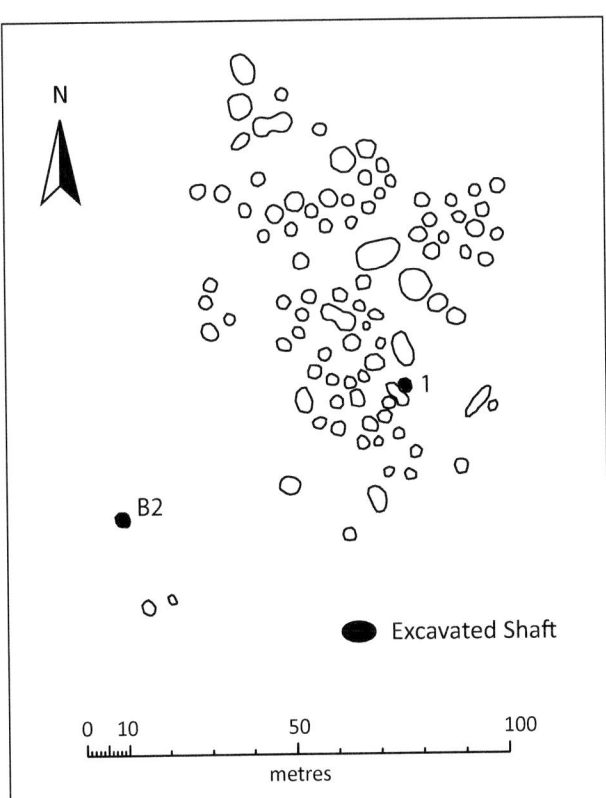

FIGURE 2.3 PLAN OF EASTON DOWN (REDRAWN FROM STONE 1931: 351)

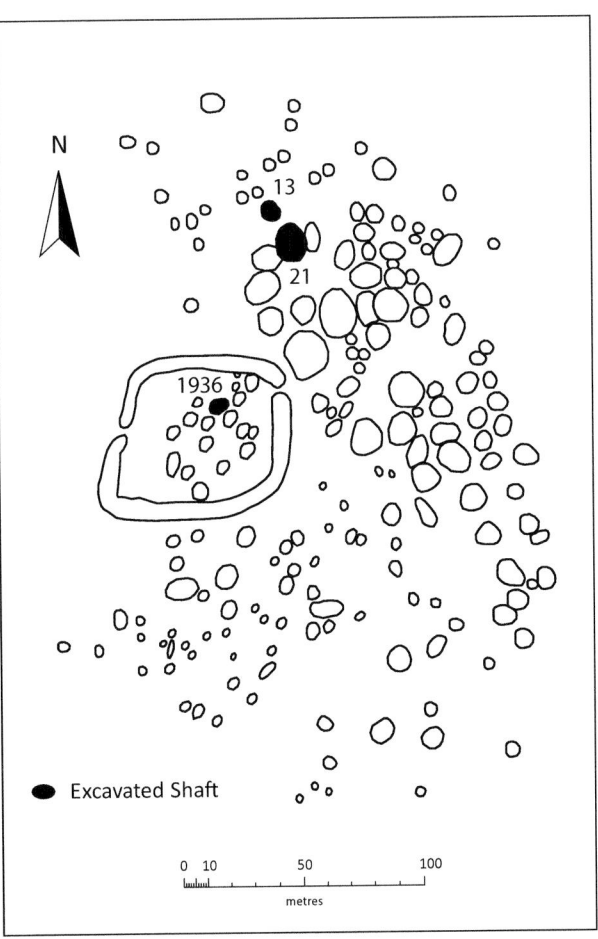

FIGURE 2.5 PLAN OF HARROW HILL (REDRAWN FROM RUSSELL 2000: 76)

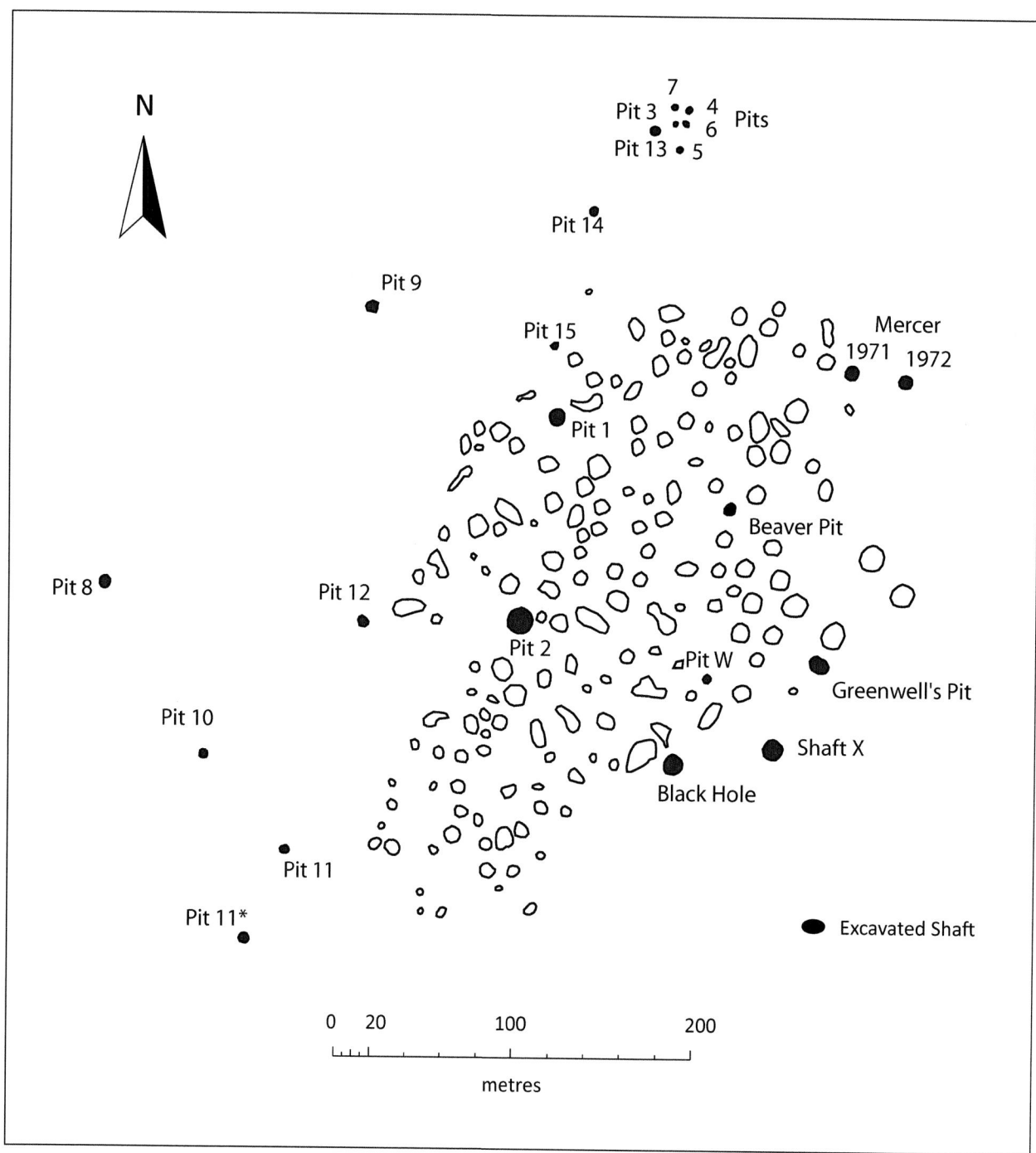

FIGURE 2.6 PLAN OF GRIMES GRAVES (REDRAWN FROM LONGWORTH AND VARNDELL 1991: FRONT PULL OUT)

2.12). However there are other factors which need to be accommodated. Some sites have been subject to extensive damage, such as Blackpatch which was bulldozed in 1950. Many sites have suffered from excessive ploughing, a situation which is still continuing at Church Hill, and consequently the total areas mined can, at most, only be conjectured.

Extraction Methods

On primary geological deposits flint occurs in seams within chalk bedrock, the depth of which can vary. Rather like a layered cake, the flint lies as a thin layer sandwiched between the chalk bedrock. The method of extraction seems to be similar for all the studied mine sites during the Neolithic period. It appears that the chalk was initially punctured with antler tines in vertical rows, and levered out in blocks (Russell 2000). At Harrow Hill punch and leverage or wedge marks were noted and photographed, and were also evidenced at Church Hill (Curwen and Curwen 1926; Russell 2001: 113). As many as three or four seams of flint can be encountered in the main shaft and the flint is extracted through a series of galleries radiating out from the bottom of the shaft.

Situating Flint Mines in Neolithic Studies

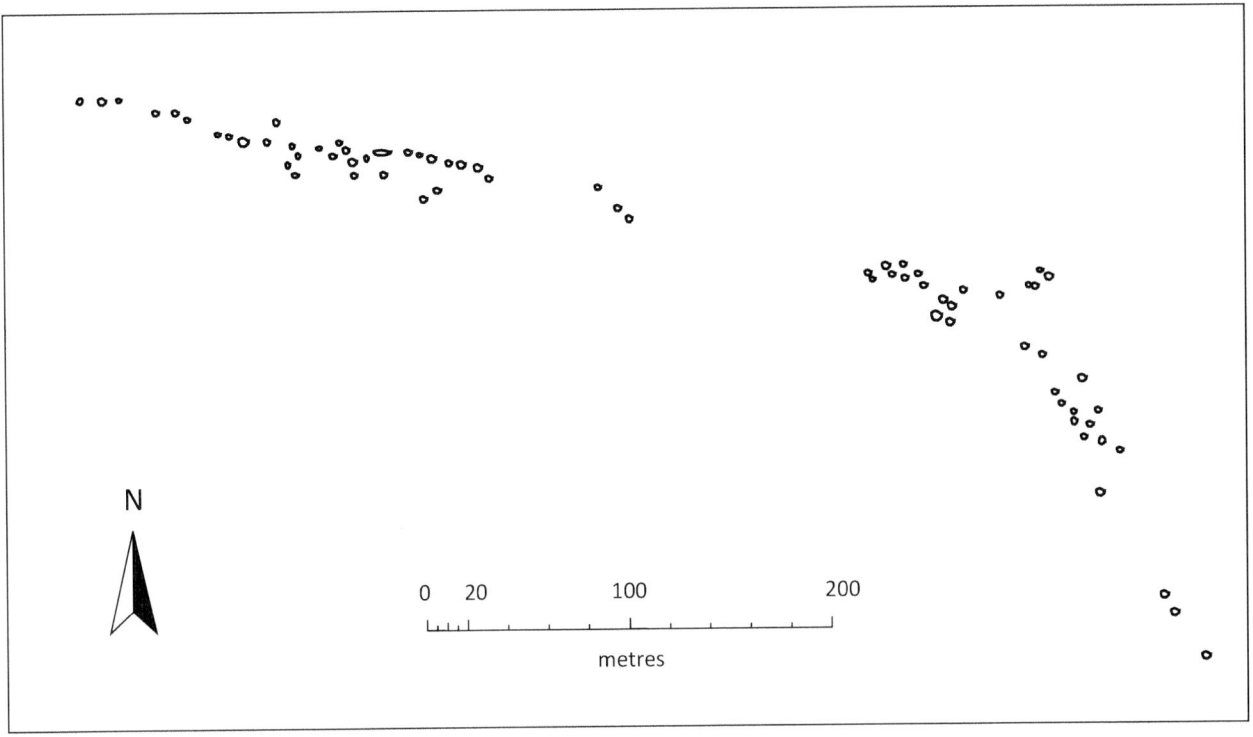

Figure 2.7 Plan of Stoke Down (redrawn from Barber et al. 1999: 59)

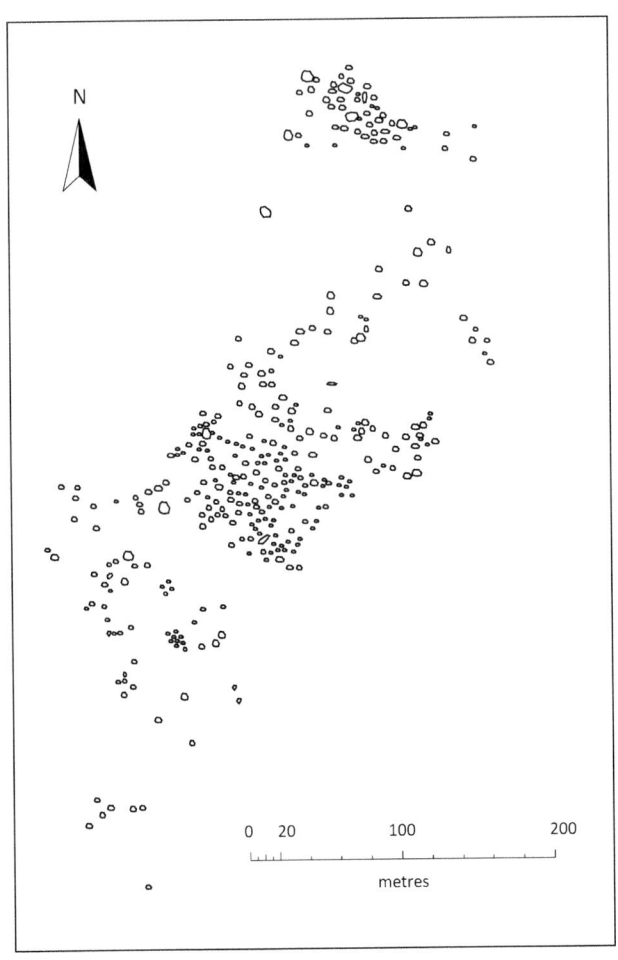

Figure 2.8 Plan of Martin's Clump (redrawn from Barber et al. 1999: 36)

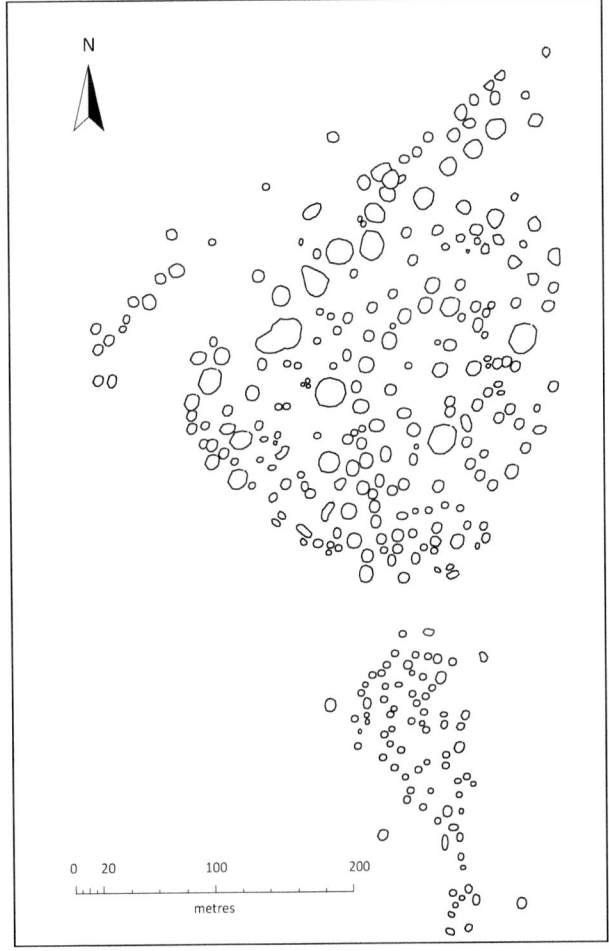

Figure 2.9 Plan of Cissbury (redrawn from Barber et al. 1999: 29)

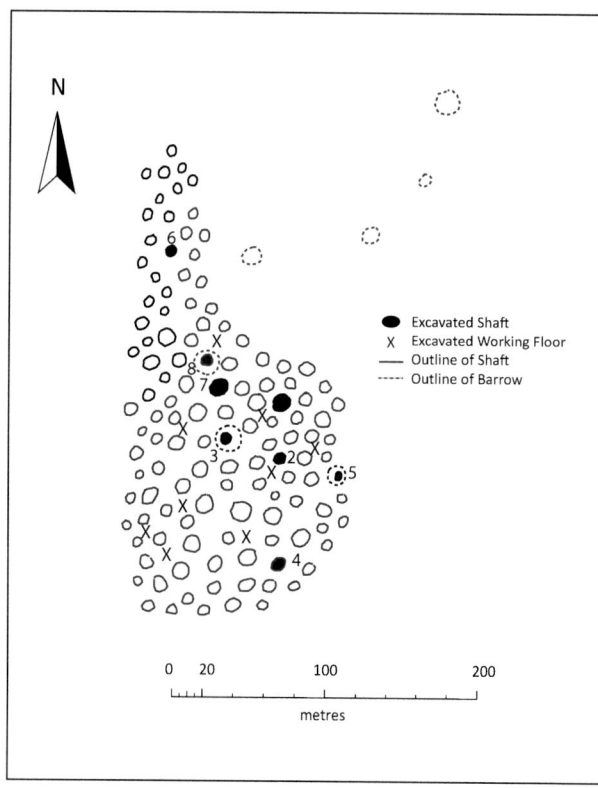

FIGURE 2.10 PLAN OF BLACKPATCH (REDRAWN FROM PULL IN RUSSELL 2001: 25-6)

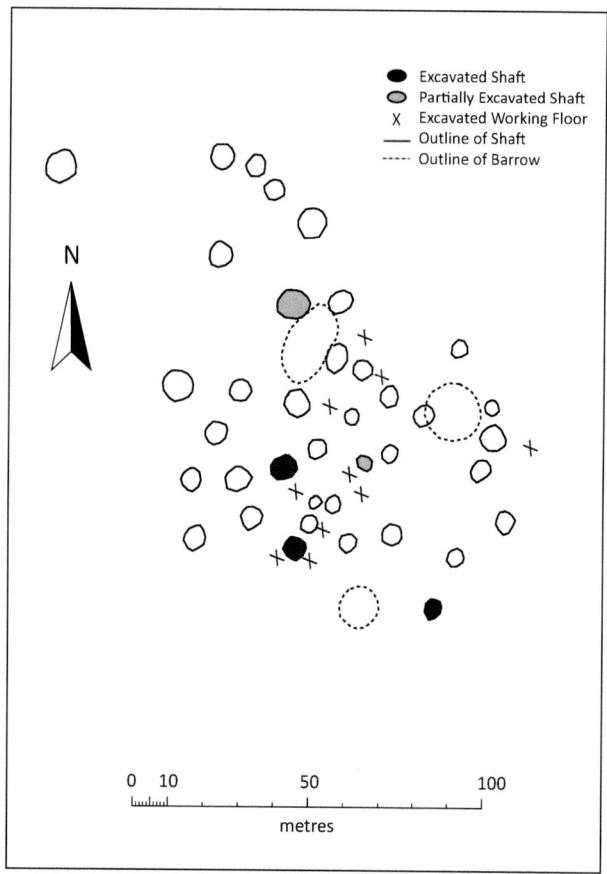

FIGURE 2.11 PLAN OF CHURCH HILL (REDRAWN FROM PULL IN RUSSELL 2001: 88)

Region	Mine	Number of Shafts
East Anglia	Grimes Graves	c. 450
East Sussex	Cissbury	c. 270
	Harrow Hill	> 270
	Blackpatch	> 100
	Church Hill	> 26
West Sussex	Long Down	> 4
	Stoke Down	> 70
Wessex	Martin's Clump	c. 1000 small pits
	Easton Down	> 90
	Durrington	> 6

FIGURE 2.12 TABLE OF POSSIBLE NUMBER OF SHAFTS OR PITS AT EACH SITE (AFTER BARBER ET AL. 1999)

When the appropriate seam had been reached, the chalk was mostly extracted on top of the flint (rather than being chipped away at from a horizontal angle) and the large nodules or tabular flint extracted from the floors of the galleries. The depth of shaft varies depending on the depth of the flint seam accessed for extraction and the stability of the surrounding chalk. Shafts can vary between being only 0.5m in depth (Durrington), to up to 13m (Greenwell's Pit at Grimes Graves). No English mine shaft has a reported depth of more than 13m (Russell 2000: 60-83, Figure 2.13). The European mines have some shafts as deep as 16 - 20 metres (Spiennes, where up to twelve horizontal flint seams were reached, Shepherd 1980: 71).

Galleries were constructed as the flint was uncovered and followed through the seam from the base of the shaft (Russell 2000: 84-117). During the excavation of galleries, it appears that a proportion of cleared galleries were filled by the extracted chalk from a new gallery, and hence some galleries (presumably the latest ones excavated in antiquity) are free of rubble, where others are not (*ibid.*). These galleries are often only wide and tall enough for one person to pass through at any time. The galleries themselves can be extensive and linked through both apertures cut through parallel galleries (which can be referred to as 'windows') or by directly opening into each other, argued by Barber *et al.* (1999: 50) as likely to be coincidental rather than planned. These apertures are seen in excavations at both Cissbury and Blackpatch and it has been suggested they allow for more light and air to penetrate the deeper galleries (Russell 2000: 101). However, galleries are not always present, or quite short as seen at Stoke Down where the base of the shaft workings represented more of an undercut (Wade 1922). Whether this is due to the instability of the chalk, or chronological or social factors prevalent at the time is impossible to ascertain. More extensive mining of upper seams has been

Depth of Shaft	DTN	MC	LD	BP	SD	ED	CH	HH	CBY	GG
< 1m	0	0	0	0	0	1	0	0	0	0
< 3m	2	1	0	0	1	3	1	2	2	0
< 5m			1	4	2	2	4	2	1	8
< 7m						1	1	1	3	1
< 9m									0	0
< 11m									1	2
< 13m									2 *	2

* *One shaft was abandoned at 12.8m depth*

DTN: Durrington; MC: Martin's Clump; LD: Long Down; BP: Blackpatch; SD: Stoke Down; ED: Easton Down; CH: Church Hill; HH: Harrow Hill; CBY: Cissbury; GG: Grimes Graves.

FIGURE 2.13 TABLE OF APPROXIMATE DEPTH OF SHAFTS AT EACH SITE (DATA SUMMARISED FROM RUSSELL 2000: 70-84)

noted at some of the Sussex sites, for example, at Harrow Hill an upper gallery was constructed and it is likely that this upper seam was mined before the flint galleries were excavated and extracted in Shaft 2. On excavation it proved extremely fragile and was subject to partial collapse (Curwen and Curwen 1926), though in general terms this is rarely evidenced.

2.6 The Context and Location of Mines

As mentioned, ten sites are defined and classed as Neolithic flint mines in the modern county boundaries of Sussex, Hampshire/Wiltshire and Norfolk. However, viewing these sites through their modern geographical boundaries seems to separate them from their local context. As the integration of mining into accepted Neolithic dialogues is a key aim of this research I have followed the route of Barber *et al.* (1999: 28, 55-7) in examining them as four groups, or clusters, which allows for a more refined analysis.

Long Down and Stoke Down are hence separated from the other group of four mine sites further east in Sussex (I have termed them the West Sussex and East Sussex groups). As can be seen (Figure 2.1), geographically they are much more distinct within their locality, forming two clusters. The East Sussex group comprise of Cissbury, Church Hill, Harrow Hill and Blackpatch which are only a maximum of 2km distant from each other on the South Downs, northeast of modern Worthing. The Hampshire/Wiltshire mines are close together and for this study could be more usefully argued to form part of Neolithic Wessex (following Barber *et al.* 1999: 28). Finally, Grimes Graves has to be considered separately due to its geographical distance.

Viewshed analyses as part of landscape archaeology have become a recent addition to the analysis of prehistoric monuments and their local inhabited landscapes. Accepting the reservations often offered in this respect of tree coverage or seasonal factors which may restrict certain views, the suggestion that obscuring or enhancing views, or the placement of sites in general terms, can provide interpretive clues as to their past meanings. Stoke Down and Long Down are placed either side of The Trundle, an impressive and extensive causewayed enclosure on this ridge of the chalk downs. The position of the mines seems to frame The Trundle and hence forms a more practical approach to this study. Russell notes that although The Trundle can be seen from Stoke Down, it cannot be seen from Long Down, and indeed the view from Long Down appears to be restricted to only Halnaker Hill, another Neolithic enclosure (Russell 2000: 141). With regard to the East Sussex group, from Church Hill the other three mine sites can be seen and all sites are intervisible with at least two others (Barber *et al.* 1999: 55-7). Each of the four mines faces towards the coastal plain, away from the Weald to the north, a situation which could have been altered through exploitation of the same hills but on a different side, in the cases of both Cissbury and Blackpatch (Russell 2000: 140-1). Of the East and West Sussex sites, all have views to the English Channel to the south and the coastal plain, being placed upon the first high ground from the sea (Barber *et al.* 1999: 55-7). Russell (2001: 141) suggests that the siting of mines on particular slopes for both the East and West Sussex groups:

> may have helped to enhance their perceived mystery by ensuring they were hidden from the majority of apparently contemporary enclosures and long mounds. The hills chosen for extraction may have been

conceptually important in a spiritual, tribal or ancestral sense to those living in this area.

As discussed these ideas of separation or seclusion are common for interpretations of the ritual significance of extraction or flint during the Neolithic. In order to explore the ideas of site location further, we need to examine preceding flint extraction activity during the Mesolithic.

Extraction in Context

Flint extraction and the production of flint tools and axes were a Mesolithic activity both in Britain and Europe and there is much archaeological evidence to support this. Therefore studying Neolithic flint extraction and axes should be viewed as a continuation of this earlier Mesolithic practice. There are many sites on clay-with-flints geology where outcrops were exploited during the Mesolithic (Care 1979). A site near Fort Wallington in Hampshire contained evidence of flint working on a large scale with axes in many stages of manufacture and is interestingly placed next to natural shafts or 'pipes' (*ibid.*: 95). Although these 'pipes' were not thought to be associated with flint extraction or mining, the excavators suggested it was possible that flint was extracted from seams close to the surface. Broom Hill is another Hampshire site where a chalk outcrop was exploited over a long period of time in the Mesolithic and a large amount of tranchet axes produced (approximately 40% of the assemblage, O'Malley 1978: 120). The axe production at flint source sites could therefore be said to have its foundation during the Late Mesolithic with the distribution of tranchet axes in many cases being a forerunner to the later Early Neolithic distribution (Care 1979; Gardiner 1990). Both authors suggest that the use of tranchet axes may continue into the Neolithic, and indeed throughout the Neolithic, which could indicate that these Mesolithic extraction sites may also have continued in use into the Neolithic.

It is established that during the Neolithic, flint extraction also occurred alongside different Neolithic monuments. Several pits were discovered during excavation for a pipe trench at the later Neolithic henge monument of Durrington Walls in Wiltshire (Booth and Stone 1952). These were little more than grubbing pits showing evidence of slight undercutting and although no dating evidence was uncovered, a transverse arrowhead was excavated suggesting a mid-late Neolithic date. Flint mining was seen at the large causewayed enclosure at Hambledon Hill in Dorset, when during the course of excavation evidence of fairly extensive mining/quarrying was found (Mercer 1987). While some bone and antler fragments were excavated, fragments of a Neolithic plain bowl in the fill suggested a contemporary date with the construction of the Hambledon Hill complex. A radiocarbon date has recently indicated the mining activity may be later, at *c.* 2460 – 2060 cal BC so the chronology is still perhaps uncertain (Healy 2004: 21). Mercer (1987: 161) suggests that as the chalk bedrock was not in the filling of the shafts (the fill being composed of weathered chalk rubble) it may have been used in the construction of a nearby timber framed rampart. Interestingly he states that there was little indication of this extraction from surface topography prior to excavation and it may occur at other monumental sites more commonly than thought. Mercer also, for the first time, suggested that tablets of bedrock chalk may have had an architectural use in building structures. This is an important concept that will be returned to in Chapter 4.

Bradley has discussed the relationship between natural shafts, flint mines and monumentality in the Neolithic (2000: 88-90). He argues that the interpretation of flint mining can be seen as more difficult than that of quarrying due to the importance of shafts and deep pits that form part of the later ritual architecture of the Neolithic in Britain. He refers to the Priddy henge monuments focussed around natural solution holes in Somerset and also the shafts at Eaton Heath near Norwich which were almost certainly natural but contained placed Neolithic deposits. Therefore both shafts and solutions holes have deposits within them, similar to deposits occurring in flint mines shafts.

The view proposed here is that Neolithic flint extraction has both a long history of practice from the Mesolithic and a wide breadth, occurring at various places within Neolithic society. It could be argued that the main difference seen with flint mine sites is the scale and concentration of such extraction in these locales. Again, I feel integration their location into a wider context is productive and this is offered below. Having situated them chronologically we can return to see how the previous viewshed analysis can be enhanced for further interpretation.

Geographical Location of Mines

The following discussion intends to refocus our concerns of the location of early Neolithic mining sites into a regional southern British narrative. This incorporates Mesolithic-Neolithic transitional changes, monumentality, and leads us away from viewing Sussex mines as somehow at the periphery of inhabited landscapes. While I have described the location of mines on the south coast and Russell's (2001: 141) interpretation that the particular hills they are situated on may have had ancestral significance, as yet I have not offered any alternative or additional views. Russell correctly includes in this interpretation that geologically the chalk bearing flint of the South Downs is fairly uniform, and hence there has been a particular emphasis on these locations for mines to be situated. Thus, with likely motivations for this already discussed such as intervisibility to other mines and views to the sea which appear to have influenced their location, I suggest there are other factors to address.

The Sussex mines are situated on the South Downs, on the first high ridge from the sea. All have views to the coast and (with the exception of the actual mining site at Harrow Hill), the Isle of Wight. The Isle of Wight appears from this distance to be connected to the mainland as a promontory. In the past, the Isle of Wight was a promontory. The

English Channel is in geological terms a relatively new phenomenon occurring after the last Ice Age. While the Channel would have quite quickly become impassable, prior to the melting of the ice caps during the Flandrain marine transgression travel across the land bridge over the North Sea to Europe for humans would have been relatively easy, becoming increasingly more difficult over time (Momber 2000). This situation is likely to have continued for a long time, with the final separation occurring at the east coast perhaps *c.*4500-5000 cal BC (*ibid.*). On the south coast, other Mesolithic sites on promontories include Portland Bill and Hengistbury Head which provide some of the best evidence for activity during this period, though this is likely simply due to their survival from sea level rises (*ibid.*: 89). Recent underwater investigations off the north west coast of the Isle of Wight have discovered evidence of a Neolithic forest at the base of a 4m cliff with evidence of flint working and hearths, at times under peat indicating the increasingly wet conditions (*ibid.*). This has been dated to approximated 7500-7000 BP (*ibid.*: 94; or *c.* 5500-5000 BC), suggesting that at least as far as the north west coast of the Isle of Wight is concerned, the now submerged land from here to the Isle of Purbeck and beyond would have been accessible by foot, connecting Dorset, Portland Bill and Hengistbury Head with the Isle of Wight at this time.

There is both Mesolithic and Neolithic activity noted on the Isle of Wight with flint working sites often bridging the Mesolithic and Neolithic periods. These have produced polished axes, arrowheads, microliths and tranchet axes (Waller 2006). A possible flint mining site at Brading Down is noted as requiring further study by Waller. In addition timber track-ways at Quarr beach have produced radiocarbon dates to approximately 3700-3300 cal BC, although an earlier date is provided from a possible fish trap in a palaeochannel at 4040-3710 cal BC (*ibid.*). The amount of evidence from the Isle of Wight is small and yet very evocative; evidence of flint working and trackways indicates that the late Mesolithic and early Neolithic inhabitants (or visitors) were attempting to both exploit the environment and manage the increasing water levels through the trackways. At the north east coast of the Isle of Wight, in the direction of Sussex, the situation is slightly more complex. The likely esturine environment on this east coast (Momber 2000) almost certainly meant that the Isle was not connected with the mainland even during the mid-Mesolithic, though the river may have been passable. If it were not passable directly, travel to the island via the Dorset side would have been easily feasible.

Tilley (1999: 197) has discussed the importance of one of the Mesolithic promontories in Dorset with extraction activity, Portland Bill, and proposes that Neolithic monumentality in the area may be referencing aspects of this. It is my intention to draw elements of his argument with Sussex monumentality and the Isle of Wight. Portland Bill, south of Dorchester, is a large promontory connected to the mainland. Chesil Beach, a 28km long and between 150m and 200m wide stretch of chert and flint pebbles from West Bay, abuts it at its north west point. While at the West Bay end it is little more than a raised beach, where it meets Portland Bill, the beach is around 15m in height (*ibid.*: 188-91). Another distinctive feature of the beach is that the chert and flint pebbles gradually increase in size from West Bay to Portland Bill, no doubt a result of wave action. Tilley discusses how this geology is quite unique and how it is said locals can determine which section of the beach they are on merely by examining the pebble size.

The Mesolithic importance of exploiting chert on Portland Bill seems evident through deposits at Culver Hill and Portland Bill (Portland site 1) with a date from Culver Hill suggesting initial occupation at *c.* 6100-5700 cal BC (*ibid.*: 191-3). Tilley also discusses the range of chert axe deposits which extend into Surrey to the east and Cornwall to the west, in addition to Cranborne Chase to the north. Care has also suggested that the amount of picks indicate that Portland was perhaps a 'quarry' site during the Mesolithic (1979: 98).

Following these arguments Tilley suggests that Maiden Castle, a nearby Neolithic causewayed enclosure, had both physical and metaphorical connections with Portland Bill in the early Neolithic which were expressed through monumental architecture. He argues (1999: 197) this is visible through Maiden Castle, enclosing the top of the hill, representing Portland itself and the construction of bank barrows (both here and along the Dorset Ridgeway) metaphorically representing Chesil Beach. Furthermore he suggests that Portland Bill provided mythological ideas of ancestral origins, ancestors from the island, which is connected with other causewayed enclosures such as Carn Brea in Cornwall, Windmill Hill (Wiltshire), Hambledon Hill (Dorset) and Offham Hill (Sussex) (*ibid.*). Tilley interprets the increasing monumentality of the Dorset Ridgeway into the later Neolithic and Bronze Age as a prehistoric understanding of the chalk Ridgeway as an ancestral beach itself (*ibid.*: 236-9). Despite all the evocative descriptions Tilley's ancestors are rather amorphous, their notoriety and importance peculiar. Why were they so important and why do ancestral islands need to be monumentalised?

In order to answer this I suggest we need to return to sea level changes. The Culver Hill midden site on Portland has been dated to slightly prior to the dates from the submerged Neolithic forest to the north west of the Isle of Wight (6100 -5700 cal BC/ 5500-5000 cal BC). Mesolithic activity of chert quarrying and exchange from Portland Bill across to the Isle of Wight and more widely across southern England, connects this underwater landscape no longer available to us. We cannot see exactly where the routeways would have been, by river or by foot, but we can judge the importance of Mesolithic coastal exploitation and with the fragmentary evidence suggesting connections between Portland Bill, the Isle of Purbeck, the areas around Hengistbury Head and the Isle of Wight.

I have discussed how the Isle of Wight can be linked by viewshed analysis to the Sussex mines, and that the Isle of Wight in turn is linked to Dorset both through both deposition of Portland Bill chert and the indications of a land connection prior to *c.* 5500 cal BC. After this date, the rising sea levels would have created an uncertain environment, where as evidenced at the Isle of Wight submerged forest, peat may have been forming. However there is some suggestion that the Isle may not have been entirely cut off from the mainland on the northwest side until the mid Bronze Age, before this time simply suffering with gradual sea encroachment (Waller 2006).

Tilley (1999: 205) argues that there are indications reflected in depositional practice of possible ritual enactments at Maiden Castle that suggest ancestor reverence in some form, and while he discusses mythology as a motivation, the reasons why the ancestors were such figures in the Neolithic landscape seem absent. I suggest that ancestors may have been revered and promontories became monumentalised because the ancestors who inhabited these lands which were no long visible or accessible; promontories were all that remained of the ancestral lands. Effectively, the ancestors had inhabited an Atlantis, a lost world literally submerged. Ancestors would have been buried in these landscapes; where children had been born, hunting areas lost: socially important places claimed by the rising sea. Monumentality in Dorset seen through Tilley's argument could have been a way of recreating the ancestral landscapes, their need to be placed in high topography to both protect them from the uncertain seas and yet stay connected to the lost lands.

The mines in Sussex could be said to be connected with this in various ways. While Tilley refers to Offham causewayed enclosure in Sussex, equally The Trundle or Whitehawk could be referencing the Isle of Wight as another promontory. Furthermore, there are indications there may have been people who inhabited both these landscapes through the exchange of flint axes proposed by Gardiner (1990; 2.4.1 earlier), though we should recognise some of the petrological analyses may be misleading. Still, this argument will be further supported in Chapter 4 and 5 where similarities in chalk artefacts and chalk art within monuments between Sussex and Dorset will be under review. Whether there was seasonal movement between the mines and Dorset, or whether several groups moved through these encroaching coastal environments largely inhabiting one place or another, what seems to connect them is shared knowledge of how to inscribe meanings into ditches through chalk art, or decorate and manipulate chalk forms. Rather than separating southern Britain in this modern county way, it may be more useful to include Sussex as part of the community of Neolithic Wessex in the Early Neolithic, in part through seeing monumentality possibly referencing off-shore promontory sites.

However, the Sussex mines are perhaps within a different understanding of landscape than those mines further inland (Easton Down and Martin's Clump). Furthermore, other aspects of location are not considered for Grimes Graves. Yet, I do not feel we need to interpret each location of each mining site in depth and attempt to discover one commonality. Sites were located in these places as they were significant.

2.7 Chronology

Perhaps the greatest challenge to this study has been chronology. The lack of many secure radiocarbon dates for such huge sites, almost all of which exhibit sporadic prehistoric activity, has rendered determinations of prehistoric use more complex than for many sites. In general terms chronologies for flint mining are rather broad. The date which heralds the start of the main phases of mining in Europe is around 4500-4000 cal BC in both Southern England and Sweden (Barber *et al.* 1999; Rudebeck 1987). This date is also traditionally seen as the beginning of the Neolithic in Britain and northern Europe. European mining seems to have started much earlier in Poland during the Upper Palaeolithic, being seen at Oronsko at 10,000 to 9,000 BC (Weisgerber 1987). During the fourth millennium BC there is dating evidence at a greater number of sites. The continuation of flint mining on the continent into the second millennium BC is likely at mine sites in France, Belgium, Denmark, Holland, Germany, Spain, Portugal, Switzerland and Sicily (Shepherd 1980: 66), though unproven in the UK.

The method of ascribing chronology for the mines has been traditionally based on diagnostic artefacts recovered during excavation. This has been problematic in British flint mines as diagnostic artefacts which can provide a chronological signature are rarely excavated, indeed only Grimes Graves exhibits any quantity of pottery in lower shaft fills and galleries. One of the first excavations by Lane Fox (1876) produced a small quantity of earlier Neolithic pottery at Cissbury in the upper fill of a shaft, a find not yet repeated within a Sussex or Wessex lower mine shaft stratigraphy. Regrettably, many radiocarbon dates obtained in the mid-twentieth century served only to confirm the general conclusion offered by flint typology; that mining occurred during the fourth millennium BC, and continued into the third. The only site to be entirely separate from this is Grimes Graves, which has produced consistently later dates indicating mining occurred solely in the third millennium BC. Recent radiocarbon dates obtained by Barber *et al.* (1999) have shown there is a possibility that at some sites such as Martin's Clump and perhaps Cissbury, mining may have started prior to 4000 cal BC. In summary, with as much confidence as can be ascribed to less than a handful of reliable radiocarbon dates and no pottery chronology, mining could be said to have taken place in Sussex and Wessex from perhaps as early as 4300 cal BC, and ceased by *c.* 3300 cal BC (Figure 2.14), with mining at Grimes Graves from *c.* 2900cal BC to *c.*2300 cal BC (Ambers 1996). In comparative terms, it is likely flint mining commenced prior to stone axe quarrying and predominately ceased at the same time (as mentioned earlier axe quarrying suggests dates fairly consistent in the

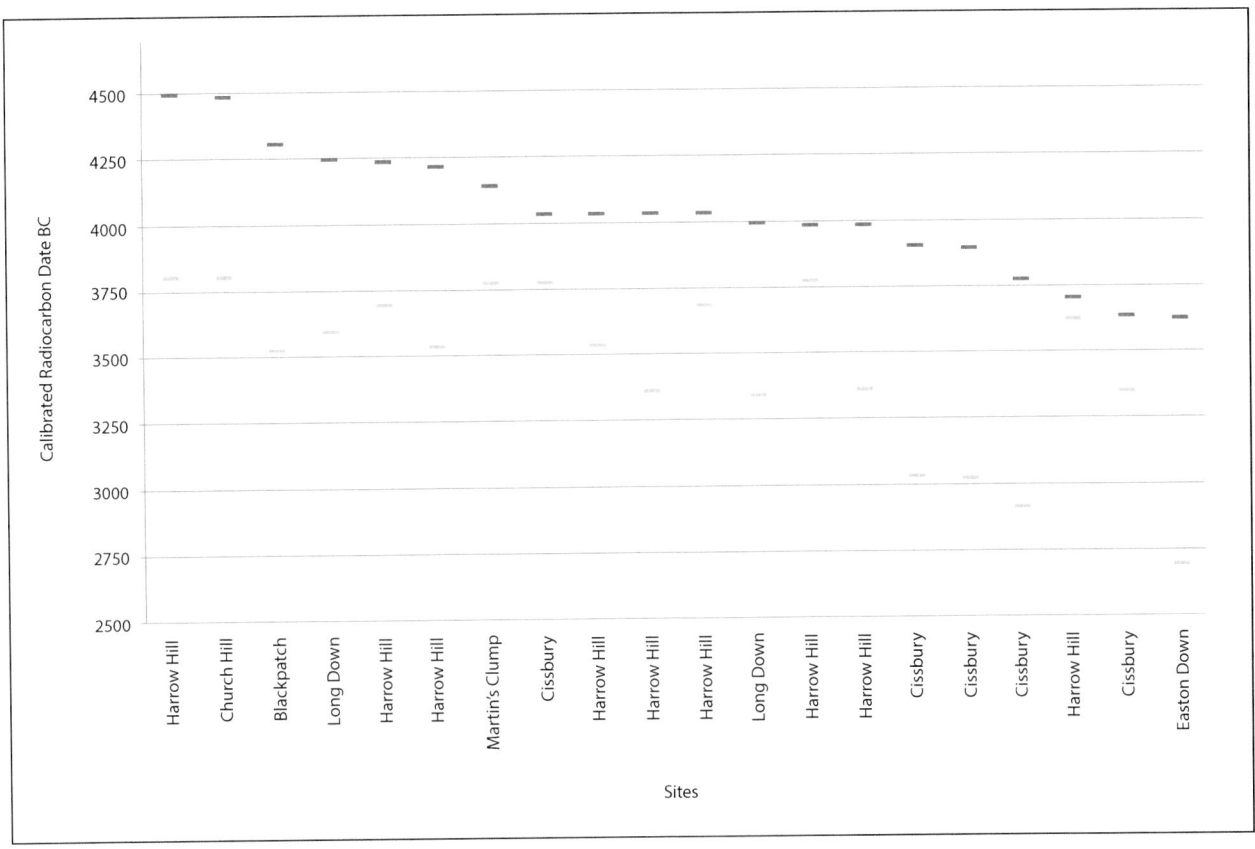

FIGURE 2.14 RECALIBRATED RADIOCARBON DATES FROM NEOLITHIC FLINT MINES (BARBER ET AL. 81-2; CALIBRATED USING OXCAL V.4.2, INTCAL 13, BRONK RAMSEY 2009)

early phase of the 400 years from c.3700cal B.C. to 3300 cal B.C.; Bradley & Edmonds 1993: 81, 106, 113, 128).

Figure 2.15 illustrates the likely range of chronological activity at each mine site, excluding Stoke Down and Long Down due to the lack of excavation and radiocarbon dates at these sites. It is possible that the group of four East Sussex mines (Harrow Hill, Blackpatch, Church Hill and Cissbury) were an Early Neolithic monumental complex where specific sites had different social emphases. This altered over time, with Cissbury almost certainly going out of use until the Iron Age and with Blackpatch and Church Hill continuing into the later Neolithic with an emphasis on burials and barrows. Activities at Blackpatch may have continued to reference Harrow Hill geographically opposite across the dry valley. It is apparent that those mines active during the later Neolithic are not those used in the Bronze Age or later Iron Age. Despite the general paucity of radiocarbon dating evidence at these sites it seems likely that this dating sequence is fairly accurate following later pottery chronologies. Later prehistoric activity often reveals greater quantities of archaeological material and had Cissbury been used during the mid-late Neolithic or Bronze Age evidence should have been forthcoming from the various excavations on the earlier Neolithic and later Iron Age evidence. Similarly at Harrow Hill where Bronze Age activity has been noted, no mid-late Neolithic archaeology has been uncovered. While little evidence exists at Martin's Clump, Easton Down certainly seems to have been a similar type of mining complex as Blackpatch with Later Neolithic and Bronze Age activity.

The unusual deposits at Easton Down in ash pits, barrows and the house structures have not been investigated in this research as they are outside of this chronological study, yet broadly these similarities with Blackpatch should be accepted (Stone 1932a, 1932b, 1933a, 1933b, 1935). While activity occurs at Blackpatch and Church Hill in the mid-late Neolithic in comparison with Grimes Graves (a complete mid-late Neolithic complex) the evidence appears entirely different in character. Had Blackpatch and Church Hill been subject to mining I would expect pottery in the later period stratigraphically lower within shafts and in galleries, as at Grimes Graves. Grimes Graves is a huge site, enduring through the Bronze Age and into the Iron Age. The extraction of flint was practiced in addition to complex and elaborate depositional behaviour into the late Neolithic but it has not been possible to extend this study into chronologically later periods. Indeed, the study of Bronze Age activity at Easton Down, Blackpatch and Grimes Graves would constitute a book of its own. In summary, the East Sussex group of mines appear at times to be chronologically distinct and this may reflect changing practices and emphases of activity from the Early to Late Neolithic, and beyond. Therefore, in Britain flint mining could be seen as the start of monumentality, prior to the building and construction of causewayed enclosures or long barrows (Barber et al. 1999).

Site	Late Meso - Early Neo	Early - Mid Neo	Late Neo - BA	LBA	IA
Harrow Hill	•	•		•	
Cissbury	•	•			•
Church Hill	•		•		
Blackpatch	•	•	•		
Easton Down	•	•	•		
Martin's Clump	•				
Grimes Graves			•	•	•

FIGURE 2.15 TABLE OF SUGGESTED CHRONOLOGICAL ACTIVITY AT MINE SITES

2.8 Deposition and Art at Flint Mines

There are three main areas of deposition at flint mines: surface features at the top of sites; the shaft fills themselves and, where present, the galleries. The flint mine sites in this study appear to have been re-occupied or subject to activity at various times in prehistory, evidenced mostly through differences in artefacts although there are some evidently later prehistoric surface features. Separating the early-mid Neolithic surface features and upper shaft fills from later prehistoric activity needs to be achieved as far as possible in order to meet the aims of this study in examining Neolithic deposits at flint mine sites.

Artefacts often inhabit the higher stratigraphy of shaft fills and associated features, termed as 'barrows', 'working floors' or 'dwelling pits'. While barrows and dwelling pits are more generally occurring archaeological features, it could be argued that 'working floors' is a term applied to certain features through an historical attachment to functional interpretations in the later nineteenth century and early part of the twentieth century at mining sites. However all these areas in particular require a review of published reports to determine the chronology of features and therefore their deposits.

The results here are less satisfactory than desired: the lack of radiocarbon dates, relatively few artefacts from secure contexts and variable quality of early excavation recording methods have combined to provide more of an impression of the date of mining activity, rather than a secure base for further study (Barber 2005: 96-7). Later evidence of activity at mining sites could suggest that mining was occurring into the Bronze Age at some of the Sussex sites, when it is still occurring at Grimes Graves (Mercer 1981a). With only one exception (Harrow Hill Shaft 13, McNabb *et al*. 1996), radiocarbon dates are from the base of shafts and galleries, not in shaft fills or in surface deposits.

Furthermore in terms of excavation, Harrow Hill and Cissbury have not been subjected to widespread surface investigations with most of fieldwork being focussed at both sites either amongst the shafts themselves, or discrete later Bronze Age or Iron Age remains respectively. The sites of Blackpatch and Church Hill both have recorded later Neolithic occupation either through specific radiocarbon dates or through the presence of later Neolithic and early Bronze Age pottery. This has led to some controversy with Russell (2001: 71) advocating that mining continued at Blackpatch in Sussex beyond the early Neolithic, a view which has been challenged by Barber (2005), which is discussed below. Therefore there are four archaeological features which are of concern and studied below; the possibility of the re-cutting of shafts in upper shaft fills, the working floors, the dwelling pits and barrows.

Upper Mine Shaft Fills

The refilling of mine shafts is thought to have occurred deliberately, using material from a freshly excavated shaft, with this process being punctuated with deposits which can occur in layers (Barber *et al*. 1999: 62; Russell 2001; Topping 2005). These deposits have been argued to follow ditch deposits at causewayed enclosures where artefacts and animal or human remains both form and suggest discrete episodic events (Thomas 1999a: 74-7; Russell 2001: 239). By referring to episodic deposition within flint mine shafts I do not mean to imply a great lapse of time between deposits, but more that each deposition separated within the fill of a shaft is deliberately spatially and temporally distinct. These deposits often consist of possible midden or curated material i.e. disarticulated animal bone, but can also include animal skulls and the articulated vertebrae of pigs.

There is no doubt from radiocarbon dates that the base and lower parts of shafts are Neolithic and yet in the upper fills of many shafts, artefact evidence can suggest much later dates. For example at Shaft 3a Blackpatch (Russell 2001: 38, 242) a spread of later prehistoric artefacts was excavated from the upper fill, and Romano-British pottery from Shaft 2 at Blackpatch (*ibid.*: 35). Furthermore cremations occur at Blackpatch and Church Hill within the upper fills and these can be associated with chalk charms (such as Blackpatch Shaft 7, *ibid.*: 41, or Church Hill Shaft 1 where the cremation is contained in a Bronze Age collared urn, *ibid.*: 92). This appears to date at least one example of a chalk artefact to an early Bronze Age date and yet charms are also excavated in radiocarbon dated Neolithic contexts (Chapter 5). However, how can this be interpreted? Does the presence of the cremation at Church Hill Shaft 1 date the shaft and mining activity to the Bronze Age?

Two methods of shaft re-filling are discussed in the literature: deliberate refilling and natural rapid silting. A rapid silt argument is favoured at some Grimes Graves shafts (Barber *et al.* 1999: 62). Silting has been argued as occurring in some shafts in Sussex, as up a metre of fine silting can be seen in some upper parts of shafts (e.g. Church Hill Shaft 6, Russell 2001: 111) and Pull argued that all shafts at Blackpatch exhibited deep layers of silt (*ibid.*: 92). However recent work suggesting deliberate deposits in shafts contradicts this. Therefore the problem remains how we can relate concepts of Neolithic deliberate shaft refilling with later activity. If shafts are thought to have been subject to structured and deliberate refilling, why would this have stopped in many cases *c.* 1-2m from the surface? Furthermore, the presence of chalk silt does not necessarily require a natural introduction to shafts; chalk silt could have been introduced as a fill type from other excavated features, or degraded chalk lumps left on surface spoils heaps. Simply, chalk silt is a description of a type of fill: silting is an interpretation.

The practice of depositing cultural artefacts within recuts is unchallenged at Grimes Graves with the insertion of Iron Age burials, one with an engraved chalk plaque in Mercer's 1971 excavation (1981a: 16-18). Thus, the re-cutting into mine shaft fills was certainly practised at Grimes Graves. I would suggest that in many cases the upper fills of shafts have been re-cut for the insertion of later prehistoric material and this can be seen stratigraphically at two Sussex mine shafts: Church Hill Shaft 4 and Cissbury Shaft 27. Shaft 27 had a void mentioned in the fill at a depth of 2.4m from the surface, at least 1.2m in length and 0.1 - 0.2m in diameter which Pull interpreted as the result of a perished timber ladder (Russell 2001: 233). However it appears at the level an over-cut which was made at the 'C' side of the shaft section. Most of Pull's section drawings exhibit fairly linear fills which Topping (2005: 79) argues may be a result of temporary roofing of the shaft during gaps in its episodic backfilling as at Zrzemionki in Poland, and perhaps at Harrow Hill Shaft 13. He argues that such roofing would prevent windblown accumulations within the partially open shaft. However the importance of the overcut in relation to the void should not be underestimated. This shaft contained the skeleton of a woman near the base of the shaft, degraded animal bone suggesting it originated from a midden context in the shaft fill, and chalk art both in the shaft and galleries (Chapter 4). It could be suggested that this void was created through the rotting out of a wooden post which served to mark the shaft and its inhabitant, to be returned to for further ritual activity at a later date. While no radiocarbon dates are available for the upper fill, a date of 3640-3360 cal BC (Barber *et al.* 1999: 81-2) was obtained from an antler pick at the base of this shaft. The stratigraphy in the upper levels may indicate, rather than a lack of silting, the deliberate re-cutting of the fill for further ritual activity.

Shaft 4 at Church Hill exhibits some complex stratigraphy in the upper levels which is close to the 'upper seam mining' which Barber (2005: 103-6) argues may not be contemporary with the lower shaft excavation. Pull refers to these upper levels fills as part of a 'living' or 'working' floor which exhibited some Bronze Age pottery. At layer VI the remains of a black poplar wooden bowl were excavated near some Beaker pottery and both a large and small flint axes (Russell 2001: 100). The lower levels of this shaft also contained chalk art and punch holes (see Chapter 4). It is likely that this later mining activity may in fact have been an over-cutting as part of a re-cut for the specific deposition of these later artefacts. That re-cutting and deliberate deposition should occur at mining site is entirely consistent with cultural practice in the later Neolithic, in common with other Neolithic monuments (such as Windmill Hill, Whittle *et al.* 1999; and Durrington Walls, Parker Pearson *et al.* 2007). Therefore, artefacts in upper mine shaft fills are regarded on their individual contexts for inclusion in analysis (Chapters 4 - 6).

Working Floors or Middens?

Working floors occur at Grimes Graves, Long Down, Church Hill, Blackpatch and Cissbury and are said to represent areas where flint-working took place once flint had been extracted from the mines in order to produce tools or axe roughouts. They vary in size and depth but are mostly over 2 metres in a circular or oval form and contain flint debris and nodules of various sizes. Pull excavated four chipping floors at Blackpatch, fifteen at Church Hill and three at Cissbury (Russell 2001) with more than fifty being excavated at Grimes Graves over at least as many years (Mercer 1981a: 4-5). In addition to flint nodules, large chippings and flakes and small chippings, many floors exhibit hearths, antler and bone deposits and chalk artefacts. Due to later activity at many mining sites the certainty with which the earlier activity can be separated from later deposits is both compromised and debated as discussed above (Barber 2005; Russell 2000, 2001). Hence the hearths which are present at Grimes Graves Floor 3 (Clarke 1915: 101) and Church Hill Floor 14 (Russell 2001: 137) appear contemporary with mining and therefore Neolithic, yet Floor 2 at Blackpatch which contained two large hearths (one with cremated human bone), and the hearth at Church Hill Floor 4 are more likely to be Bronze Age (Russell 2001). Chalk artefacts are found in 'working floor' contexts with a chalk lamp originating from Floor 4 at Grimes Graves (Clarke 1915: 104) and a chalk 'egg' from Long Down Floor 4 (Salisbury 1961).

Three difficulties arise when viewing these features as 'working floors'. Firstly, the deposits are not solely flint; secondly, it would be physically uncomfortable to stand on chipped flint and they are more likely to be flint 'dumps' rather than areas where flint working was taking place and thirdly the discrete nature of the floors suggest that some fencing may have been in place to contain the feature (e.g. Floor 12 at Church Hill, Russell 2001: 241). Russell tentatively indicates that these may suggest the remains of settlement activity (*ibid.*) though he does not elaborate in what form.

It is more likely they may represent a form of occupation which was possibly middenning rather than settlement. By investigating the nature of other Neolithic middens some further analysis can be offered. The midden spread on the West Kennet Avenue at the base of Waden Hill revealed a spread of worked flint and pottery *c.*100m x 40m (Smith 1965a: 210-216). The worked flint and debitage was densely packed, approaching 50 pieces per square metre (Pollard 2005). Garrow (2006: 111-13) has suggested that concentrations of flint at Over north of Site 3 may suggest evidence of a midden which provided the material for the clustered pit deposits. The working floors present at mine sites do not contain pottery, though this could be said to be indicative of the general practice of excluding pottery from the area surrounding extraction activity. While a great deal of Beaker pottery is recorded from Easton Down and Blackpatch, and Grooved Ware excavated at Grimes Graves, very little Neolithic pottery occurs elsewhere at mining sites. Furthermore, of the little pottery found at the mining sites, I have not been able to trace any deposits of it within the lower levels of shafts or within galleries. The pottery which occurs is almost exclusively Beaker from recuts into the tops of shafts and therefore is not contemporary with the radiocarbon dates from shafts (Barber *et al.* 1999: 81-2). Tiny amounts of early Neolithic pottery have been excavated from two locations: the fill of the Large Pit at Cissbury (Lane Fox 1876) and from a probable house slot on Easton Down, in between two later Beaker 'dwelling pits' (Stone 1933b: 232).

Therefore the reasons working floors may be midden deposits has been argued on the basis of their discrete form and their deposits which constitute more than simply flint chippings, showing hearths and chalk artefacts. Once we accept early-mid Neolithic pottery *may not be present*, these floors appear more akin to midden deposits. Therefore when conducting the analysis of artefacts in this study, working floors are viewed as areas for deposition which may have Neolithic deposits and therefore are assessed individually.

Dwelling Pits

Dwelling pits consist of oval or elongated depressions, 2-3m in length and no more than 0.5m depth. They often have external stake-holes and contain fragments of pottery, flint implements and flakes, animal bones and pot-boilers (Stone 1933b: 229). This type of pit was also excavated at Blackpatch and appears to be Late Neolithic/Early Bronze Age (Russell 2001: 82). The nature of these deposits is suggestive of domestic activity, though similarities to the midden at Durrington Walls Southern Circle should be emphasised (Wainwright and Longworth 1971: 38-41). The dimensions of this Durrington Walls midden are more similar to the working floors (being 12m by 6.7m) yet it is contained within an oval depression with external stake-holes at each end. It contained a large amount of pottery, flint and animal bone within ashy and charcoal deposits and recent work excavating Neolithic houses at Durrington Walls suggests that this Southern Circle midden may be the remains of a house (Parker-Pearson *et al.* 2007).

The initial interpretation of these dwelling pits being occupied by people may be valid and construe settlement evidence, though not necessarily evidence congruent with mining. They are more likely to represent episodic settlement during the re-cutting and ritual activities taking place during the Late Neolithic/Early Bronze Age. Therefore where dwelling pits do not contain pottery they are interpreted as possibly being Neolithic in date; where Late Neolithic/Early Bronze Age diagnostic pottery is present artefacts are included a this later period in analyses, yet where Bronze Age or later artefacts occur in contexts, they are excluded from the study.

Barrows

The Blackpatch 'barrows' could be said to be some of the more complex surface archaeology to interpret at flint mines. The difficulty in recording such complex structures means that much simply cannot be fully understood from the records, and as the site was bulldozed in the 1950s for post-war agriculture these answers will never be obtained through re-excavation. Piggott had argued that some Blackpatch barrows were almost certainly likely to be Neolithic (1954: 49), thoughts echoed more recently by Barber (2005: 96-7). Piggott (1954: 49) specifically proposed Barrows 3 and 12 to be of an early phase. However some of these mounds contained definitive Late Neolithic/Early Bronze Age dating material with internments, and assigning an appropriate date can appear less complex (e.g. Barrow 1, Russell 2001: 51). Barber (2005: 107) argues that the main phase of mining occurred during the early Neolithic with the later activity focusing on burials which 'underlines the continuing significance of both the flint and the place itself'. However, on closer examination the relationship between stratigraphy, dating material and mining activity provides conflicting evidence which has initiated some interpretational controversy (Russell 2001; Barber 2005). The heart of this problem is that many of the 'barrows' contain mined flint in large quantities either as a capping over the mound, or as platforms within the mound. This could indicate either:

- Some mined flint was buried at the surface to prevent 'market saturation' of prestige flint, and/or mining was taking place during the Late Neolithic/Early Bronze Age and into the Bronze Age (Russell 2001) or

- A significant quantity of Early Neolithic mined flint was unutilised for tool manufacture and left on the surface for construction of these features (Barber 2005).

In terms of attempting to provide indications of chronology for chalk artefacts and with some of these interments being associated with chalk charms, it is necessary to make conclusions regarding the individual 'barrow' features and deposits. One important factor is the suggested early-mid Neolithic prohibition on depositing pottery within shaft fills or galleries, and the common practice of doing so in the Later Neolithic and beyond. Hence, if a feature has burials with this later pottery I have interpreted it as the later dates, however if the integrity of the feature and deposit appears uncompromised and without pottery deposition I have interpreted it as contemporary with early-mid Neolithic mining.

Using this methodology, I can concur with Piggott and Barber that some of these mounds are Neolithic and large quantities of mined flint seem to have been excavated for construction of these features. Figure 2.16 suggests the period at which the primary construction of the individual features was undertaken following depositional evidence (Russell 2001). Some Late Neolithic/Early Bronze Age artefacts are present in the features I ascribe to the earlier period, but appear to have been inserted at a later date as they are not present in the primary or central deposit of the mound. This data has been used to inform artefact chronology as studied in Chapters 4-6.

In summary, settlement evidence from the early Neolithic can be characterised through interpreting the working floors as middens where the there was a strong cultural segregation of ceramics and flint extraction. Pottery was probably present, but excluded with great effect from mining and midden-mining contexts in the early-mid Neolithic. Though rather ephemeral, the suggestion of contemporary settlement activity with mining can be argued through this. While settlement evidence is more concentrated in the later Neolithic and Early Bronze Age two factors appear chronologically distinct in interpretation: the cultural exclusion of pottery appears to have relaxed from the mid-Neolithic and the dwelling pits or houses may indicate a move from mining settlement to settlement more generally at Blackpatch and Easton Down.

Blackpatch Barrows	Neolithic Construction	LNeo/EBA Construction	LNeo/EBA Insertion
1		•	•
2	•		•
3	•		
4	•		•
5			•
6			•
7		•	•
8		•	
9		•	
11		•	
12	•		

FIGURE 2.16 TABLE OF PROPOSED DATING OF BLACKPATCH 'BARROWS' INCLUDING CHALK ARTEFACTS PRESENT

2.9 Conclusion

This chapter has attempted to summarise a history of excavation and interpretation on British flint mines sites, drawing out the parameters of this study and the possible problems that exist in analysing artefacts from them. I have proposed that the functional focus on sites and on axes (their size and origin) has led to a lack of attention to deposition and examination of architecture at the flint mines. In effect, this separation of artefact from site has resulted in a lack of cohesive, integrated study. This has been further compounded due to the paucity of radiocarbon dates and the publication omissions, only partly rectified in the last seven years. Moreover, the interpretations offered often appear to be a reflection of interpretations gleaned from other sites, particularly axe quarries. The work completed on axe quarries has been more widely available and possibly this sole factor has been crucial in their analogical interpretations being applied onto mine sites. However, this does not mean that the interpretation of flint mining in England has been advanced through reflecting these interpretations, or inverting them. Indeed, one could argue that it has detracted from a chronological principle - that flint extraction has Mesolithic roots and flint mine sites are situated within existing and continuing important landscapes.

This focus on flint and functionality has also effectively excluded other artefact analyses. While the amount and type of flint waste has been discussed in various ways, other types of deposition have rarely been mentioned. There are common misconceptions regarding these which have also been discussed: the authenticity of chalk artefacts and art being a major concern. It has been assumed through the reporting of the Grimes Graves 'goddess' and phallus that chalk artefacts both dominate the assemblages from mines and may be fraudulent. Furthermore, the use or prevalence of these artefacts has mostly been removed from wider discussion and hence unconsidered. There have been few articles in the past 60 years that have explicitly discussed chalk artefacts or chalk as a symbolic substance (N. Thomas 1952; J. Thomas 1999b; Varndell 1991, 1999). Varndell's (1991) work in constructing a chalk typology is subject to much discussion in Chapter 5, and should be applauded for its lone attempt to tackle this category of substance. Neolithic art and decorated chalk blocks are subject to a full chapter of analysis (Chapter 4) and portable chalk artefacts are analysed later in Chapter 5. However, chalk artefacts are not the only deposits in mines which have been ignored: fossils, iron pyrites and animal bone have also suffered from a lack of cohesive analysis and a study of fossil and natural substances is presented in Chapter 6. In the next chapter I will discuss how our theoretical discourses have also hindered the inclusion of this material and propose ways in which we can move forward.

Chapter 3

Addressing Functionality with Materiality and Phenomenology

No artefact ever truly dies, in that as long as we can recognise it as an artefact at all it is networked in a series of complex ways with all of the other artefacts which have ever been (Thomas 1996: 61).

3.1 Introduction

The previous chapter outlined the history of flint mine excavation and interpretation. This has shown how a functional approach to both the archaeology and artefacts encountered underpinned the understanding of these sites as functional extractive sites. Functionality offers us only a common-sense approach to the archaeological record. This is problematic and has resulted in much of the less obvious archaeological evidence in mines being largely ignored. It has also created a dichotomy in the discipline in both analysis and interpretation between 'functional' and 'non-functional' artefacts which I argue can be traced back historically to the earliest archaeological studies. The aim of this research is to integrate mines and their deposits within current British Neolithic dialogues by reassessing their architecture and material culture; the theoretical and methodological issues involved in this are discussed in this chapter.

In this study there are concerns with how we identify artefacts for interpretation. In some cases within mining contexts, certain deposits have hardly been acknowledged as constituting part of the archaeological record at all. The aims of this theoretical discussion are twofold: that we should attempt to allow for all types of artefacts and contexts to be a constructive part of the archaeological record and be able to receive interpretive understandings as a result; and also that past artefacts should be recognised through the context of their deposition and not only their form. I consider that the deliberate placement of certain artefacts in an aesthetic way and within certain contexts, which could be argued as 'art', form some deposits within flint mines and suggest that we re-examine our theoretical approach to them. I propose that we view them as deposits that can be interpreted and reinterpreted through each of the significant features noted from both their form and placement. The basis of this is that artefacts are a cultural category of understanding and not simply a physical one. We do not need to recognise an artefact as consisting of a particular form, we simply need to recognise it as being part of the archaeological record and review all facets of its complexity as thoroughly as possible during interpretation.

I propose that this is best achieved within a broad phenomenological approach following directly from the work of Tilley (1994, 1999), Thomas (1996, 1999a) and Pollard (1995, 2001, 2004). While these authors have approached the archaeological record emphasising aspects such as architecture, landscape and deposition using phenomenology, I have brought these elements together and attempted only a minimal separation in a phenomenological interpretation. In discussing evidence in this way it seems impossible to state what might be classed as an artefact, or a deposit, or architectural factor, when each term might be equally relevant to the same context. Hence this chapter discusses my approach to the nature of artefacts and context in the archaeological record both theoretically and methodologically. Theoretically, materiality is used (see 3.4) not as a way of examining one aspect of an assemblage in relation to others, but rather as an integrated approach to artefact, context, deposition and substance. In attempting to incorporate these different types of evidence, consideration is given to how we both identify and interpret contexts and artefacts, which commences with a history of past approaches (3.2) before examining the relationship between artefacts and the interpretive tools of personhood and materiality (3.3, 3.4). Furthermore, the architecture of mines has never been considered as an active space but rather space simply created as a by-product of extraction activity. Identifying artefacts within archaeological spaces allows us to use structured deposition as both a theoretical and methodological tool, reinterpreting architectural aspects to deposition (3.5). Using structured deposition provides particular benefits in this way which will be outlined in detail.

In methodological terms, recognising artefacts has been a practical activity in this study, the results of which form the analysis in Chapter 4, 5 and 6. How chalk artefacts have been recognised and categorised or discounted and excluded is discussed together with the other methodological issues in 3.6. In conclusion I propose that the theoretical basis of this research allows for a structured encompassing study of the archaeological record following broad disciplinary norms. Yet, the approach I outline enables the consideration of previously unstudied artefacts in our interpretations of the British Neolithic.

3.2 A History of Artefact Studies

It is suggested that within archaeology the way artefacts are studied is initially through their function and then form. This appears to have had a historical origin, with the construction of artefact as a category being discussed further in 3.3. In this section I outline how if an object had a perceived past 'function', it was classed as an 'artefact' and as such formed the core of modern understandings of typology and context. It is proposed that functionality for an artefact is only ever inferred through analogies to either a comparable society's artefacts or other artefacts from the same society and illustrate the problems encountered with this approach.

The Creation of Functional (Practical) and Non-functional (Ritual) Artefacts

The fifteenth and sixteenth century collectors of curiosities made no distinction between artefacts originating as a result of human activity or geology (Trigger 1989: 47). It was not until the later sixteenth and seventeenth centuries that cross-cultural analogies were beginning to be used to infer the origin and use of stone axes, a process which continued over more than a hundred years (*ibid.*: 52). Therefore function was initially a way of recognising archaeological artefacts through analogy as separate from natural geological objects. As human activity was the secondary interpretation of these artefacts, it is rather unsurprising that the early modern studies of objects commenced with classification systems brought to archaeology from primarily geological and palaeontological frameworks (*ibid.*: 92).

While functionality may seem a simple concept, this use of analogy created a particular interpretive framework in which functionality was understood. Socio-cultural evolutionary ideas had followed swiftly from the biological evolution argued in Darwin's publication of *On the Origin of Species* in 1859. Tylor and Morgan both argued in the 1860s that technology indicated the social development of societies from savagery to civilisation. The work of Lubbock (1865) intertwined this vividly with cross-cultural generalisations to compare past prehistoric societies with those of modern (in many cases recently encountered) tribal societies (Trigger 1989: 92). These cross-cultural generalisations held the belief that artefacts and their technology will improve over time, as cultures and people evolve. Therefore the axe, seen in flayed, expanded, chipped, cast types is first defined as an 'axe', which is used for the same purpose in cross-cultural terms and then defined through substance (stone, flint, bronze, iron etc). Societies could therefore be differentiated, based upon their states of enlightenment or savagery, through both technology and substances used: a metal axe would indicate a more advanced society than a society that used stone axes. Function is therefore intrinsically linked with subsistence and technology; the purpose of functional artefacts is to aid subsistence hence the most technologically advanced artefacts were seen to be indicative of a more complex culture. Lubbock also created a scheme of religious hierarchy within his analysis suggesting that societies would move through stages of religious belief dependant on their cultural evolutionary stage, encompassing 'atheism, fetishism, totemism, shamanism, anthropomorphism and ethical monotheism' (Insoll 2004: 43). Other artefacts were acknowledged as being part of ritual or religious systems, but viewed as part of a different interpretive structure solely understood in those terms (*ibid.*: 43-4).

In summary, from this earliest period in the discipline, functional (practical) artefacts were seen as belonging to different comparable analogical structures than non-functional (or spiritual) artefacts. Therefore we could argue that artefacts themselves within each society studied are firstly subject to this conceptual division. This division appears to have been accepted within the discipline until very recently. Frequently discussions of non-functional artefacts were concerned with finding evidence of religion or spiritual activity and belief in the past. For example, Childe changed his view on religion throughout his career. While understanding the importance of what religion can add to interpretations through ethnography, he eventually concluded that determining questions of belief in the past would be difficult. He instead advocated that a study of technological matters (hence technological objects) would produce practical results rather than conjecture (Trigger 1989: 262). 'Ritual' was used as a term by Childe (1940: 51) implying regular practices suggestive of religious connotations, hence the division of technology and more ethereal concerns of the past was both quite clear when confronted with archaeological material, and rather obtuse at the same time. In practical terms, technological artefacts were obviously functional, and religious artefacts non-technological or 'non-functional'. Or 'non-functional' artefacts were, by definition, indicative of ritual or religious activity.

The narrative structure of culture-history included cross-cultural analogies in narrative form and often led to rather grand statements on religion and ritual in prehistory. Religion, mortuary ritual and other belief systems were seen as unattainable through archaeology, though they were acknowledged as concepts which would have been present in prehistoric societies. Artefacts which had not been recognised as functional began to be seen as possibly indicative of these societal uses. For example, Christopher Hawkes's proposed 'ladder of inference' (1954) explicitly rather than implicitly argued that technological and economic questions were more easily answered than religious ones, and it is a rare example of explicit archaeological attention to religious questions for this date (Insoll 2004: 46). He believed that religion could be inferred archaeologically though only after technological questions had been answered. However, many authors used ritualistic or religious terms to describe artefacts encountered as both individual types and deposits. While a full detailed discussion of these is out of the scope of this chapter, a few examples in the literature include an amber amulet discussed as being part of upper Palaeolithic hunting-magic (Bibby 1959: 176), fossil sea urchins thought of as 'sun-symbols' in burials (J. Hawkes 1951: 52) and a later example of the presence of fossil sea urchins in a Whitehawk burial seen as 'spells' (Jessup 1970: 72).

The New Archaeology of the 1960s brought a systemic approach to the operation of culture, bringing a systemic approach to artefacts. Binford divided objects into three types: techonomic artefacts which were used by the society to manage their environment; sociotechnic artefacts for operations within the social system; and ideotechnic artefacts relating to ideological concerns (Trigger 1989: 298). Binford (1962) accepted that certain objects may contain one or more of these traits and while he argued that determining each of these artefact category's function within a past social system is similarly challenging, and that the role of an artefact be it symbolic or practical should be easily read, he accepted that archaeologists at that time needed to be ethnologists in order to infer social and religious concerns from the archaeological record. In other words he queried the skill base of archaeologists to achieve this at all. The hypothetico-deductive method he advanced enabled work on burial practices, previously seen as religious and hence unstudied. Yet later in his career he became more pessimistic and there are two examples of Binford's own work where ideotechnic artefacts or architecture were ignored: the shrines of the Nunamiut; and the presence of red ochre at four sites in Michigan (Insoll 2004: 48-9). To summarise, while he divided artefacts into three conceptual types from which different interpretive methods could be employed, functionality was only ever returned to as an interpretive category through both sociotechnic and technomic artefacts: ideotechnic artefacts were still largely ignored in interpretation.

At a similar time, Grahame Clark took a different approach to investigating the past (Trigger 1989: 266). He preferred to focus on ethnographic analogies but did not accept that societies at particular stages of evolution would be similar enough to each other for cross-cultural generalisations. Crucially for our purpose, he determined that *analogies had to be drawn only between individual artefacts rather than whole cultures* (*ibid.*). This was refined in the Star Carr report where he stated that it was appropriate to draw analogies between different contexts if they are technologically and ecologically comparable (Clark 1954). He argued they should only be treated as suggestive analogies rather than definitive ones yet in many senses he is simply diluting and reiterating the cross-cultural generalisation of Lubbock, not in cultural evolutionary terms, but in taking a rather piecemeal approach to the use of analogy.

Marxist archaeology, a concept which Childe also advocated in the 1950s, became more widespread in the 1970s and 1980s as structural Marxism in British archaeology. Its perception and approach to artefacts, and their role in past societies, provides an important stage in the development towards current approaches to artefacts. Marxist archaeology is similar to New Archaeology in seeing artefacts as components within a social system in a functional manner and this is often reliant on ethnographic analogies with work by Marxist anthropologists. Following Marx the approach focuses on the forces of production (artefacts) and relations of production (social aspects; workers and managers). Hence, the ideologies of a community are the outcome of their daily experience, an experience which is structured by the way they work and subsist. This includes the production of artefacts and their way of being produced as part of daily practices, practices which reinforce the dominant ideology. While Marxist production schemes were at the core of some debate within anthropology during this time regarding scales and scope of production within kin or non-kin, agricultural or hunter-gatherer based systems, all emphasised the presence of a dominant ruling class (be it clan based or familial) which could be viewed through comparative conspicuous wealth (Layton 1998: 138-147)

In this view, artefacts are not only systemic and produced by individuals, but crucially are divided into 'prestige' and 'normal' artefacts, indicative of functional distinctions within a given society. Instead of being just parts of a system, classified and structured in an economic, functional or ideological (ritual/religious) way, through Marxist archaeology they become, in a sense, internally ranked within their own classification system. In simple terms, there are 'prestige' functional, 'prestige' economic and 'prestige' ideological artefacts, where prestige affords them a sense of commodification – they can be exchanged within a society. Therefore, artefacts themselves are subject to a system where certain artefacts afford more power than others within a society through their ability to be exchanged. Non-functional or ritual artefacts are still defined as a separate category and can be subject to a further internal division of ranking. While Insoll (2004) argues that we need to place religion at the centre of our analysis, I would suggest that we simply need to understand artefacts differently.

In summary, I propose that while there has been a great deal of change in the theory the outcomes are surprisingly similar in the creation and maintenance of functional and non-functional artefact categories. Due to early cross-cultural generalisations and later use of analogy, functional artefacts only exist within a framework of non-functional artefacts and vice versa: they support each other. However, early studies on artefacts also led to a different focus on artefacts: typology.

Substance, Typology and Context

Typological studies began following the categorical separation of geological objects and humanly made artefacts. The work of Montelius in the 1880s in creating typologies of archaeological artefacts across Europe was fundamental, with a goal of this being to devise a chronology (Trigger 1989: 155-6). Thomsen advocated an approach to determining chronology through the typology of 'closed finds' and was very influential; 'closed finds' representing objects found together in burial, hoard or other grouping which suggested they were deposited at the same time (*ibid.*: 76). At this early time context and object were seen by the Danish archaeologist Müller as relational, and Müller argued an artefact should not be encompassed within a typology without a secure context (Hodder 1999: 86). Context at this early stage is therefore simply an acknowledgement of the contemporaneity of a group of artefacts.

These three concepts, typology, context and substance, therefore often met interpretively with the goal being chronology. Chronological studies at this period were largely within theoretical understanding of social evolution. Hence, the main component part of typologies was substance, as substance (bronze, iron or stone) was seen as a way of assessing how civilised a group was. Substance is therefore a key component to understanding function. Different substances formed the basis of these early typological structures in order to quantify this initial social evolutionary question.

Few writers of any period have returned to this debate and the discipline is currently structured following this early typological separation. While we broadly adhere to categories of substance in our physical analyses, I will propose our artefact and substance categories are perhaps interpretively normative and as a result, restricted. Renfrew (1976: 159-60) does discuss interpreting substance following Marxist thought and proposes how prestige goods can have an historic or association value and an intrinsic value which is based on substance. The substance can have a higher intrinsic value due either to the rarity of the substance or the amount of labour required in its manufacture. Furthermore, Renfrew specifies that a prestige good made of a commonly acquired substance is usually indicative of a ritual artefact. He is therefore illustrating two beliefs: the rarer the substance the more socially important the artefact, yet a ritual artefact may have social power even when constructed of a ubiquitous substance. Artefacts are still divided as non-functional (ritual) or functional, with substance constructing part of the reason for this separation.

These approaches to the past resulted in interpretations of the British Neolithic based on the commodification of artefacts. Hence, as prestige artefacts can be exchanged, the distribution of artefacts, the methods by which that may occur and the social distinctions they may indicate became prevalent discourses in archaeological interpretations of the late 1970s and into the early 1990s, especially with regard to flint and stone axes. As chalk is an ubiquitous substance, easily available, easily worked in small amounts and there is no evidence of exchange (though this could be a result of the lack of study), chalk artefacts do not meet the interpretive logic of structural Marxism as being acknowledged as prestige, exchange goods. Hence, following Renfrew's argument that it is only usual for ritual artefacts to be made of a ubiquitous substance in order to be classed as prestigious, chalk artefacts became classed as ritual artefacts. This is in essence an interpretation based of their apparent lack of functionality through their substance.

Summary

The argument that 'most, if not all archaeological argument from artifact typology to evolutionary theory, is based on analogy and comparison' (Hodder 1999: 47) creates a serious situation with regard to the acceptance of objects as artefacts. The historical factors discussed above influenced the discipline from its inception, yet I also suggest that analogy as a tool has played a pivotal role in the non-acceptance of chalk artefacts within interpretations of the British Neolithic. Analogies still form a determined core in archaeological interpretation. Wylie's (1985: 93). discussion on analogy explicitly examines how analogy works in practice: 'analogical inference consists of the selective transposition of information from source to subject on the basis of a comparison that, fully developed, specifies how the "terms" compared are similar, different, or of unknown likeness'. She discusses this as 'relevance', where there is a re-structuring of source and subject to enable further connections to be made between them and hence produce 'relational analogies' (*ibid.*: 94-5). However, all analogy requires the first initial step of an indication of similarity between source and subject. It is likely that objects which could not be compared ethnographically through analogy (as they did not occur in other tribal societies, or at least not widely) have been simply dismissed. Stone axes, found in many societies allow us to imagine similar societies in the past, the use of non-functional materials was often not seen as related to the same analogical schemes. This lack of integration through ethnographic analogy is only part of the reason chalk and other substances have not been included as artefacts – the way we construct 'artefact' as a category for interpretation is also a crucial component of this problem.

3.3 Defining Archaeological Artefacts and their Ambiguity

The following section seeks to deconstruct into stages how we view artefacts. Whilst the process of excavation seeks to extract all artefacts contained within archaeological features, not all objects are perceived as artefacts. I will demonstrate how both bias and a disciplinary emphasis on specific questions influence how we interpret at many levels within the discipline.

Artefacts as a category form a theoretical cornerstone of archaeological interpretation, being the material conditions of past social life. Opinions on artefacts therefore differ while encompassing how we treat them categorically, scientifically and philosophically. It is widely assumed that we recognise artefacts as being the result of humanly altered materials within an archaeological context (but see later discussion). Additionally, artefacts are seen as being similar to objects, and the words 'objects' and 'artefacts' are often used interchangeably, being applied to specific recognisable forms. These forms have been initially determined by their form (or morphology) and are historically based on perceptions of past use (with use being determined by form). While we may imagine there is a traditional terminology for studying specific substances, or nomenclature, our investigative structure is not substance based although it is presented as if it were. I suggest instead that it commenced through a focus towards the perceived use of an object (or function) in the past, achieved through ethnographic analogies. Nomenclature is a useful and necessary part of building structure and meaning within the discipline. However, within any categorisation system there can be assumptions and weaknesses which have impacted on the study of chalk artefacts and other material remains from the Neolithic. This is best explained through examples.

Fired clay remains can be termed variously as pottery, pottery vessels, pot sherds, pot fragments, fired clay and baked clay. Pottery is in itself a cultural term, implying the process of potting (the creation of vessels) and when this is applied to excavated objects that resemble pottery vessels, the prefix 'pot' or 'pottery' is included in its description. However, while all pottery vessels consist of 'baked' or 'fired' clay, those terms are only used when referring to objects that do not resemble vessels. From Neolithic and Early Bronze Age sites these are usually clay balls but some pieces may be suggestive of daub. Hence, they do not appear within the site reports as part of the pottery assemblage but occur in a separate section, as at Etton (Pryor 1998), Mount Pleasant (Wainwright 1979: 180) and Durrington Walls (Wainwright & Longworth 1971:188). Specifically, this suggests they are not studied by pottery specialists (as they are not vessels), yet they are materially of the same substance. If the material produced from fired clay was instead of balls or pieces of daub, beautiful structured clay plaques, it is likely they would be included for further study by pottery specialists as they would be seen as a cultural artefact. This raises the question: is a clay ball less of a cultural artefact than a pottery vessel?

Similarly, faunal remains are studied as examples of past consumption patterns and can provide suggestions regarding economic strategies such as herd management or hunting. This bias continues in the division between 'wild' and 'domesticated' species apparent in site reports, especially at the perceived economic divide of the Mesolithic-Neolithic transition. The emphasis on domesticates omits by default the many questions we could ask of faunal remains, such as to what extent did wild species contribute to socio-economic strategies? Did they play any part in ritual or symbolic life? Furthermore, certain categories of faunal artefact are not well studied, such as antler or bone combs, as their function is ambiguous. These again occur in separate sections of excavation reports yet no studies have encompassed their presence nationally during the Neolithic. Hill (1995) has criticised the dichotomy which exists between the interpretation of human and animal remains where the former are seen as 'ritual' and the latter economic. While comparing the culture : nature dichotomy of objects to the wild : domesticated dichotomy of animals is not without its problems, I am simply suggesting here how these discourses function within the discipline. Bones can be (as clay balls) arguably cultural artefacts in their own right, yet are sidelined in favour of economic arguments, or in another term, function. Human remains and their associated deposits are always seen as more critical to interpretation than other types of bone evidence. Thus, in summary, we can argue that in terms of perceived importance to interpretation in the British Neolithic, human remains are most important followed by domesticated animals, bone products and then wild species. How did this type of ranking appear in the discourse, and is it helpful in interpreting the archaeological record and context?

This process can also be extended to flint products which are viewed in a more complex way. While flint is investigated in some senses in a similar way to pottery (yet with debitage studied), flint can also be seen as forming architectural features within the archaeological record. Hence flint axes, knives, scrapers and waste flakes are examined as cultural artefacts, yet the raw material (nodules) forming created 'platforms' or specific deposits are not considered as active artefacts. The strategy of examining nodules is not fixed within the discipline; nodules are often simply mentioned as contributing to features or contexts and so quantifiable data is absent. The ubiquitous nature of flint nodules within the subsoil of the chalklands of southern England has, I believe, led to some confusion with regard to how seriously we should view these and it can be argued that occasional flint nodules in archaeological depositions are a result of accidental inclusion. However, within identifiable contexts as platforms or flint cairns or cappings, little attention is given to the past retrieval strategies of flint for that purpose. Why do we regard the same substance in such a different way: why is the source of a flint axe a more important question than the sourcing, transportation and creation of a flint capping on a barrow? A wider question might be: when does (in form) a naturally occurring object become a cultural artefact? How do these objects imply context, if at all?

In one of the rare discussions on the physicality of material culture, Thomas argues that while an artefact is buried, it is never completely de-contextualised from its past social context and 'it will still give indications to its discoverers of its character *as an artefact*, of some kind' (1996: 61, his emphasis). He continues:

> when we come to interpret archaeological evidence, we will rarely find ourselves looking at something which outwardly *appears* so completely 'Other' that it escapes being immediately recontextualised through our prejudices and assumptions, before we have any opportunity to interrogate it analytically. No artefact ever truly dies, in that as long as we can recognise it as an artefact at all it is networked in a series of complex ways with all of the other artefacts which have ever been (*ibid.*: his emphasis).

Thomas is therefore acknowledging the importance of recognition as an interpretive tool and that both the context and artefact need to be recognised. Hodder also discusses artefacts, referring to them as objects explaining that 'objects only exist within traditions of inquiry' (1999: 15). For example, during excavation sieving objects of a smaller size than the sieve would result in them being lost and not acknowledged. He also adds that the specialisation of archaeological science has permitted a fragmenting of the discipline and therefore what Thomas refers to as analytical interrogation, may involve many people and processes (Hodder 1999: 12-3). Returning to the relationships between artefact and context Hodder continues: 'at the primary level of data analysis, interpretive *theory constructs objects* in a number of ways' (1999: 84, his emphasis), and '*theory also constructs context*' (ibid.: 85, his emphasis). Or to summarise, '*So definition of objects depends on interpretation of contexts and definition of contexts depends on interpretation of objects*' (ibid..: 86, his emphasis).

This relationship between object, artefact and context needs to be seen as relational and reflexive. I argue that (following Hodder), as it is a reciprocal hermeneutic process, when one part of this relational process is weak it impacts on the whole process of defining both the artefact and the context. One can see that this is another pivotal part to understanding the problems associated with examining chalk objects (or rather, chalk artefacts) in addition to other materials previously unconsidered. I have argued that the current categorisation system of artefacts has been static since late Victorian times and that this has permitted both a loss of non-functional materials in scientific archaeological analysis, and also a loss of the understanding of their depositional context. Thus, in Thomas's terms, the chalk objects, fossils, iron pyrites and other material discussed in this book have not been recognised as artefacts. It is possible that they are seen as completely 'Other' and so do not reach the next stage he mentions of analytical interrogation, or as that they have already been acknowledged as natural fossil or chalk they have been categorised as non-artefacts due to the lack of an archaeological typology.

In Hodder's terms, this also influences the archaeological perception and recognition of the context. Hence, the application of the term 'artefact' to any material is a theoretical problem based on the theoretical relationship between context and object. If we do not recognise the context we do not recognise the artefact, or vice versa. As our discipline has been founded on analogy and comparison (Hodder 1999: 47), we could argue that in many senses our theoretical limits have been similarly constricted in that perhaps we have only recognised ethnographic contexts within archaeological ones.

3.4 Theoretical Basis of this Study: Integrating Materiality and Personhood

I have outlined some problems that exist within the discipline with regard to both identifying and categorising artefacts. Throughout this I have suggested that the functional and non-functional categories have resulted in an unbalanced approach to studying artefacts where some categories or sub-categories of archaeological evidence are seen as more relevant, or easier to interpret, than others. This bias could be argued as producing an unnecessarily closed interpretive system which excludes some artefacts and hence also some interpretations. I propose to approach these theoretical problems in several ways. This research aims to interpret deposits in flint mines which requires specific sequential stages: identifying artefacts; interpreting their status as part of a typology; and interpreting them in relation to other artefacts, deposits and architecture. While the theoretical approach advocated here has influenced the identification of artefacts and interpreting their typology, it has mainly involved methodological concerns which are addressed in detail in section 3.6. Once identification is complete, interpretation necessitates a consideration of both spatial depositional analysis and the possibility of deliberate structure in deposits, yet also how the artefact or deposit as an active component may aid interpretation of Neolithic cultural understandings. Or simply, what the combinations of artefacts and deposits may have meant in the past and how that relates to differing scales of analysis at the site and intra-site level.

Theoretically attention needs to be given to matters of both a philosophical and practical focus. I have chosen to view philosophical human engagement with artefacts through concepts of materiality and personhood, which are themselves seen through the broader perceptions of phenomenology. In practical terms I have followed structured deposition, an established practice seen in more recent Neolithic studies (3.5). Hence the understanding of artefacts I propose follows a consideration of materiality and personhood, with how I propose to view and interpret deposits following a consideration of structured deposition.

Defining Materiality

The most complex part of archaeology is the integration and interpretation of the relationship between person and artefact in the past. The way of expressing this mediation is both theoretical and philosophical. This discussion therefore moves between explaining materiality and how this relates both to persons and artefacts.

Materiality could be argued to be a seductive term, in that it is so often used in differing contexts within archaeology that its meaning is difficult to qualify. The Oxford English Dictionary states that materiality considers the matter, not form, of reasoning. Therefore, what follows is that reason and structure are shown through materiality, but meaning is not. However, while certain approaches are more similar than others, the initial interpretive separation is that between the scientific and theoretical approaches to materiality and could be said to form two main branches of analyses. The first is a data driven approach in defining the physicality of the artefact in terms of bounded scientific schemes (argued by Meskell as stemming from material culture studies), which does not 'automatically engage with social relations' (2005: 2). In being scientific it seeks to define the actuality of substance of the artefact, the defining chemical properties of the constituent elements of it. In this way, materiality is reducible to a defined set of facts and any social interpretive element may or may not be included. The theoretical approach examines the role that the substance of the artefact has in relation to the society it appears within, or as Meskell (*ibid.*) suggests 'the unstable terrain of interrelationships between sociality, temporality, spatiality and materiality'. While the substance is acknowledged as important, materiality is essentially conceptual in that it is a physical manifestation (artefact) of an understanding of substance in the singular, and substances in the plural. Thus, materiality as a concept is used both in encountering and defining substance objectively and interpreting the social placement of the substance as active within the society studied.

DeMarrias *et al.* (2004: 2) argue that there is a further division within theoretical materiality approaches, the materialist approach. This directs an interpretive emphasis towards 'the ways that power and authority develop through control over material and symbolic sources' and so have their history within Marxist approaches to material culture. The materialist approach is one which has been extensively used within studies the British Neolithic and was discussed earlier in 3.2 and will be further in 3.5. Again, these theoretical definitions of materiality have tended to diversity rather than cohesion (Jones 2002). Hence, for example, Schiffer (1999) sees people and things as separate, materiality encompassing all things including matter and energy. However he sees these as devices for communication: interactors, and the main body of his work focuses on how things create interactions between people through performance in different settings. Jones's (2004: 330) later suggestion that materiality as a concept 'encompasses the view that material or physical components of the environment and the social practices enacted in that environment are mutually reinforcing' is rather objective, a view seen as too simplistic by Needham (2005: 194-5) as other factors within the society are not considered.

Gosden (1994) suggests people encounter the landscape and artefacts through their bodies; a view shared by Tilley (1999) following the phenomenologist Merleau-Ponty. Phenomenologically, materiality as a concept considers substance, the substance of things and human reason, but not meaning. Yet, once we understand something as a substance, it has meaning (Thomas, pers comm.). Pollard (2004: 48) defines materiality as 'how the character of the world is comprehended, appropriated and involved in human projects', so extending the idea of materials into a cosmological understanding. In this study I follow these approaches, which define substance as socially active within a society and part of a human-encountered experience. A full review of phenomenology or phenomenological approaches within archaeology cannot be accommodated here, however the interpretations argued in this work as artefacts being materially active in their substance, in addition to being socially active in respect to their use and deposition, require further discussion.

Situating Materiality within Phenomenology and Personhood

The first step within this is to define the parameters and structure of at what level a person encounters an understanding of substance. This consideration fundamentally lies at a philosophical level through both theories of personhood and phenomenology (how people reason with materials, architecture, nature and so on, is based on their experience of engagement with them). These understandings are complex and create a sympathetic and yet multi-layered tension between the physical properties of substance, the cultural understanding of that substance (and how that is either created or somehow pre-existing), and their cultural expression through form. These theories therefore meet at both the person and the artefact.

Phenomenology has a greater history in this regard and personhood could be said to be reliant on this approach. Brentano was ancestral to the phenomenological tradition and in the late nineteenth century began to describe 'descriptive psychology' as a way of understanding and describing 'cognitive acts', rather than a study of neurological processes (Thomas 2006: 44). Brentano's use of 'intentionality' states that mental processes are directed at conscious activity where they are 'connected to each other relationally which makes them comprehensible' (*ibid.*).

Husserl refined this in using phenomenology as the separation between things with are understood by 'intuitive' means, ie. that something becomes apparent because it is recognisable, and a 'phenomenological reduction', where we aim to challenge our intuition by exploring the means to which we came to our intuitive understanding. Thomas (*ibid.*) explains this as moving away from what Husserl describes as a 'natural attitude', or intuition, through 'reduction', self-questioning our perceptions in order to illuminate the processes to which we come to understanding the significance of an object. Mediations have been offered by later philosophers to argue how this operates, with Merleau-Ponty arguing that the human body is pivotal in this relationship. Tilley's study of the Dorset Cursus, encountering other monuments and natural features while moving around it, follows Merleau-Ponty's view that the human body 'provides the fundamental mediation point between thought and the world' (Tilley 1994: 14). Once this is established, Tilley argues that his body (and through it) his thoughts and feelings on traversing the Dorset Cursus can allow for interpreting the thoughts and feelings of people in the past.

Theories of personhood argue that the notion of individuality is not universal and that people do not always understand themselves as being separate entities either from each other, or from other animals, or substances, or artefacts (Fowler 2004). Hence, the human body which Merleau-Ponty sees as a translating structure is not perceived of as a cultural boundary and therefore the conscious (or habitual) thought or mediation is simply not present when encountering the world. In effect, phenomenology is an argument of how humans understand their environment through their cultural (and social) placement from birth. Personhood has grown from this premise with the acknowledgment that what constitutes a person is also culturally specific. Hence, materiality used here seeks to integrate humans with artefacts in both a practical anthropological artefactual way and also a method of attempting to discover how these types of artefacts were understood by humans during their use in the Neolithic.

A Phenomenological Materiality

Materiality and personhood have provided avenues with which to further explore artefacts interpretively. Anthropology has had a key role in the understanding of artefacts, as without living people to talk to about their material world and how they understand themselves in relation to it, we would find it difficult to begin to use phenomenological reduction and view artefacts as 'human' or active in any but the most practical functional ways. The important suggestion which links artefacts and humans is that societies construct people the way they construct objects (Kopytoff 1988: 90), a view which has enabled archaeologists to try to interpret this inversely. Tilley (2004: 218) recognises this same concept through the dialectical thought of Hegel and Marx. So, the social construction of a past society can be seen through the social construction of artefacts: if we can access the social construction of artefacts it can give us clues to how the society was constructed. Ingold has followed the phenomenologist Heidegger in promoting a 'dwelling' perspective in terms of human engagement with the world. He sees materiality as an engagement where objects are created through the substance encountered (e.g. Ingold 2000: 339-348). In this cited example, Ingold talks of weaving a basket, and discusses how the basket can be said to 'become' a basket rather than have a cultural idea impressed upon it. Therefore, artefacts are 'created', and at a depth through the engagement of the person with the substance – artefacts are not simply stamped with a cultural blueprint.

However, in terms of how human engage with materials these approaches could be argued as being historically situated. Within chronologically differing studies one cannot escape the implications of both chronology and societies' access to differing substances or approaches to material culture. While Renfrew (2001; 2004) has argued that this 'sapient paradox' represents the elaboration of material culture which appears at the start of agriculture (rather than at the appearance of anatomically modern humans) and is hence concerned primarily with a philosophically broad approach to humankind and cognition, at the other end of the spectrum historical archaeologists and historians examine fetishism with specific artefact types, such as the toothbrush in nineteenth century Bogotá (Ammann 2005). It cannot be denied that the wealth of materials and survival in later and contemporary anthropological or archaeological research, historical records and past sedentary environments, influence our interpretations. In many cases it is likely different approaches to materiality were prevalent at different times, and our interpretations reflect the scale with which we examine materiality. The way people use materials to reason with will alter dependent on their environments (social and physical) and we should not attempt to define one approach which is correct or all-encompassing.

Ingold (2007) has argued for a return to studying materials in his approach to materiality. He believes that will increase the effectiveness of studying materiality by discussing the change substances can embody through their existence within a cultural world. Hence he invites the reader to collect a pebble, immerse it in water and leave it to dry while they read his text. He uses the metaphor of the wet stone slowly drying to imply differences in its visual interaction in a cultural approach to materiality (*ibid.*). However, his arguments have sparked criticism from archaeologists and anthropologists alike (e.g. Tilley 2007a; Knappett 2007) which are perhaps caused directly through these general approaches advocated to encompass both archaeological (historic and prehistoric) and anthropological debates. Ingold's call to direct more attention to materials than materiality suggests we take an almost autistic dialectic view with interpretation. If within each interpretation or discussion of artefacts or 'things' we are required to reassemble the scientific materiality of one particular substance in all its individual mutable forms, we will simply create multiple mutable interpretations. This in many senses may be an admirable wish, but is it feasible? Interpreting substances within materiality is an important part of interpretations of materiality, but for archaeologists the placement, use and chronological implications of artefacts are on what the discipline is necessarily based. We therefore need to balance the theoretical requirements of the discipline within the practical parameters of discourse. We need to acknowledge that substance is an important factor both solely and as part of artefact construction (similarly including physical, metaphorical and cultural concerns). These nested scales of interpretation with regard to the relationship between substance and artefact are essential. Yet again, as archaeologists we necessarily need to return to the artefact itself.

Summary

I have argued that chalk objects were not wholly classed as chalk artefacts and do not have a typology and classification system primarily because they did not appear relevant in ethnographic societies encountered during Victorian times. I have also argued that as chalk is not seen as a functional substance, it is not considered that chalk objects should be properly classed as artefacts and moreover, not examined as equally meaningful to other artefacts (with few variations, see 3.5). This initially followed socio-cultural evolutionary thought and then Marxist beliefs on production and social value. Furthermore, chalk has often been considered as a by-product of other activities: the creation of banks from ditches, spoil heaps from mining – a passive rather than active substance. For example, the human perception of chalk in the Neolithic has often been discussed within an understanding of the importance of monumentality in the chalklands of southern Britain. These arguments often work inversely; chalk is important because it is white and will allow a visual impact to be made in monumental terms and hence it is the visuality of chalk which marked it as important. However, Thomas (1999b) has referred to the digging of chalk and its re-deposition as a form of reciprocity with the earth and while his argument concerns chalk it may equally be applied to other sub-soils where pits or monuments are present. Bender (1998: 47-55) follows Thomas in arguing that chalk as a substance forms the base of later monumental elaborations incorporating other substances such as earth, wood and stone. In following Madagascan ethnography Bender argues that while wood was seen as once living, chalk and stone may contrast with fertility, and hence chalk and stone may have been seen as infertile (*ibid.*: 45). Parker Pearson and Ramilisonina have also used this ethnography to discuss that Neolithic understandings may have treated stone as affiliated with the dead and wood with the living (1998). And yet, if this is the case, how would the understandings of wooden monuments on the chalklands differ to those off the chalk? Can chalk be understood as dead like stone, or 'once living' like wood?

Tilley (2007b: 339-40) has argued that while the visuality of monuments in the Neolithic was integral to their positioning in the landscape, he proposes that chalk was important as it contained flint. Hence as chalk produces oddly shaped flint; flint which may look like bones, flint may have been perceived as ancestral bones and been incorporated into monuments deliberately as a part of deliberate deposition. The importance of chalk is therefore understood as it being visually distinctive (though the same could be said of, for example, orange clay subsoil) and containing another substance which had ancestral significance (flint 'ancestral' bone), but where does the materiality of chalk itself form the base of these understandings? Flint also occurs in clay-with-flint geological deposits hence the materiality of clay could also be included. Tilley's argument perhaps relates more to the materiality of flint, than chalk.

For this study an understanding of chalk as a substance is required. It is the substance encountered during flint extraction and in doing so the mines, as entities, are created from it. Artefacts are made from it, architectural forms built from it. Marks are made on the chalk walls and deposits are made within the chalk voids. The materiality of chalk as a substance is necessary for this study, as this study rests upon chalk being understood in cultural terms. Thomas (1999b) discusses how the materiality of objects may influence their understanding in bringing elements of their substance; qualities and influences which add to their embodiment. He further proposes that chalk artefacts are related to transformative activities at causewayed enclosures and hence chalk artefacts may be related to human bone and polished flint axes as key symbols in the Neolithic (*ibid.*). While these arguments combine materiality and embodiment, the meaning of chalk is still elusive with a concept of materiality and indeed the only interpretive progressions made are through depositional relationships. These will be explored in more detail with regard to chalk artefacts within this book.

Other substances found in deposits have also been widely ignored: fossils, antler picks and iron pyrites; while conversely the traditional artefacts of flint, pottery and bone have been subject to increasingly elaborate scientific methods of study to still answer economic or functional questions. Tilley refers to this separation of materials, that there are things which are made (artefacts) or encountered (unaltered materials) (2007a: 19). I challenge this in two respects. Firstly, *encountering* is a specific type of engagement. Tilley's wish to separate these is not reflective of changing practice but rather our fixed perceptions of what artefacts are. One encounters other people, animals and the weather. We encounter experiences we do not control. In an archaeological sense, we might encounter new monumental forms or landscapes as we participate alongside the experience of engaging with them. If we contrast this with artefacts, humanly made and constructed from substances, this is a type of action one controls. We create artefacts and they become socially significant through this process. However, we cannot encounter a fossil we have excavated from chalk because in order to interact with it, we have extracted it. We do not encounter iron pyrites as sentient beings, we experience them as physical deposits. Antler is retrieved from a shed site, or cut from the skull of a dead deer. Our actions in containing these substances create them as artefacts. We control them, and our experience of them is bounded through this. We create their significance through the social norms and values we inhabit. This is reinforced through following Hodder (1999) that context constructs artefacts as artefacts construct context. Hence, a fossil is an artefact as much as a flint blade, and we can recognise this archaeologically provided it is subject to a contextual relationship seen primarily through deposition. These problems of recognising objects as artefacts, expanding context and exploring substance will be discussed further below.

The challenge of this study therefore is to integrate the various levels at which I am trying to define materiality. In effect, I am moving from the perception of substance, to artefact to use, to deposition and the wider implications of this chronologically. Unlike Ingold's example above where the fibre makes the basket, and the basket becomes itself and takes form, I argue for the understanding of the natural world and substance, how the cultural 'norms' of that substance apply and are used through form and decoration, and how the social cycle of the substance meets an 'end' within deposition. Hence this study is not a study in art, or style, or deposition, but a study in *materiality*. I propose that materiality can be more fully envisaged and explored through structured deposition. By investigating the depositional relationships of chalk artefacts, following Thomas (1996; 1999b) we may be better able to discuss the potential symbolism of this class of artefact.

3.5 Applying Structured Deposition

I have proposed that structured deposition provides both a theoretical and methodological framework through which we can examine materiality. In simple terms, structured deposition supposes that archaeological artefacts are deposited within contexts in a meaningful way. They are not simply accumulations of material, or refuse tips, or accidental, but rather relational to each other. Hence deposits can also be seen as expressions of moments in the past, or temporality. This section relates a history of structured deposition and how it can feed into the methodology.

How Non-Functional Artefacts Became Ritual: An Overview of the Basics of Structured Deposition

Early advocates of structured deposition within archaeology were Richard Bradley, Colin Richards, Julian Thomas, JD Hill and Joshua Pollard, with each author focussing on prehistoric material. Colin Richards' BA dissertation analysis, with additional later study by Julian Thomas was published in the paper *Ritual activity and structured deposition in Later Neolithic Wessex* (Richards and Thomas 1984). Focussing on deposits within Durrington Walls, Wiltshire, they argued the construction of deposits was indicative of structured practice resulting from repetitive ritual behaviours in the past, and termed this phenomena structured deposition (*ibid*.: 191). Specifically, different decorations on Grooved Ware occurred in different areas of the site and there was a preference to deposit flint flakes or pottery sherds in particular areas (*ibid*.: 205). They suggested that the more intensively decorated vessels occur with greater depositional emphases in certain areas, which may indicate those areas were for a restricted use of certain activities and/or persons (*ibid*.: 197). There is explicit attention to design and symbolic meanings with reference to the decoration of Grooved Ware, where they argue that similar motifs will have had enduring significance within ritual activity even when those meanings in the past may have been ambiguous or at times disputed (*ibid*.: 191).

While they approach the results through a largely structural Marxist perspective, at the heart of this study lie several different ways of interpreting artefacts and their deposition by viewing them this way. These are:

- At some sites, the placement of artefacts was a result of highly structured and repetitive activities which were probably ritual in nature.

- Designs on ceramics (or other material culture) may embody complex ritual ideas which were condensed into the design (*ibid*.: 192).

- As in the case of flint flakes and pottery sherds, different substances may be deliberately placed in combination with, or exclusion to, other substances as a result of ritual activity or prescription.

- Yet, deposits in certain areas indicate activity in that area; hence movement around monuments and in particular places may be indicated through depositional activity.

This work became pivotal in both the acceptance of structured deposition as a concept and its relationship to ritual (or non-functional) activities during the Neolithic. In many senses this early study combined a detailed approach to spatial analyses with an acknowledgment of anthropological approaches to space following Van Gennep and Bloch and Turner (*ibid*.: 190-1) though in practical terms it allowed a ritualistic interpretation of the use of monuments built upon data driven foundations. It also contained reference to textual metaphors as a way of ascribing meaning to artefacts. Following textual metaphors, artefacts have been said to embody meaning and can be read like text, though within a wider framework of meaning and context (Tilley 1991).

This innovative integration of archaeological data, spatial deposition of material culture and social anthropology led to further studies by Pollard (1995) on Woodhenge, and Thomas (1996, 1999a) on Mount Pleasant. All these studies formed part of a larger argument concerning the architecture and spatiality of the monuments in general. Hence, Thomas's (1999a) study on Mount Pleasant Site IV and later work on the Southern Circle at Durrington Walls use structured deposition to imply areas of ritual deposition and the access to them, within a broader argument about social control and hierarchy. Thomas argues for Durrington Walls that:

> Just as a social division may have existed between those taking part in activities inside the henge and those observing from the outside, some distinction may have been drawn between those in the centre of the circle and those being encouraged to process around them (1999a: 58).

This view is popular and Bradley argues that 'the monuments of the later Neolithic period provided a structure according to which existing traditions of deposition could be organised' (2000: 131). This idea of tradition and history reflected in deposition is engaging. However, while Bradley reflects that the late Neolithic draws these earlier practices together, the question of when these practices commenced and how they related to each other at the time is lost. Pollard's interest in the meaning of structured deposits, while including a spatial architectural element, is more subtle, in particular regarding the deposits at Windmill Hill near Avebury and Woodhenge. He acknowledges that specific deposits in certain areas at Woodhenge may reference aspects of Neolithic life, and while they may be indicative of movement and use, they are of great complexity. He states:

> In many respects the form and content of the monument could be seen to present a microcosm of the Neolithic social world, expressed through a process of orchestrated "connotative geography", with individual areas of the structure being ascribed different references through deposition and their relation to an overriding cosmological order (1995: 152).

Hill's (1995) study concerning Iron Age pits had a slightly different focus in showing that the wild remains of animals were not simply accidental inclusions in pits but rather deliberate depositions. His work therefore integrated wild animal remains into interpretations of the British Iron Age so widening the focus of research in this period of prehistory, and also suggested a new interpretation for pits which were initially only seen as domestic refuse pits. This study therefore tackled the perceived appropriateness of material culture, or in other terms, what one expects to find within particular archaeological features. Integrating non-domestic species as being archaeologically relevant is more challenging as one explores different chronological periods, from hunter-gatherer societies to agricultural societies, with differing emphases. We have expectations as to what is appropriate, relevant or in other terms 'functional' for each society based on their economic strategies. Hill therefore uses structured deposition to challenge assumptions regarding functionality.

To summarise, in its early form structured deposition argued for the inclusion of all deposited artefacts as relevant and their integration into architectural and spatial analyses as a result of ritual activity. Deliberate deposition of artefacts in particular places can provide a further avenue for consideration which has been used for architectural and monumental arguments on the use of space. Importantly, challenging the assumptions we hold about artefacts and their functionality have been refined further by Thomas and Pollard in different ways: Thomas advocating an 'economy of substances' in order to contextualise different artefact groups; and Pollard's 'aesthetics of deposition'.

Recent Approaches to Structured Deposition

Thomas's approach to an economy of substances has been argued through much of his recent work (1996; 1999a; 1999b). In this he suggests that the combination of different classes and types of artefacts in Later Neolithic deposition may constitute a cosmology where artefacts have embedded meaning and can be brought together in different contexts to produce a specific meaning for that context (1996: 166-7). Thus, worked bone and stone axes occur in Grooved Ware pits and burials, yet not henges or Peterborough Ware pits; marine shell occurs in henges and Grooved Ware pits but not burials and Peterborough Ware pits. Later he expands on this lack of apparent universal rules or constraints on the combination and types of artefact included in specific depositional events, despite general trends being evident (1999a: 78-9). He contends that this constitutes a *bricolage*; that there are many materials available in the Neolithic hence the interplay, contrasts and contextual application of them varies and can evoke and emphasise specific meanings at different times. He also highlights the performative nature of deposition suggesting that certain deposits, or combination of different artefacts, may be the result of improvisation during deposition. In doing so, he distances himself from the more hierarchical structuralist Marxist interpretations and draws temporality as a pivotal structuring theme.

Furthermore, Thomas has investigated the possible meaning of chalk as a substance, its associations with depositional contexts and also the place of chalk in a wider social context in the Neolithic (1996, 1999b). He has noted that not only is carved chalk often deposited in primary contexts, but also suggested that the carved chalk within the Sussex mines highlight areas of transition and segregation (1999b: 80). In discussing the flint mine burial at Shaft VI at Cissbury, excavated by Lane Fox, he has argued that this and similar burials with chalk blocks (at Whitehawk and The Trundle) suggest that, in the Neolithic, chalk as a substance seemed to be associated with the human body. Therefore this economy of substances could be said to be a cosmological ordering within the Neolithic, artefacts being embedded with meaning perhaps represents a symbolic and metaphorical understanding of material things and their position in Neolithic society. Following these phenomenological perspectives, Thomas has also approached the meaning of artefacts. He argues that the point at which a material or substance becomes an artefact is culturally specific and members of any society have 'pre-understandings' which 'form part of our cultural equipment, the inheritance that we acquire by being born into a particular community at a particular time' (*ibid.*: 199). In a philosophical sense this is returning to Hill's work on Iron Age pits and can be seen as a way of expanding our views of what artefacts are.

Pollard's research into the aesthetics of depositional practice provides a new dimension to this argument of structured deposition in the British Neolithic in further describing *how* deposition can be structured (2001). He argues that structured deposits can have an aesthetic quality evidenced in hoards and uses an example of how pottery fragments may suggest this when they have been impressed upon the sides of pits. Moreover these deposits often occur in between layers, not within them, implying they were placed prior to the infilling of the next layer (*ibid*: 323, 327). Pollard uses aesthetics to argue for both knowledgeable social action (Gosden 1999) in addition to things which appeal to the senses, or what may be termed 'art'. In a later paper, Pollard (2004) illustrates that substance (or artefacts/deposits) are not fixed and can be transformed through time and decay, hence the meaning of a substance may not be fixed either at its time of deposition or at its retrieval archaeologically. Ingold's (2007) metaphor of the stone drying, as discussed in 3.4.4, in many ways mirrors this, emphasising the way even what one considers might be a static substance may embody transformation. Pollard (2001: 325) cites examples of deposits at the Coneybury 'Anomaly' and Roughridge Hill where deposits were arranged in clusters of bone and pottery sherds at the base of pits which would have required specific placement. Furthermore layered 'clean' soils are seen in the deposited fills at Yeavering, Northumberland and Cassington, Oxfordshire with similar layering interspersed with artefacts at Woodlands, near Amesbury (*ibid.*: 327). Pollard's central argument is that the placement of deposits, in addition to other social meanings (such as a process of signification, ritual, inalienability of artefacts and so on), may include an appreciation of aesthetics – deposits as 'art'. He cites Gell (1996) in stating that 'the difference between "art" and mere "artefact" is often very fragile, resting upon the reactionary premise that one is interesting or beautiful and the other simply 'functional' (Pollard 2001: 328). Pollard (2004: 50) later argues that this distinction between 'art' and artefact should be simply denounced as it is interpretively unhelpful.

However, as any method, structured deposition is not without its problems. Under Marxist thought, ritual is seen as a mechanism which can perpetuate particular social relations and therefore the intentions and subjugations of social 'actors' within this framework could be seen as a discourse in power relations between varying elites. The failing of structured deposition is that it is too easily married to structural Marxism in this manner and leads towards the prestigious aspects of artefacts. In doing so it becomes embedded with ideas of hierarchy both in regard to particular artefacts and their social importance. While this was evident in some early examples (Bradley 1984; Richards and Thomas 1984; Thomas 1984; Thorpe and Richards 1984), and is lacking in the more recent considerations of it, the problem remains as to identifying the form of ritual authority without leaning on Marxist societal structures.

In addition, comparing the archaeological record to that of static 'text' or components within a linguistic context is helpful, yet comparison to language suggests that, as words, the significance can be arbitrary or ambiguous (Thomas 1996: 59). Furthermore, the use of textual metaphor tends to generalise artefacts and essentially, the artefact could be anything and everything, but the nature, form and composition of the object is secondary. This has been highlighted by both Jones (2004) and Gosden (2005), that in the reliance on the role of text in understanding meanings of objects, the nature of the object itself became lost. By using the textual metaphor which enables us to take individual deposits apart and compare them, material specialists within the discipline can compare one artefact class cross-context and both inter-site and intra-site. Hence, structured deposition which both enables the creation of context, artefacts and interpretation, can be also be responsible for the removal of the context altogether. Therefore paradoxically, in long term processes, deposition can appear to be merely systemic and the use of a textual metaphor can emphasize the division between an artefact and its interpretation as it is filtered through a problematic interpretive scheme.

Yet, both Thomas and Pollard provide sophisticated arguments for reviewing structured deposition from a phenomenological perspective. While Thomas's arguments allow us to review substances in an inter-related way, Pollard's aesthetics proposed detailed analysis of specific types of deposit and their arrangement. These authors direct us to examine deposition in more detail and could be said to follow this impression of past 'pre-understandings' of material culture. What is culturally specific and what is not in a past society can only be gained archaeologically through deposition, because context and deposition are our only tools. Therefore, by applying structured deposition as an interpretation, we can access contexts and artefacts which may be otherwise lost. Furthermore Brück (1999) has discussed the relationship between our understandings and past understandings of depositional rationality, arguing that any unfamiliar deposits to us may not simply signify a ritual motivation by past people. By taking a methodological approach to all artefacts, we can deconstruct 'ritual' deposition in its constituent parts, enabling a *construction* of interpretation rather than an *assumption* of one.

3.6 Methodology

Based upon the concepts outlined in this chapter this methodology is constructed in two parts: the interpretive methodology and the practical methodology. Combining context, substance and artefacts is a relational interpretive enterprise and I have argued, following Hodder, that there is a hermeneutic relationship between artefact and context. Hence, the recognition of an object as an artefact is crucial to the recognition of context, both as a fact and as a component part of structured depositional arguments. I have proposed that in theoretical terms we include previously unconsidered substances and objects as artefacts, and hence how I apply that theory to the practical aspects of this study is crucial. This section seeks to demonstrate how I have recognised context, substance and form and consequently how they were studied in practical terms.

Interpretive Methodology

I have suggested that we need to reassess what constitutes artefacts within excavated contexts. The hermeneutic nature of this means that while it was approached in three different ways (context, substance and form), the results of these investigations fed back into each other within the study. Therefore while in many cases the recognition of the context as being relevant for study was a primary consideration, without recognising artefacts within that context, its recognition was meaningless. Without recognising substance, categorisation of artefacts or correlations of contextual deposition could not be analysed. I will discuss how interpretively I recognised context, substance and form, and in the following section how this was applied practically.

Recognising Context

Context is approached through structured deposition which allows us to examine both single deposits, and combinations of deposits, as significant in the archaeological record following a textual approach as previously outlined. Hence, structured deposition gives us the premise that at sites, the placement of artefacts was a result of highly structured and repetitive activities which were probably ritual in nature. This contributes to recognising context by allowing us to presuppose that all archaeological contexts could be of importance.

Recognising Substance

Substance is of further consideration within this argument and relates to the material the artefact is constructed from or when appropriate, a combination of different materials. Substance needs to be categorised in order to categorise artefacts. In theoretical interpretive terms I take two premises: that different substances may be deliberately placed in combination with, or exclusion to, other substances as a result of ritual activity or prescription (and may therefore participate within an economy of substances within the Neolithic); and all materials should be considered as part of depositional activity and not only those we expect to perceive as 'functional'.

Recognising Form

There are two aspects to recognising form in this study: 'art' and artefacts. The interpretation of 'art' as noted earlier by Pollard is problematic and I propose to alleviate this by ignoring the division between 'art' and artefact and simply treating 'art' *as* artefact. This enables us to access the context of the art. Alongside studies interpreting archaeological art are often concerns of style and execution. Hence where art is encountered, in hermeneutic terms we should be able to move between all contexts or areas of information in order to interpret meaning. By this I mean that we can study the context and content of the art whilst perceiving its socially significant nature without judging its form as relating to our cultural norms. While this may be seen as simplistic, a common misconception of archaeological 'art' in many of the forms encountered in Neolithic Britain is in its lack of recognisable 'aesthetic' quality or fine execution of design. These are modern Western conceptions which do not aid our analysis.

Recognising form in artefacts has taken a slightly different approach. Form must relate to a recognisable quality in a phenomenological sense yet some artefacts are of a natural origin. Hence where form is recognised it is noted, whether a humanly-constructed artefact or an artefact which is of a natural origin. In referring to flint nodules as possibly resembling human ancestral bones in the Neolithic, Tilley (2007b: 339-40) is effectively proposing that these flints were perceived of as material components of life to Neolithic persons, or perhaps we should say, artefacts? Collections of fossils, iron pyrites and animal material (such as antler), occur in deposits. The only method by which we can acknowledge this material is by banishing the nature: culture dichotomy that exists in recognising artefacts. *An artefact is a cultural concept, not a physical one.* If the material an artefact is made of is wholly natural and unmodified, its deliberate placement can structure it culturally as an artefact.

Structured deposition using textual analogies also permits us to suppose that designs on ceramics (or other material culture) may embody complex ritual ideas which were condensed, manipulated or formed through their social use and application on different substances. Hence by noting the content and context of the designs we can begin to interpret when certain designs or forms may be suitable for sharing and in which media, and when these indications are absent. The form of designs is therefore important to categorise effectively.

Practical Methodology

Recognising Contexts

Context in the flint mines may include shafts, galleries, walls, floors, rubble or fills and hence each has been interpreted as a possible individual area of focus for deposition. Therefore in all cases where a substance or artefact may be encountered, a context is acknowledged.

The accidental inclusion of fossil or iron pyrites as natural inclusions within the chalk cannot be fully discounted for every context. However I believe that unless we have practical archaeological indications that there is a lack of intention, we should assume it exists. By this, I mean unless there are clear indications through stratigraphy that objects have been washed into a feature or otherwise may obviously have arrived within a deposit by natural occurrence, their deliberate placement should be assumed. The lack of detail in many reports has rendered this difficult to ascertain and hence all substances which may be considered artefacts have been included with the exception of deposits of snail shell, which have been seen as natural inclusions following advice from Mike Allen (pers. comm.).

Recognising Substance

I have recognised substance in a phenomenological way: through encountering it physically. The aim of the recognition has been for the purposes of categorisation, so that through the analysis conducted I was able to group substances, constituent artefacts, and their contexts for interpretation. The substances are materially different: chalk when compared to flint, fossils or iron pyrites is pliable. It smears. When wet it becomes sticky clay; when dry it is dusty and can leave impressions of itself on other surfaces, and your hands. Flint is hard, can be flaked or ground only with effort and skill. Iron pyrites are hard and can produce sparks when struck; they look almost metallic. Fossils resemble sea-creatures and can be fused and hard, or easily broken (as fossil shell). Substance has therefore been recognised in a relational way, through comparing it to other materials present in archives and relating them to the excavation reports. Hence all substances are recognised through artefactual recognisable 'norms'; substances categories are necessarily consistent. There was one chalk-like substance I was unable to identify from Harrow Hill and having no parallels is consequently excluded from this study.

Recognising Form

The recognition of artefacts forms an important part of this study, yet this has only rarely been conducted by myself. As the study consisted of the analysis of both written reports and museum archive material, artefacts and material groupings or forms were already highlighted as significant by their excavators. In this respect it has been my theoretical approach which has interpreted many artefacts as artefacts rather than a recognition of new artefacts. Indeed, the very presence of this material in archives could be said to have identified them already as artefacts, they were simply not analysed as part of an archaeological assemblage. While concerns of authenticity have been raised about some examples, these are considered individually where relevant (for example the Grimes Graves Pit 15 group, as discussed in Chapter 2).

Recording and Synthesizing Data

On completion of my initial investigations of published material on the flint mine excavations, I ascertained that the main collections available for study were held at the following six museums and I visited them during 2004 and 2005 to examine their chalk and other artefact collections: Salisbury Museum, Norwich City Museum, Chichester Museum, The British Museum, Worthing Museum and Lewes Museum. Regrettably I was unable to access the chalk material for logistical reasons at the following locations; The British Museum, Thetford Museum and Brighton Museum. In all cases their material was off site due to storage issues and/or rebuilding work. I visited the museums in order to engage directly with this material. As the aims of this research are to attempt to integrate the materiality of the mines with contemporary Neolithic monuments, artefacts from a sample of monuments within these regions needed to be studied together with mining examples and to aid my analysis I also visited the Alexander Keiller Museum at Avebury and Dr Martin Green's private museum at Down Farm, Dorset. Materials were studied from both mining and contemporary sites in identical ways in order to quantify and qualify the chalk artefacts and other types of deposits. In some cases, artefacts that I expected to find in the archives had been misplaced or removed. In these cases textual information is all that remains and forms the basis of the interpretations. All available artefacts were identified and studied as to their substance of composition and their form. They were measured and digitally photographed and then assigned a classification within a typology, noting the chronological aspects in particular. It was not possible to examine any in situ art and all study in this area has been based on textual sources.

The material encountered took three forms:

- Chalk artefacts, fossils, antler and iron pyrites which were noted in reports and found in museum collections.

- Chalk forms, fossils and iron pyrites which appeared to be part of the excavated material and retained in the archive but which were not noted in reports.

- Chalk forms which could have been artefacts but were unmarked or categorised as such, though they were curated.

Having considered this material, in practical terms, portable artefacts and marked chalk on walls or large blocks produce different interpretive questions. Root (1983: 209-212) has proposed that portable and non-portable information operate differently in societies, where portable information can be encoded through styles and be widely shared; non-portable information conversely implies a restriction in sharing information. While these premises can be (and even by Root have been) argued as only relevant in particular circumstances, dividing the material for analysis in this way seemed sensible. Portable material culture can be easily carried and concealed - it is socially active in different ways. Hence where artefacts are less than 20cm in length at any point they are termed portable; with large blocks, fixed or semi-fixed architecture with markings classed as non-portable. This study has therefore been separated into three analysis chapters which are divided as follows: Chapters 4 and 5 examining non-portable and portable chalk artefacts respectively; and Chapter 6 integrates natural substances as artefacts studied through their deposition.

3.7 Conclusion

Throughout this chapter I have attempted to illustrate the difficulty that pervades the discipline in terms of nomenclature and hierarchical approaches to material culture. These factors, arising from various sources but with Marxist approaches as a key addition, have all led to confusion with regard to widening our archaeological categories. One could say that while we cannot agree on what is important and the ranking of it - fragments, deposition, form, detail of expression - we are missing what could be. Furthermore I have highlighted that the hierarchical approach to material culture is supported both by the material specialists in UK institutions and some early structured depositional approaches. Theoretically and practically there are methods by which researchers actively decide which questions to ask of the archaeological record. Approaches to materiality have tended to focus on specific artefacts, monuments or substance themes rather than integrating them into wider views of substance.

I have also suggested that chalk objects have not been classed as chalk artefacts and do not have a typology and classification system as initially they did not appear relevant in ethnographic societies encountered during Victorian times. While metaphor allows us to compare dissimilar things, analogy permits us to suppose if one or more similarity between things is present, then other similarities are likely to be present also. Stone axes, found in many societies allow us to imagine similar societies in the past, yet as ritual and religious artefacts and aspects of societies encountered were seen as secondary to technological and evolutionary questions, it became easier to (broadly) ignore them. They have, along with other non-functional artefacts, been seen as part of a different analogical interpretive scheme. Furthermore, as chalk is not seen as a functional substance, it is not considered that chalk artefacts should be meaningful apart from within ritual or religious interpretations. This largely follows Marxist thought on production and social value. Chalk has been considered as a by-product of other activities: the creation of banks from ditches, spoil heaps from mining – a passive rather than active substance. There have been few articles in the past 60 years which have explicitly discussed chalk artefacts and chalk as a symbolic substance (N. Thomas 1952; J. Thomas 1999b; Varndell 1991, 1999). J. Thomas's (1999b) interpretation of chalk being metaphorical in some senses to the human body in the Neolithic is very useful as there are human representations that occur in chalk which may indicate that understanding in the Neolithic. However can we see anything else in chalk deposition?

Turning to substance, in relational terms chalk is extracted in the same context as flint, fossils and iron pyrites. It is bedrock, in that it literally has these other substances embedded within it. The cultural separation of the substances flint, fossil and chalk and then deliberate physical use in practices (which may include a modification of form) enables greater schemes of interpretive relationality. Their modification, reassembling and re-deposition could form part of the *bricolage* suggested by Thomas. As discussed earlier, under phenomenology in order for a substance to be recognised a meaning is already present. Hence there is an underlying similarity in cultural meaning between artefacts made from the same material or substance which underlies Thomas's economy of substances. The inherent symbolism of stone has been discussed by Tilley (2004), that by examining different stone types in monuments we can see that there was a great discernment practised in their selection and construction. I propose that we can only truly interpret these meanings through the wider appreciation of the different types of substance manipulated and deposited within a cultural context. So, while stone can have a myriad of meanings, as can pottery (clay), or flint, how do these categories relate to each other? Furthermore if artefacts become part of a material 'language', signifying particular elements of life metaphorically (Tilley 1999), the inclusion of naturally occurring artefacts (such as fossils or iron pyrites) alongside humanly created artefacts, expands the metaphorical cultural signature of the 'language'. This can broaden our understandings of both structured deposition and the past society. Many of the chalk artefacts discussed in this research can only have been created from sub-surface chalk and so the extraction of raw material must have been part of the process. Phallic symbols, chalk cylinders, carved blocks and marked blocks have been created through the use of past human action. There is indeed a gradient of precision in execution, some objects are finer and have more detail than others. Yet, *all are artefacts*.

Hodder (1999: 39) states that in general archaeologists reason through 'accommodative arguments' and 'we contextualise and fit together all the bits of evidence available. When bits do not fit we worry at them and try to reduce the inconsistencies'. I have argued that these accommodative arguments are in essence restricted through our view of what constitutes an artefact. I have attempted to bridge this gap by arguing that following Hodder, the relationship between context and artefact is co-dependent and that we can only determine archaeological context or artefacts in relation to each other. For if we do not recognise a context, anything within that context will not be recognised as an artefact. Furthermore, if we encounter objects and do not interpret them as artefacts, we may miss the context. Hence, I proposed that 'artefact' is a social category and not a physical one. Studying the structured deposition of artefacts and examining their additional aspects of aesthetics and substance allow a finer level of analysis. These concepts are explored through examples in the following chapters of this book. The questions it aims to address are how do these artefacts and substances relate to each other? What artefact forms are more prevalent at different chronological times? How does the presence of art and decoration influence interpretations of flint mines? How does this reflect back on interpretations of the wider Neolithic? Finally, can we interpret anything in addition to extraction for the southern British flint mines?

Chapter 4

Non-Portable Chalk: Art and Artefacts

Rolleston argued 'that he thought they might very reasonably be supposed to have been made by one of the savages in some moment of fidgety restlessness, such as savages of all kinds were subject to' (Harrison: 1877b: 438).

4.1 Introduction

The above quote embodies the impression of chalk art which has persisted for over a hundred years; a lack of recognition of its value for study. While it has been viewed in this manner, including examples from flint mines within wider Neolithic discourses has not appeared of relevance. However, in the last twenty-five years further examples of chalk art have been seen during excavation from other types of Neolithic monument and these, having been excavated under modern conditions, have influenced the acceptance of chalk art as authentic archaeological evidence. Yet, in many senses these recently discovered examples are excluded from cohesive interpretations without the supporting evidence from flint mines. As the aims of this work are to incorporate flint mines within wider discussions of the British Neolithic, the inclusion of chalk art forms from mines in such a comparative study seeks to also aid understandings of chalk art from non-mining locations.

The previous chapter outlined the theoretical and methodological approach used to study and interpret chalk artefacts, art and other types of 'non-functional' deposits found in the flint mines. This proposed several ways of expanding our categories for analysis by reviewing the accepted norms for context and artefact. Hence art is studied as an artefact, the approach also used in examining chalk art and unmarked blocks. By viewing this evidence as artefactual, we can bring a greater level of analytical weight to it. After reviewing the ways chalk art has been seen (4.2) I propose how to study chalk art through its form, style and context (4.3). In section 4.4 art in the flint mines is discussed with an analysis of examples in contemporary monuments following (4.5). Understanding chalk art and artefacts is discussed in section 4.6, before the main points are drawn out in conclusion (4.7). Initially the study commences with a consideration of the current interpretations of chalk art and chalk blocks.

4.2 Chalk Art as Functional and Non-Functional Evidence

Chalk art and marked chalk blocks are categories of evidence which have been viewed as possibly having a functional meaning in addition to being seen as non-functional expressions of Neolithic archaeology. This non-functionality has taken two forms – either in respect to it not being acknowledged as a class of evidence, or as evidence which solely enlightens ritual or religious aspects of the Neolithic.

Chalk art was first encountered during excavation at Cissbury flint mine, encompassing in situ markings on chalk walls, decorated or marked chalk blocks and smaller portable chalk artefacts. Initially one man in particular Harrison (also referred to as Park Harrison in records) made considerable effort to investigate already excavated shafts (such as Tindall's Pit, Lane Fox's various shafts and Willett's Pit; Harrison 1877a: 263) to search for markings and it is through his research and papers between 1877 and 1878 that we have some useful details of the art and some accompanying illustrations (1877a, 1877b, 1878). He argued that chalk art may have had a functional use, but was perhaps rather over-enthusiastically in favour of it being an early form of writing or cuneiform (*ibid.*: 265, 270). This was the cause of some dissention and rejection of the art among his peers. Other opinions suggested they may be functional makings to count the amount of flints retrieved (*ibid.*: 271). Hence early views were polarised; either they were functional markings as writing or type of accounting or alternatively were simply marks made out of the boredom of miners (Harrison 1877b: 438).

The first half of the twentieth century saw further examples of attempts to understand this phenomenon. Clarke's (1915: 73-5) excavation of Pit 2 at Grimes Graves uncovered two sets of linear art at gallery entrances and he offered a functional view for these. He proposed one set represented 'Tally Marks', (a count of flint obtained) and the second set a 'Sundial', suggesting that it may have been functional for assessing time passing time when in the shaft. Excavations by the Curwen's (Curwen and Curwen 1926) at Harrow Hill discovered a number of examples of chalk art; both in situ and on marked blocks. They avoid any direct interpretations but describe them as 'graffiti' hence implying a temporal motivation by a bored individual rather than a deliberate social activity. During the 1940s and 1950s, Pull discovered art at Church Hill (Shaft 4) and Cissbury (Shaft 27). Although no interpretations were offered for the Church Hill markings, they were thought genuine (Russell 2001:102). The art at Cissbury Shaft 27 is slightly more complex as some symbols are unique in Neolithic Britain and this is discussed later (Russell 2001: 188).

Recent interpretations of chalk art have focussed more on the non-functional ritualistic aspects to it, though with functional leanings. For example it has been argued that art placed at the entrance of galleries may have been made to 'impart information about those galleries to anyone entering the shaft' (Barber *et al.* 1999: 65). Topping (2005: 69) suggests that they may be part of 'post-extraction prayers and offerings' following comparative analysis to North American ethnographic evidence. In addition, Barber *et al.* (1999: 65-6) compare the linear motifs depicted within the Cave Pit at Cissbury with decoration on a Grooved Ware bowl from Tye Field, Essex.

Paradoxically, chalk art in other Neolithic monuments has received a different interpretation emphasising their similarity to rock art designs. The decorated areas in ditches at North Marden, Sussex (Drewett 1986) and Flagstones, Dorset (Woodward 1988; Healy 1997) have been affiliated with the passage tomb art traditions of Ireland and Scotland. Furthermore, the decorated chalk blocks excavated at the Monkton Up Wimborne shaft and pit circle have also been argued as similar to this tradition (Green 2000: 83). This is undoubtedly due to the more recent excavation of these monuments when within the discipline there is a well established discourse on the types of rock art designs and placement within the western Atlantic of Europe (e.g. Shee Twoig 1981; Bradley 1997; Beckensall 1999). In many senses rock art is viewed as non-functional in a ritual/religious way yet the complexities involved in discussing chalk art through rock art warrants further discussion and is returned to later in this chapter (4.8). Initially, how we examine chalk art within the theoretical parameters outlined in Chapter 3 will be investigated.

4.3 Considering Chalk Art and Deposits as Artefacts

Chalk art cannot productively be analysed under the types of non-functional assumptions discussed above. These approaches are misleading in two ways: they lead us to discuss art as separate from other archaeological evidence and often negate the types of rigorous analysis conducted on standard artefact types. 'For example, artefacts made from flint are initially subject to classification and typological analyses to categorise them, e.g. labelling them as 'transverse arrowhead' or 'scraper' and so on - it is only when this is complete that any individual artefact is compared to others. This chapter aims to begin the process of viewing chalk art and non-portable chalk blocks as 'artefacts' by approaching them in a similar methodological manner.

One of the areas to be examined here is the materiality of chalk, and how is it to be viewed as a substance. Geologically, chalk is a rock. If we view chalk as a type of rock, and as a rock we apply the same interpretive categories to chalk art and artefacts we do to stone art and artefacts, we access a firm history of discourse and theory within Neolithic studies that is not simply based on design parallels. Having established that chalk art and rock art have similarities, chalk art can be examined in the tradition of studying rock art. The term 'art' encompasses all types of decoration on chalk following rock art analysis. As argued by Bradley (1997: 4-5), 'the term 'rock art' is unsatisfactory, but, as happens with so many technical terms, it is too late to look for an alternative now'. He continues (*ibid.*: 5) that rock art 'describes the distinctive practice of painting or carving natural surfaces in the landscape', though his analysis also includes rock art within monuments. Moreover, we can begin to challenge some assumptions. This difference in the literature in the interpretation of stone and chalk indicates an interpretive dichotomy between accepting chalk as a necessary and ubiquitous part of the landscape yet imagining that it may have had cultural importance. This is an argument not applied to the study of stone monuments; stone is accepted as difficult to quarry, transport and erect. However, chalk has been seen as a polar opposite: ubiquitous, light and accessible. That chalk rubble or blocks were used in the construction of banks for long mounds, henge monuments or barrows, need not be indicative of its lack of social importance as a material, or as a form, nor necessarily its use as a ritual substance (Chapter 3). We do not view any stone monuments as by-products of other activity.

Consideration can therefore be given to those chalk blocks which are not modified but given specific depositional placement in the mines, as unmarked standing stones are. Furthermore it can also include chalk architecture found within the mines, both in terms of the architecture created through extraction and through applying chalk blocks in different ways to create certain forms (enclosures, platforms, walls, standing blocks etc.). It is common for all types of stone artefacts to be included in analyses, even when they are poorly understood (e.g. Edmonds 1995). By following traditional discourses of stone monument building, or the enhancement of place through architecture we can expand our interpretations of chalk in a familiar way, within common Neolithic discourses.

I propose to do this by studying the form, type of decoration (style) and archaeological context of non-portable chalk art. In terms of form, non-portable chalk has been categorised and studied in three ways:

- Carved or marked chalk blocks above 20cm in size, of any shape.

- Chalk art - marked chalk in situ within the architecture of monuments on the natural chalk wall.

- Non-marked chalk blocks are discussed in terms of their architectural/contextual placement.

I have argued that a chalk block over 20cm in any direction is non-portable as this roughly represents the size at which it could not fit in an average person's hand and be moved.

Large blocks are unlikely to be active in the types of social engagements represented with smaller portable objects, which are the focus of Chapter 5. This type of separation has been used in rock art studies where markings which are in situ or on large stones are analysed as 'non-portable', following Root (1983) and Bradley (1997) where a cultural difference is seen ethnographically with portable and non-portable information and artefacts.

The use of style in determining usual cultural norms is practiced in all artefact analyses. As re-examining the in situ chalk art in mines cannot be conducted, this study has used published illustrations and descriptions provided, an approach also applied where decorated blocks were not available for analysis. Following this, the authenticity of markings is a subject requiring some attention. From the first excavations it was suggested that markings may have been produced by workmen or casual visitors adding their marks to the galleries and shaft walls. Indeed this seems to have been common practice with workmen and excavators carving their names into the walls at the end of a season, in addition to any visitors contribution - 'William Penfold', being specifically mentioned (Harrison 1877a: 270). Conversely, this modern graffiti highlighted some differences between the newly made marks and those which could be archaeological, giving credence to the antiquity of the many chalk markings. The newly made marks differed in colour from the archaeological ones, being whiter and fresher, with older marks exhibiting a yellowish coating within the marks in common with the chalk surface surrounding them (*ibid.*). Regrettably, this type of coating or crystallisation does not occur uniformly within in situ markings and many marked chalk blocks excavated in more recent years appear fresh. In general the presence of a carbonate coating within marks may be indicative of antiquity, but its absence is unlikely to confirm any markings as fraudulent. However I do not see the possibility of fraud as problematic within this style analysis. Chalk art has never been well published or categorised, hence any fraudulent markings are unlikely to be consistent with the style or placement of genuine Neolithic chalk art. It is anticipated that the analysis conducted in ascribing styles will highlight those markings which do not appear consistent within Neolithic style norms. Reservations have already been expressed over examples from Pull's excavations at Cissbury (Chapter 2; Russell 2001: 188).

The designs have been divided into four types which constitute that seen within art or on chalk blocks. These types are linear designs, circular and semi-circular markings, cups or perforations and figurative animal markings:

- Linear Designs. The linear scrapes or parallel lines on chalk blocks/art are incised in many cases by a sharp flint, although some wider marks may have been produced through the use of a broader, rounded tool such as a bone point or wooden stake. There are indications on some pieces this may have been done with the addition of water. The designs are abstract and not representational.

- Circular or semi-circular designs. These can be wholly round or fashioned as a semi-circular motif and appear on in situ art and on decorated blocks. The design and execution vary and at times can be present with linear designs.

- Perforations or cup designs. Perforations occur both on large blocks and portable chalk artefacts but rarely exhibit evidence of suspension through rope marks.

- Animal markings. These are representative of both large mammals and fish, only being noted at Cissbury by Pull.

The context of art is discussed in several ways. As artefacts, their placement is argued as a relevant part of analysis and therefore this is discussed both architecturally and relationally to other deposits. Within such contexts as the mines the depositional placement and relationship to other artefacts can be expressed three dimensionally where the evidence allows. This approach is a fundamental part of both standard spatial analyses and structured deposition. How relevant the placement of art is within the mines is discussed in the following analyses and has been conducted with reference to examples of chalk art from contemporary Neolithic monuments. By referring to evidence from contemporary monuments, the relevance of these types of artefact and deposition can be assessed both regionally and nationally, placing chalk art studies and flint mines within wider Neolithic discourses.

4.4 Chalk Art in the Flint Mines

The following section discusses the nature and placement of chalk art. The analysis is necessarily divided into particular shafts in order to describe the context of each example effectively. In situ chalk art in the mines by shaft is reviewed with two shaft complexes (shafts which interconnect through the galleries and hence are interrelated contexts) analysed separately. Following this, decorated and undecorated chalk blocks which do not form part of contextual relationships but which appear to form architectural features in particular shafts or galleries are analysed. A summary of the evidence from the mines is given, with a discussion concluding this section.

Art in the Mines: Chalk Art studied by Shaft

The following descriptions of chalk art and other features are supported by accompanying illustrations which have been redrawn from published sources. Some art has been interpretively drawn from descriptions provided.

No 2 Escarpment Shaft, Cissbury (Figure 4.1)

The second escarpment shaft had scoring at the entrance of the south gallery and a lattice pattern at the entrance of the west gallery (Lane Fox 1876: 374) with further markings discovered by Harrison in 1876 (1877a: 266). A double cross and associated 'pick hole' were found on the south wall of an inner chamber of the gallery, near the roof of the chamber noted on the illustration (*ibid.*). From the description and excavation plan it appears that this chamber is likely to be the gallery indicated. Harrison notes it would have been difficult to make repeated blows with a deer horn in the same place with this angle (*ibid.*) and is perhaps more likely to have been made by other means. A heavily decorated chalk block was also found in this gallery but has not been illustrated and is now lost.

Shaft 27, Cissbury (Figure 4.2)

Pull notes art as being present 15 feet (4.58m) down on the shaft wall to the east, though this was not illustrated or described (Russell 2000: 189). Art was also discovered in galleries 7 and 8 as noted and illustrated. It is probable that these in situ graffiti marks are linked with an unexcavated

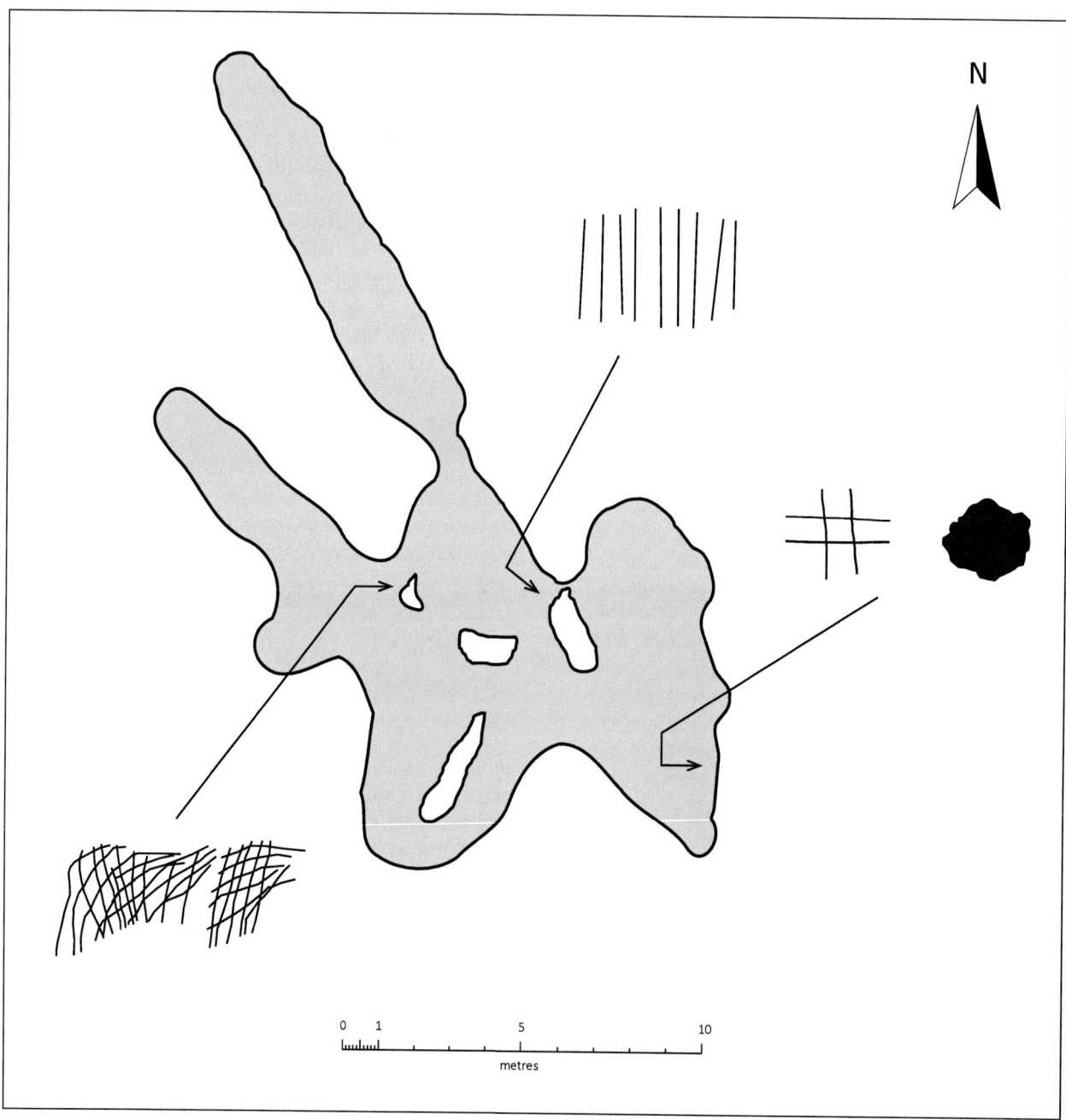

FIGURE 4.1 NO 2 ESCARPMENT SHAFT, CISSBURY (AFTER LANE FOX 1876). SCORING WAS AT THE ENTRANCE OF THE SOUTH GALLERY AND A LATTICE PATTERN AT THE ENTRANCE OF THE WEST GALLERY. A DOUBLE CROSS AND ASSOCIATED 'PICK HOLE' WERE FOUND ON THE SOUTH WALL OF AN INNER CHAMBER OF THE SOUTH GALLERY, NEAR THE ROOF OF THE CHAMBER (HARRISON 1877A: 266; LANE FOX 1876: 374). SHAFT APPROXIMATE SCALE, ART NOT TO SCALE. ART REDRAWN FROM PUBLISHED IMAGES OR RECONSTRUCTED FROM DESCRIPTIONS OF MARKINGS

shaft to the north east on the above plan. The graffiti within Shaft 27 at 15 feet (4.5m) is only a metre above the shaft floor at 18 feet (5.5m) and opposite to the skeleton (found in the west gallery) and could be referencing that burial. The 'Great Nodule' in gallery 1 is an unusual deposit within the same gallery as the burial.

Regarding the art, Russell is inclined to view all markings as authentic; stating that their discovery seemed to be made by different excavation members at different times (Russell 2001: 189). Pull states they were filled with 're-deposited fluffy carbonate' to argue for their Neolithic origin. On balance however, I have concerns about the integrity of these unusual markings. Firstly, the two representations of deer and one fish are misplaced in this period of prehistory, with no other recorded images of this type and their striking resemblance to Palaeolithic cave art (Russell 2000: 50). Secondly, the use of the term 're-deposited fluffy carbonate' is almost the same phrasing used with the arguments concerning authenticity of graffiti in earlier excavations, where Harrison was at pains to argue that markings cannot have been fresh due to discolouration of the markings and ingrained dust (Harrison 1877a; 1877b). That Pull was familiar with these texts is evidenced by

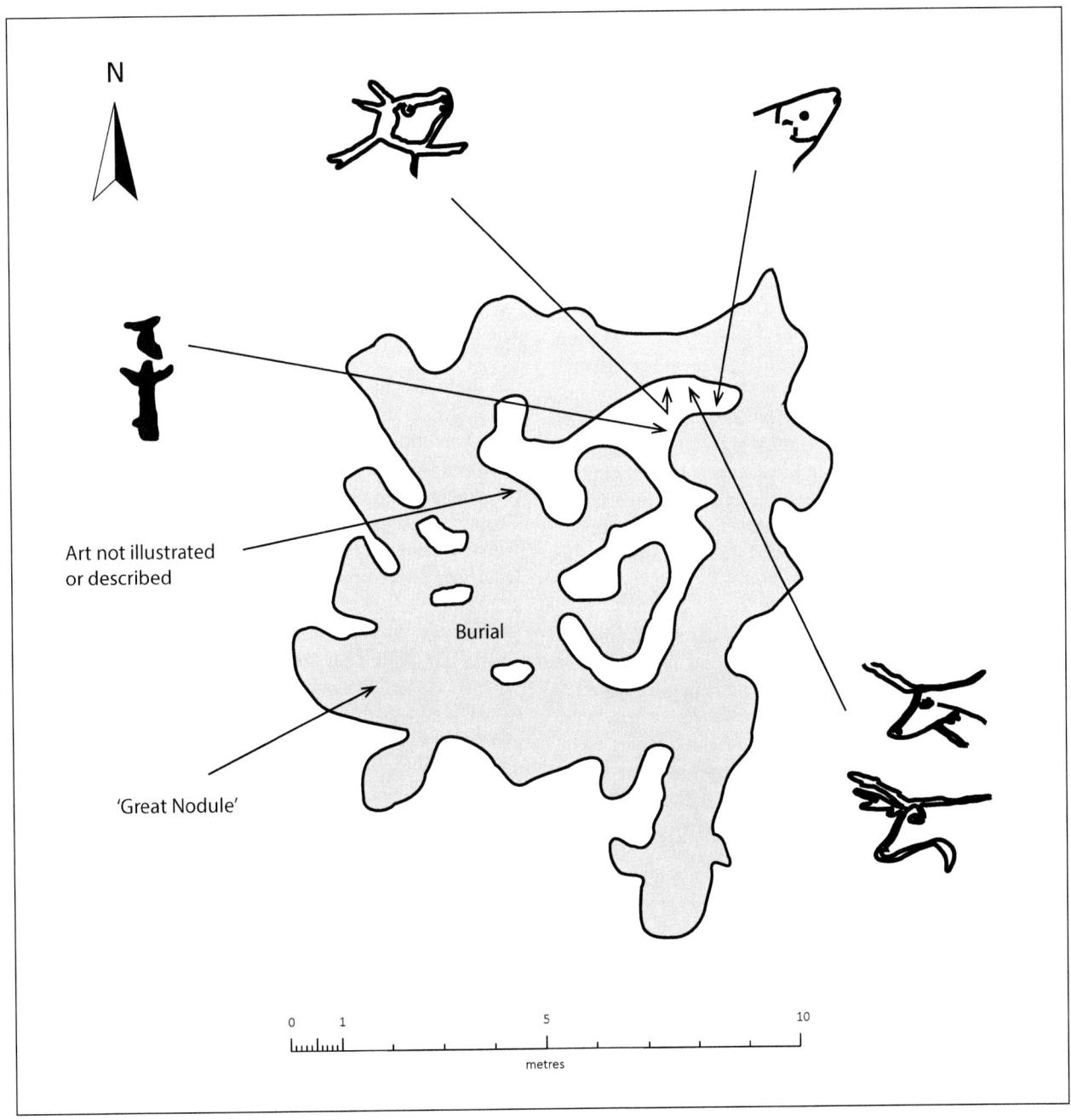

FIGURE 4.2 SHAFT 27, CISSBURY (AFTER RUSSELL 2001, 112; 170). ART WAS PRESENT 15 FEET (4.58M) DOWN ON THE SHAFT WALL TO THE EAST, A METRE ABOVE THE SHAFT FLOOR AT 18 FEET (5.5M) AND OPPOSITE THE SKELETON (FOUND IN THE WEST GALLERY), THOUGH THIS WAS NOT ILLUSTRATED OR DESCRIBED (PULL IN RUSSELL 2000: 189). ART WAS PRESENT IN GALLERIES 7 AND 8 AS NOTED AND ILLUSTRATED. SHAFT APPROXIMATE SCALE, ART NOT TO SCALE. ART REDRAWN FROM PUBLISHED IMAGES OR RECONSTRUCTED FROM DESCRIPTIONS OF MARKINGS

his reproduction of the markings from the Cave Pit in his notes on Church Hill and the graffiti he uncovered from Shaft 4 there during 1946-48 (Worthing Museum Acc. No 61/1584).

Pull seemed to be aware that these markings were inconsistent with what was known of Neolithic art at this time and furthermore, was almost certainly familiar with the widespread concern over the animal markings found on flint by Armstrong at Grimes Graves in the 1930s (Varndell 2005). Pull had had problems in the local archaeological community following disagreements on the publication of the first excavation at Blackpatch. This very public feud with members of the Worthing Archaeological Society in the early 1920s was evidenced in the local press and Pull refused to be a part of the society again until the late 1940s (Russell 2001: 265-272). In 1953, the year of the discovery of these Cissbury markings, he had also suffered some embarrassment concerning the 'Cissbury ivory fish' found near the skeleton in Shaft 27. Pull had strongly argued it had to be Neolithic as the site was secure, even though the shaft was left open for over a year while excavations took place during most weekends (Russell 2001: 184). As noted by Bickerton in a letter, Childe was hesitant about accepting the fish as Neolithic or Early Bronze Age and it was suggested it represented a local type of Medieval bone gaming piece (*ibid.*: 279). To add to further embarrassment for Pull, the Inspector of Ancient Monuments, Dunning, compared the fish to another held by one of the main critics of Pull in Sussex, Curwen (*ibid.*), a fact likely to have been widely acknowledged in local archaeological circles. While no records indicate this, the previous uncertainty over Pull's excavation methods and interpretations may have been reignited – this was his last excavation as site director.

Given this background accepting such unique designs as genuine is difficult. It is possible that within this mine such representations were acceptable. The more familiar abstract marking (the Miner's symbol) was discovered first, with others following a week later and further examples eight months after that (August 1954). It appears from Pull's notes at the time that the excavation of these galleries was proceeding well and they were not heavily filled with rubble, meaning access would have been easily obtained (Worthing Museum Acc. No 1961/1584). Varndell (2005: 57) argues that these markings are 'difficult to judge' and confirms that even at the time Joan Sheldon, a lecturer at the Institute of Archaeology London, stated on the that they were '*impossible to pronounce*' (*ibid.*; her emphasis). Having voiced these concerns, and without recourse to re-examine them, the decision whether to include them or not within this analysis is difficult. However, it seems churlish to deny them within this study without firm evidence of forgery and it is hoped in the future this may be resolved more satisfactorily. The presence of art at Cissbury is comparatively prolific and the locations of the Shaft 27 shaft wall art a consistent context within this.

Shaft 4, Church Hill

Three designs were noted as appearing at gallery entrances although which of the five galleries they were over was not recorded (Russell 2000: 102). The design of circular depressions and linear lines are entirely consistent with other art.

Pit 2, Grimes Graves

Two sets of linear art at were found at gallery entrances by Clarke (1915: 73-5). They were named as the 'Tally Marks' and the 'Sundial' and discussed earlier.

Chalk Art Studied by Shaft Complex

The two sites of Cissbury and Harrow Hill have had several shafts excavated in close proximity to each other which display both art and interesting architectural features. It seems appropriate to discuss them as shaft complexes rather than individual shafts with cohesive descriptions and illustrations which are more informative. In all likelihood these shafts were opened simultaneously or sequentially during their use.

The Cissbury Cave Pit Complex (Figures 4.3 and 4.4)

Six shafts are interlinked through the galleries at Cissbury, evidenced in the excavations of the 1870s. Four of these have been fully excavated and are known as Willett's Pit (or Shaft 1), Shaft II (the Cave Pit), Shaft V and Shaft VI (the Skeleton Shaft). Shafts III and IV were unexcavated. The art is discussed initially accompanied by Figure 4.3, with architectural features and deposition being discussed latterly and accompanied by Figure 4.4.

In Willett's Pit (Shaft I), above the entrance to the east gallery yet within the gallery itself and 2 feet 6 inches (76cm) above the ground, Harrison noticed the art resembling a reversed numerical '4' with an additional vertical line (*ibid.*: 264). Two additional markings, having a similar appearance to an 'L' and a '1' were found near this mark but on the exterior of the wall. The motif appearing similar to '16' was discovered at the entrance to the north gallery. A pierced detached chalk block was found at the entrance to gallery 6, opposite the art noted above (Willett 1875: 345). It is interesting to note that in this shaft the entrances to the north and east were specifically marked, with a further block at the south-west. This shaft is linked to the Cave Pit (Shaft II). The Cave Pit is named due to the presence of a chamber at the bottom of the shaft constructed with chalk blocks. Art was noted in various places: over the entrances to galleries B (three linear lines) and C (diagonal lines); the west jamb of the entrance to gallery B and within the gallery a block decorated which may have had two separate phases of markings with one over another and what was later described as perhaps representing a 'rude human figure' and now lost (Harrison 1877b: 434; 1878: 415).

The top fills of this shaft contained many marked chalk blocks with motifs. Harrison noted that no marked blocks were found at a depth below 16 feet (4.88m) from the surface and those found were almost exclusively on the east and south-west parts of the shaft (1877b: 433). One block, at a depth of 5 feet (1.52m) from the surface had

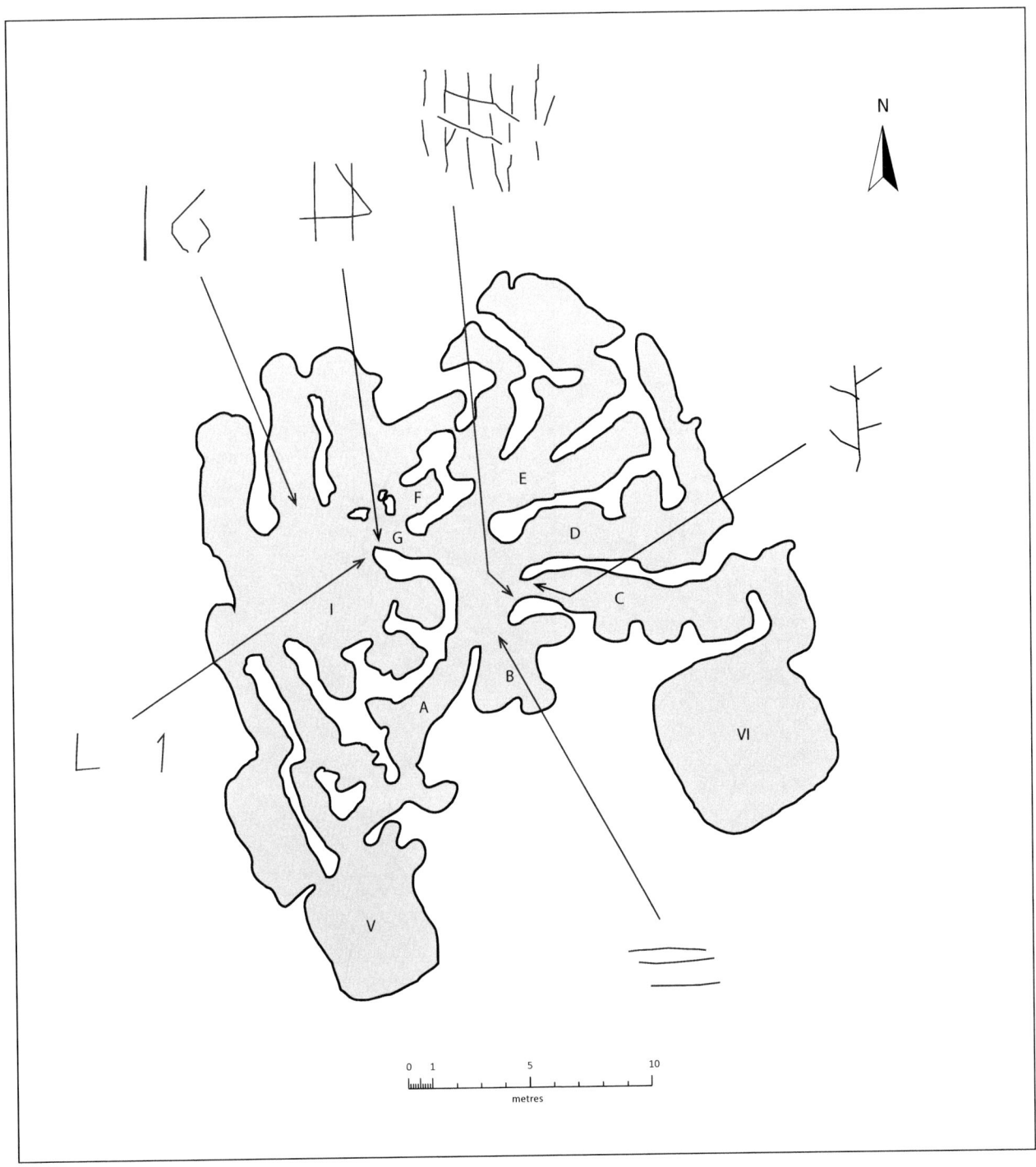

FIGURE 4.3 THE CISSBURY CAVE PIT COMPLEX ART (AFTER BARBER ET AL. 1999: 50); A REVERSED NUMERICAL '4' WITH AN ADDITIONAL VERTICAL LINE WAS IN SHAFT I ABOVE THE ENTRANCE TO THE EAST GALLERY YET WITHIN THE GALLERY ITSELF AND 2 FEET 6 INCHES (76CM) ABOVE THE GROUND (HARRISON 1877A: 264). MARKINGS, HAVING SIMILARITY TO AN 'L' AND A '1' WERE FOUND NEAR THIS MARK BUT ON THE EXTERIOR OF THE WALL. THE MOTIF APPEARING SIMILAR TO '16' WAS DISCOVERED AT THE ENTRANCE TO THE NORTH GALLERY. ART WAS NOTED IN VARIOUS PLACES IN SHAFT 2 (CAVE PIT): OVER THE ENTRANCES TO GALLERIES B (THREE LINEAR LINES) AND C (DIAGONAL LINES); THE WEST JAMB OF THE ENTRANCE TO GALLERY B AND C (HARRISON 1877B: 434, 1878: 415). SHAFT VI CONTAINED CUP-LIKE ART MARKINGS ON THE WALLS OF A GALLERY AND DISTINCTIVE LINES MADE WITH A FLINT OVER THE ENTRANCE OF A GALLERY (NOT ILLUSTRATED) (HARRISON 1878: 432). SHAFT APPROXIMATE SCALE, ART NOT TO SCALE. ART REDRAWN FROM PUBLISHED IMAGES OR RECONSTRUCTED FROM DESCRIPTIONS OF MARKINGS

four marks together and other marks are illustrated in Harrison (*ibid.*). When this evidence is combined with the placement of the marked chalk blocks in the fill and the presence of platforms or apses created on the east and south shaft walls it seems to imply that this shaft was used as a communal, possibly ritual, space. The platforms, 9 feet (2.75m) and 14.5 feet (4.4m) below the surface, face towards the cave giving the impression of the shaft being similar to an amphitheatre (Harrison 1877b: 432), and while the east, south and southwest have concentrations of art or marked blocks, the north is entirely excluded from the presence of art.

Shafts V and VI offer a contrast. The upper fill of Shaft V apparently contained many marked blocks but sadly these have never been fully described or illustrated and are now lost (Harrison 1878: 420, 422). Shaft VI contained cup-like art markings on the walls of a gallery and distinctive lines made with a flint over the entrance of a gallery (Harrison 1878: 432). Unfortunately no other detail was given. This

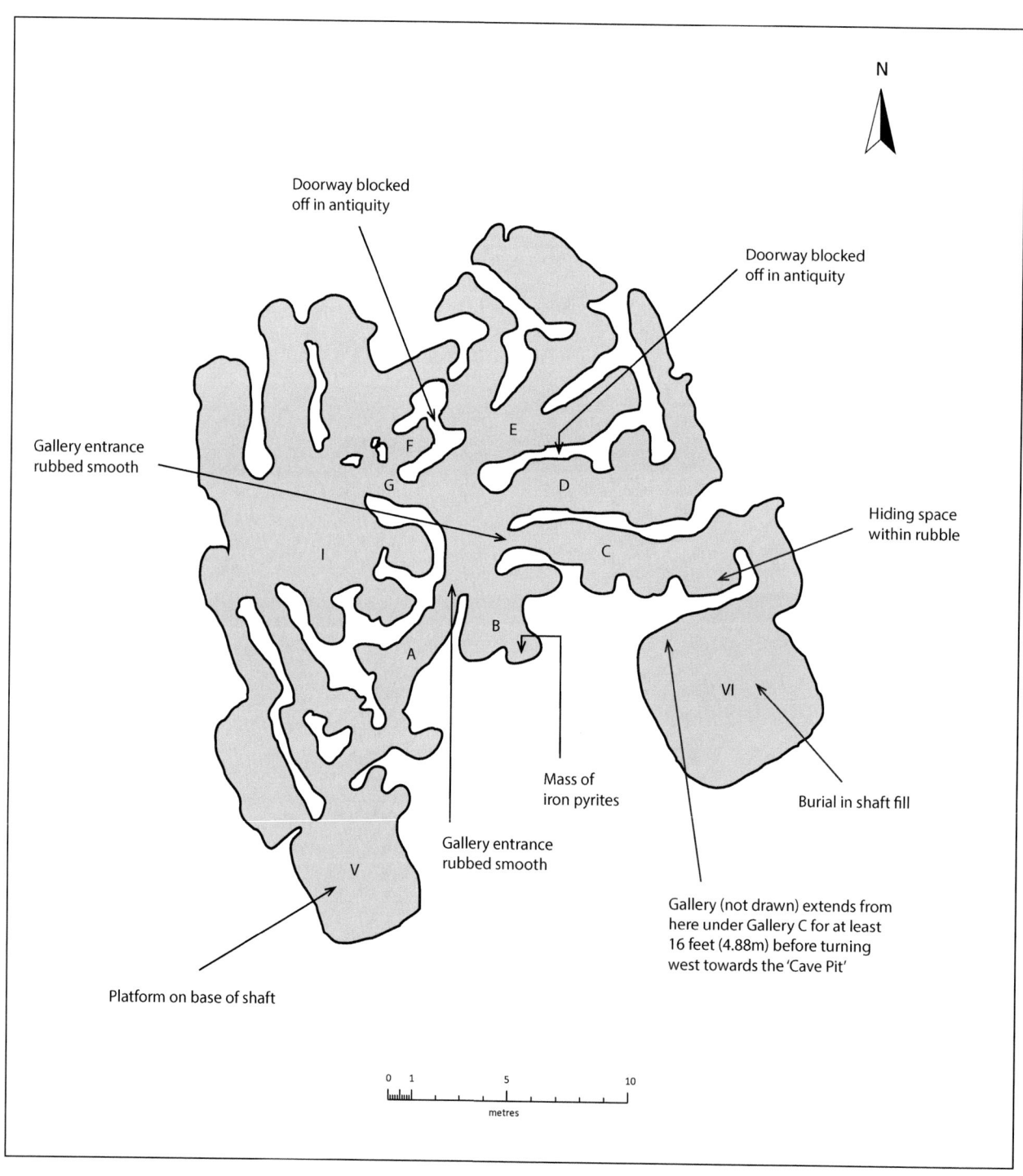

FIGURE 4.4 THE CISSBURY CAVE PIT COMPLEX, ARCHITECTURAL FEATURES (AFTER BARBER ET AL. 1999: 51; SHAFT APPROXIMATE SCALE, ART NOT TO SCALE)

is almost certainly due to the excitement surrounding the burial found in the shaft fill at 16 feet (4.88m), about half way down the 30 foot (9.14m) shaft (*ibid.*: 431). This is one of the earliest recorded discoveries of a burial surrounded by chalk blocks, other examples being excavated from Whitehawk and the Trundle causewayed enclosures (Thomas 1999b). The burial at Cissbury was placed with a flint axe near the knees, eight snail shells, six small flint tools, a chalk disc and a pebble marked by burning (*ibid*).

In architectural terms, the Cave Pit complex provides one of the most exciting internal spaces seen in British Neolithic studies. The 'cave' in the Cave Pit was constructed of chalk blocks and measured 7ft by 5ft 6" (2.1m x 1.6m), resembling a 'large baking oven, such as one often sees in farm-houses' (Harrison 1878: 413). It was in association with a chalk platform and, seemingly, integral with a hearth which had evidence of use. They connect in many places and yet there are at least three examples of the prehistoric blocking off of interconnecting galleries, seen with the accumulation of fine chalk concretion around the clean blocks (at the rear of E-F and in the middle of D-E, Figure 4.4). The Cave Pit itself had an entrance from Willett's Pit which was subsequently blocked off. The entrances to two galleries were rubbed smooth suggesting they were accessed more than the others (A leading to the Shaft V gallery system and C leading to Shaft VI). Gallery A was however completely full of chalk blocks initially and therefore any use through this entrance must have taken place for some time before it was filled with chalk rubble.

Within gallery B, referred to as a triple cave with a 'great central ceiling height', the small centre chamber, being only 46cm in height, contained a mass of iron pyrites which resembled a 'large reptile' on the south wall (*ibid.*: 415, Chapter 6). Other deposits are rare although many hundreds of flint flakes were found near the iron pyrites in Shaft VI (*ibid.*: 438; Chapter 6). Other areas are described as having high ceilings: Galley E which seems to have been heightened and the 'antechamber' F. Some galleries were left free of rubble completely although in gallery C, which connects the Cave Pit with Shaft VI, while rubble mostly covered this gallery, in the rear right chamber a space was left free of rubble and described by Harrison as 'an area of concealment' (1878: 416).

At the base of Shaft V, a platform was left raised from the base of the shaft (1ft 3" and 3ft wide, 38cm x 92cm) curving around to the centre on the south east at the base of the shaft where there were two cut steps. Embedded within this platform was a large chalk block, 1ft 6" in height and 2ft 5" in length (46cm x 74cm) from which a wide rubble wall to extended either side of it, leaving a narrow passage between it and the shaft wall and in this space was evidence of a small excavation hole (Harrison 1878: 421-2). Harrison also describes his puzzlement that the flint in the shaft was of good quality and there would have been no reason why it could not have been utilised. Although not mentioned specifically, this suggests that the platform was made of flint, or that there was flint elsewhere in this shaft. It is impossible to discern the exact nature of this platform. While flint occurs in layers they are not always entirely linear hence the platform could have contained both deposits.

The Shaft VI galleries are not illustrated yet they are described in Harrison's brief description as a postscript to the 1878 paper. To the east of the shaft two caves were seen between which there was a small doorway, only 1ft 3" high and 1ft 2" wide (38cm x 36cm). Chalk blocks were placed in the southernmost cave. Harrison describes how at a depth of 30 feet (9.15m), a gallery runs northwards from the shaft *under* gallery C for approximately 16 feet (4.87m) before turning westwards towards the Cave Pit (1878: 432-3). As he states, this is the first instance of a gallery being seen to extend underneath another gallery and it has not been evidenced in other more recent excavations. The Cave Pit's depth was recorded at 20 feet (6.1m), and hence it seems likely that Shaft VI was excavated after the Cave Pit.

Harrow Hill Shaft 21/13 Complex (Figure 4.5)

A total of seven examples of chalk art were found in Shaft 21 in addition to one carved chalk lump referred to as being 'bun-shaped', likely to be similar to a chalk ball with a flattened base (Curwen and Curwen 1926: 121, 126). Regrettably the chalk from the Curwen's excavations was not present for study at the Sussex Archaeological Society at Lewes Museum, and there are photographs only of the chalk blocks Graffiti 1, Graffiti 5 and Graffiti 6 which were copied for use in the figures. The illustrations of Graffiti's 3, 4 and 7 have been completed by the author through descriptions provided.

Graffiti 1 was placed in the upper gallery of Shaft 21 and demonstrates one of the commonly occurring motifs of parallel lines. A fracture in the chalk to the right of the piece shows that while part of the top layer of chalk has broken off, this is prior to the application of the decoration. The linear lines are present on only part of the block, as seen in others below, and also extend the full length of the block. While a scale is not provided on this photograph there is one present on the Curwen & Curwen (1926) Plate VI photograph and measures approximately 22.5cm in width and 30cm in length. While size is not specifically mentioned I have interpreted this as being of a similar size. Two of the chalk blocks were found at the base of the shaft with two examples of in situ art and are placed in opposition to each other on a north-west/south-east trajectory, Graffiti 7 was placed 60cm above the shaft floor also forming part of this opposition but in the reverse direction of north-east/south-west orientation to Graffiti 4 placed almost on the base of the shaft. No marked chalk is found on the approaches to the west galleries, yet these galleries lead in the direction of the Shaft 13 art. Some of the galleries in this shaft had been subject to collapse during prehistory and the roof in several places had been supported by additional chalk blocks (Galleries I, IV, V & VI, Curwen and Curwen 1926: 112). Graffiti 4 had been placed near a small flaking floor and hearth 15cm above the floor of the shaft. That the oppositional placement had been made during the backfilling of the shaft, while referencing the earlier block placements, is suggestive of structured practice.

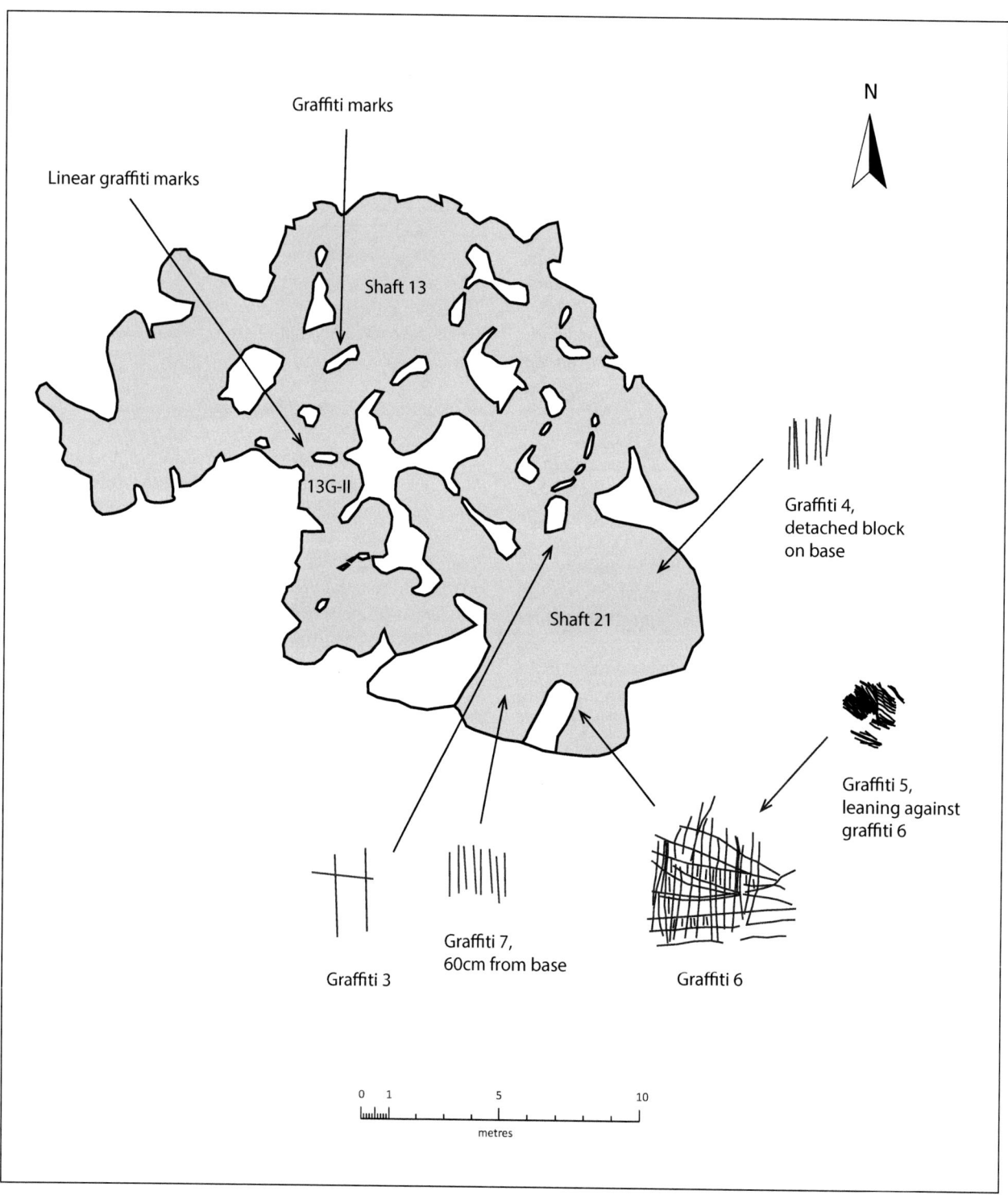

Figure 4.5 Harrow Hill Shaft 21/13 Complex (after Barber et al. 1999: 51; Curwen and Curwen 1926; McNabb et al. 1996). A total of seven examples of chalk art were found in Shaft 21 (after Curwen and Curwen 1926: 121, 126). Graffiti 7 was placed 60cm above the shaft floor; Graffiti 4 was placed close to the floor. Graffiti 6 was extracted from part of the gallery wall. In Shaft 13, chalk art was at the entrance to Gallery III, and within 13G excavated in 1982, near datum point 447 which appears to be at the north east, just inside Gallery 13G III (after McNabb et al. 1996: 24, 25). No illustrations of either art have been published. Shaft approximate scale, art not to scale. Art redrawn from published images or reconstructed from descriptions of markings

Graffiti 5 exhibits a combed decoration present on other chalk pieces and appears to have been made with a serrated flint blade dragged across the surface of the chalk. These occur in opposing directions, creating a raised and triangular, chevron appearance. In this type of decoration the linear lines are created by a different method to that shown above, the motif much more condensed and of a striking nature. The opposing faces suggest a desire to highlight this particular part of the block.

Graffiti 6 is the only block shown from this site which has been extracted from part of the gallery wall. The complexity of design illustrates different, additional actions in its creation. As can be seen from Figure 4.7, the vertical and horizontal lines in the main were made as a result of single actions to the length of the decoration, but additional lines have been added later at the third and eighth horizontal rows. The third horizontal row has single lines added in where the eighth has two in each square. In addition to these two rows being added to, the horizontal lines deliberately create points and triangles – they are not as chessboard, but much rather a fluid design incorporating wider squares or rectangles and very much smaller ones. Two of these points end at the fracture of the chalk block (at the second/third horizontal row and at the fourth/fifth/six) perhaps suggesting that this fracture was present during the application of the design.

Moving on to Shaft 13, chalk art was mentioned as occurring in Curwen's excavated Shaft 13 (at the entrance to gallery III), and within 13G excavated in 1982, near datum point 447 which appears to be at the north east, just inside gallery 13G III (McNabb *et al.* 1996: 24, 25). No illustrations of either art have been published, merely their placement at gallery entrances being noted. No marked chalk blocks are published as arising from this later excavation at Harrow Hill (*ibid.*).

Shaft 13 is a central shaft with many associated smaller shafts on its perimeter which were not visible on the surface prior to excavation. McNabb *et al.* (1996: 25) argue that many of these smaller shafts are likely to predate the excavation of the large central Shaft 13. The radiocarbon dates for Shaft 13 and associated shafts have wide margins and three dates have been produced from carbon samples from which contamination is possible. Broadly, the six dates allow for a time span between 4500 cal BC to 3370 cal BC (Barber *et al.* 1999: 81), although probable dates cluster around 3800cal BC. The sole recent date for Shaft 21, Gallery II is 4880 +/- 30 BP or calibrated covers the range 3780 cal BC to 3540 cal BC (Barber *et al.* 1999: 82). As this gallery extends almost to the base of Shaft 13, we can assume that this date effectively dates both shafts. This gallery entrance also exhibited sides which were rubbed smooth through use (Curwen & Curwen 1926: 114), indicating continued use of this gallery, also seen at the Cissbury shaft complex.

Marked and Unmarked Chalk Blocks by Shaft

Marked and unmarked loose blocks are discussed here where they do not appear in relation to other chalk art examples already reviewed.

Blackpatch

At the centre of the base of Shaft 1, large stacked blocks of chalk were placed which rose 4 or 5 feet high (1.2m–1.5m) but left enough room for all the galleries to be accessed (Goodman *et al.* 1924: 73). The structure of this fill is rather unusual as mostly chalk blocks were placed into mined galleries and it appears to have represented some architectural feature which may be a platform.

Cissbury

Tindall's Pit was excavated by Tindall in January 1874 (Willett 1875: 341). No galleries were present, the shaft tapering to 10 feet (3m) at its base, having been 18 feet (5.48m) at the top (Lane Fox 1876: 364). Four pear-shaped pierced blocks of chalk, pierced at the smaller end and weighing around three and a half pounds each (1.6 kg), were discovered in the shaft but regrettably no indication is given as to their actual location. From the general description it is probable they originated from the lower levels of the shaft fill (Harrison 1877a: 341). No illustrations are given for these pierced blocks but it is stated that around the holes 'are signs of thongs or strings having cut into the soft chalk by fraying' (*ibid.*: 346). These four pierced blocks are therefore the only large chalk blocks to exhibit this type of use wear evidence.

Harrison writes that many marked chalk blocks were discovered in this shaft by Tindall and kept by a local man, Ballard, with a very detailed carved chalk block being given to Rosehill by Tindall (Harrison 1877a: 267). This block was seen by Harrison who measured and described it. The dimensions are 7 inches by 5 inches (18cm by 13cm) and due to its size (being under 20cm) it is examined as a plaque (Chapter 5).

Harrow Hill (Figure 4.6)

Three decorated chalk blocks were uncovered during Holleyman's excavations of three shafts during 1936 and are held at Worthing Museum, although their contexts are unrecorded (Holleyman 1937). Another chalk block from Harrow Hill is held at the Keiller Museum at Avebury, labelled as having been given as a gift to O.G.S. Crawford though unfortunately there are no records as to the origin of it. All four blocks are illustrated but as no further details exist for their origin or placement no further discussion can be offered. One block from Harrow Hill exhibits two deep holes, one exhibits linear scratches and the third linear lines which appear to have been made with a rounded tool. The block at the Keiller Museum only contains one deep groove.

FIGURE 4.6 PHOTOGRAPH OF CHALK BLOCK FROM HARROW HILL (PHOTOGRAPH AUTHOR; © WORTHING MUSEUM AND ART GALLERY)

Grimes Graves

A very large chalk block (1ft 8inches by 8 inches, or 51cm x 20cm) was excavated from the base layer (X) of Pit 1 (Clarke 1915: 52). The workmen referred to it as 'Grime's Tombstone'. Clearly this was an unusual find but cannot be further commented upon as while Clarke states it was below one of the 'hearths' (or more probably charcoal depositions) in layer X, this context is two separate fills at the base of the shaft, hence even conjecturing placement is impossible. It is not mentioned as being decorated.

Chalk Art and Artefact Summary

Figure 4.7 draws together for the first time details of chalk art within the flint mines studied. It illustrates that the main component of chalk art across the mines is composed of linear designs or scratches. These can best be described as abstract, or rather, unrecognisable as representational art. There is one instance of art being described as being akin to a cup-mark, and the designs at Church Hill Shaft 4 had circular motifs. All the decorated blocks within the mines exhibit linear decoration. Also included in the table are shafts where loose decorated blocks are found. This has been completed in order to highlight those shafts where both art and decorated blocks occur and can be seen with reference to any gallery markings present.

All the shafts at Cissbury with art also have examples of art within one or more associated galleries and three of the five also contained decorated loose blocks. Where Church Hill only had one shaft with art out of at least eight excavated, art seems more prevalent at Harrow Hill with three in situ examples. The art at Grimes Graves is quite surprising as in relation to the amount of shafts excavated, chalk art rarely occurs. If chalk art were a regular social practice one would expect more examples. Two radiocarbon dates exist for two shafts mentioned in the table: 3780-3540 cal BC for Harrow Hill Shaft 21 and 3640-3360 cal BC for Cissbury Shaft 27 (Barber *et al.* 1999: 81-2). Just two shafts exhibit only decorated blocks, Tindall's Pit at Cissbury and blocks retrieved from Holleyman's 1936 excavations of Harrow Hill of which regrettably no written records survive. Omissions to this table are noticeable, with no markings present at Blackpatch, Long Down, Stoke Down, Easton Down or Martin's Clump. The lack of excavation at most of these sites does not allow for further conclusions to be drawn, but the Blackpatch data is interesting in its absence. At least eight shafts were excavated here and the lack of markings surprising.

Situating Chalk Art and Blocks in Flint Mines

The placement of chalk art, decorated and non-decorated blocks appears to have had significance within flint mine sites during both the early-mid Neolithic in Sussex and the later Neolithic at Grimes Graves in Norfolk. The paucity of evidence from rarely excavated sites such as Easton Down and Martin's Clump in Wessex, and Long Down and Stoke

Site	Shaft	Shaft Base - Linear Decoration	Shaft Base - Cup Mark	Shaft Base - Circular Design	Markings within Galleries	Decorated Blocks with Linear Design	Animal Markings
Cissbury Cave Pit Complex	Willett's Pit	●			●	●	
Cissbury Cave Pit Complex	Cave Pit	●			●	●	
Cissbury Cave Pit Complex	Shaft VI	●	●		●		
Cissbury	No 2 Escarpment Shaft	●			●	●	
Cissbury	Shaft 27	●					●
Church Hill	Shaft IV	●		●			
Harrow Hill	Shaft 13G	●					
Harrow Hill	Shaft 13	●					
Harrow Hill	Shaft 21	●				●	
Harrow Hll	Holleyman					●	
Grimes Graves	Pit 2	●					
TOTAL		11	10	1	1	5	5	1

FIGURE 4.7 TABLE OF FLINT MINE SHAFTS WITH ART

Down in East Sussex may not exclude the presence of this social practice in these locales.

The range of styles of decoration is fairly restricted, being in the main limited to linear and abstract markings. Both in situ markings and decorated blocks appear in many shafts to be in opposition to each other or deliberately placed within fills (at times up to 1 metre or more from the base of the shaft). This could indicate both an intention to place the art in particular places in addition to a planned and orchestrated refilling of the shaft. In two cases oppositional decoration is suggested as being incorporated into mortuary ritual (Cissbury Shafts VI and 27). The repeated presence of art at the base of shafts is the most common expression and does not appear in galleries where it has not appeared at the base of a shaft. Hence it seems likely that the shaft base markings are somehow a primary manifestation of this practice; art in the galleries being expressed as an elaboration, or secondary manifestation. The oppositional markings expressed at Harrow Hill Shaft 21 provide fascinating information due to the care of the Curwen's excavation methods. This complexity in both the level of deposits and indications that certain marks were ' added to' (as Graffiti 6) confirm impressions from the shaft walls which were rubbed smooth, that the shafts and galleries were repeatedly returned to. This rather contradicts the functional argument of shafts being opened purely for the extraction of flint.

In terms of the four East Sussex flint mine sites as a group, the presence of art at Harrow Hill, Cissbury and at one shaft at Church Hill and the corresponding lack of any art at Blackpatch poses a quandary. Chalk art was not a required, socially prescriptive part of flint mining itself or the creation of these sites; it was manipulable, both in its presence and in its elaboration within this geographical space. Without more secure dating it is difficult to argue for a chronological variation in social practice. Although Blackpatch has evidence of Later Neolithic and Early Bronze Age activity, this is also seen at Church Hill where art occurs in one shaft. Furthermore, variation in site use seems a difficult argument to sustain when flint was clearly extracted from all sites with similar practices.

Repeated access by different groups with varying approaches to art would concur with Topping's (2005) approach to land tenure, where groups may have access to the land for mining their individual shafts. However this could lead us to allocate separate groups to different shafts and I am reluctant to expand this argument when there is such a lack of chronological sensitivity; the evidence could support different regional groups visiting Sussex at a temporally similar time, yet could also support chronological differences. In terms of chronology two shafts with art can be dated: 3780-3540 cal BC for Harrow Hill Shaft 21 and 3640-3360 cal BC for Cissbury Shaft 27 (Barber *et al.* 1999: 82). Hence at the date which the overlap occurs (c. 3500 cal BC) chalk art has social relevance for this East Sussex group. The dating of Grimes Graves is in general terms during the third millennium BC and hence at least 500 years later than these examples. The presence of it at Grimes Graves is surprising in the respect it only occurs in one shaft but is equally limited to both the base of the shaft, over the gallery heads and comprises of the incised, mostly linear, scratches.

Unmarked chalk blocks have been shown to have depositional placements in delineating space, either through surrounding a body or the creation of internal architectural features. Chalk art and both decorated and undecorated chalk blocks therefore appear to be socially significant in both delineating space providing architectural features (such as the platform at the base of Shaft V, Cissbury and Grime's Tombstone, in Pit 1 at Grimes Graves). In order to situate this research into Neolithic discourses more fully, regional comparisons follow.

4.5 Comparisons with Contemporary Monuments

As discussed in 4.1 and 4.2, as chalk art and decorated chalk blocks have never been studied as an artefact class in Neolithic studies and this is the first time that this evidence has been brought together. This study has only focussed in detail on Dorset and Sussex, being areas which exhibit chalk art, decorated chalk and architecturally placed chalk blocks, in order to provide a context with which to examine similar evidence from flint mines. While no examples encountered have been excluded from this analysis, their presence at deposits in other counties (Wessex and Yorkshire) should not be fully discounted.

Chalk Art and Unmarked Blocks from Sussex

North Marden

Two decorated chalk blocks were excavated from Ditch 2 during the excavation of this oval barrow in 1982 (Drewett 1986). One contains a cup mark, perforation and a semi-circular hole at one side, the second a cup mark and linear scratches on one side (*ibid.*: 37-39). Three in situ art markings, all linear, were found on walls of the ditches although the location of them was not recorded.

The Trundle

The Trundle is a Neolithic causewayed enclosure on the South Downs to the west of the Sussex flint mines, close to the Goodwood racecourse. Three excavations have taken place here (Bedwin and Aldsworth 1981; Curwen 1929, 1931) with each producing carved chalk artefacts and the later two excavations, chalk blocks. The first block (Figure 4.8) was discovered by Curwen (1931: 104) at the base of the inner ditch cutting III near the centre, together with a chalk cup and a perforated chalk block, in turn associated with many large chalk blocks and an amount of charcoal. The first block has been highly decorated with a flint (*ibid.*) with a semi-circular design radiating out from the carved hole. The inside has been smoothed and even with the uneven edges it seems unlikely to have ever been completely circular, however to the left of the block, the decoration is slightly broken indicating some damage and reduction of the piece. The interior of the design has a lipped appearance, or ridge, running around the central hole. The design itself is linear carved lines expressed in segments, reflecting a purposeful design. The impression of the design is similar to a fossil ammonite and fossils. Fossil casts or fossil shells are often encountered during the extraction of chalk.

A further block was fully perforated but unfortunately there is no scale on the photograph and it was unavailable for study. However, in situ photographs taken during the excavation indicate it is of a similar size to the block above (Curwen 1931: 107, Plate III). The complete perforation of this block shows it is possible to create designs such as this even in large blocks and the lack of any extra decoration suggests that this perforation was a complete design motif in itself.

Bedwin and Aldsworth excavated another decorated block in 1980 (1981: 211, Figure 4.11). An extension of the ditch excavated by Curwen in 1928 was uncovered inside the west entrance to the hillfort and this chalk block was discovered on the floor of the causewayed enclosure ditch, within a fill of angular chalk blocks (*ibid.*: 208). The block has been squared off to two sides and exhibits linear lines incised into the chalk on one side. These fork out from a central line and again extend to the end of the chalk block. Where these meet the end of the block, a funnel has been made into the chalk, which would allow water or another liquid to drain down it. In terms of architecturally placed blocks, the burial of a woman was discovered under a cairn of chalk blocks in the outer ditch, with a further incised chalk block nearby which was unavailable for study (Curwen 1929: 48).

Whitehawk

Whitehawk causewayed enclosure on the South Downs produced four decorated chalk blocks (and other carved chalk artefacts which are discussed in Chapter 5). Two were perforated chalk blocks found in the circle of chalk blocks around the body of a young woman and baby, the

NON-PORTABLE CHALK: ART AND ARTEFACT

FIGURE 4.8 PHOTOGRAPH OF THE TRUNDLE CHALK AMMONITE (PHOTOGRAPH AUTHOR; ©LEWES MUSEUM)

FIGURE 4.9 PHOTOGRAPH OF THE TRUNDLE INCISED BLOCK (PHOTOGRAPH AUTHOR; © THE NOVIUM [A SERVICE PROVIDED BY CHICHESTER DISTRICT COUNCIL]. ALL RIGHTS RESERVED)

other two perforated blocks came from underneath the body (Curwen 1934: 110). In addition, the body of a child of about 7 years old was found in a hole with a post beside it and in the upper fill an incised chalk block (Curwen 1936: 72). Only one chalk block is still available for study following Curwen's excavations of the 1930s from Ditch II Cutting 1. It is a roughly half circular block with a perforation at the centre.

Chalk Art and Unmarked Blocks from Dorset

Dorset has been included as a region due to the examples of chalk art at both Monkton Up Wimborne and Flagstones. Maiden Castle has some well published chalk material which has also been included. Regrettably it was not possible to conduct a review of all chalk material in Dorset as it is outside the parameters of this study and only Martin Green's Down Farm museum in Dorset was visited. Hence this information is largely from textual sources only.

Maiden Castle

Maiden Castle is a causewayed enclosure near Dorchester, Dorset where in total four chalk blocks were discovered. A chalk block was excavated by Wheeler between 1934 and 1937 (Wheeler 1943: 2). It measures approximately 21cm by 18cm at its widest points and while Wheeler refers to it as a loom weight, the photograph shows no evidence of suspension wear on the chalk perforation. It was excavated from the Neolithic level of the 'town ditch', underneath the long mound (*ibid.*: 86-89), the 'town ditch' likely to be an outer causewayed ditch. The other three examples were excavated as follows: one nearby in a slightly higher but Neolithic stratigraphy (whole) and two in the long mound material which were fragments (*ibid.*: 183).

Flagstones

While exhibiting a rather unusual form and only partly excavated, Flagstones is classed as causewayed enclosure (Healy 1997). Four engravings were discovered on ditch walls not more than 50cm above the base of the ditch. Two are comprised of spirals, one a linear lattice pattern and one linear, parallel lines. They were on the external walls of some of the segmented ditches and on a terminal of one ditch. No carved or marked chalk was recovered from the ditches.

Monkton Up Wimborne Shaft

The Monkton Up Wimborne pit circle is situated on Cranborne Chase, Dorset, less than 500m from the Dorset Cursus. Within this a shaft was dug into a sunken pit, 10m in diameter and 1.5m deep into the solid chalk (Green 2000: 78). Within the pit is a raised platform, built up of chalk debris and midden material and in turn this pit is encompassed by a circle of pits. Within the shaft, two chalk blocks were excavated in addition to other chalk artefacts mentioned in Chapter 5. The shaft is 6.6m deep with one block excavated from the base of the shaft and one from 1m above the base of the shaft. The first chalk block was found at the base of the shaft. It is a large irregular rectangular block, approximately 30cm by 15cm, containing a carved, half-circular void to one side. The second chalk block, found 1m from the base of the shaft, is flat on one face and domed on the reverse. The flat side has a circular hole (or cup mark) approximately 10cm in diameter and the outer surface has a pecked decoration on one side near a groove in the chalk. This piece illustrates the completion of a chalk hole, but not extending to a full perforation seen with other pieces. At this level within the shaft, polished axe marks had been made on the shaft wall. While these are not mentioned as appearing in other contemporary sites or earlier flint mines, similar marks do occur at Grimes Graves and are discussed later. In another part of the sunken pit, a quadruple burial was placed in a pit filled with chalk blocks (Green 2000: 78).

Summary of Chalk Art in Contemporary Monuments

The data is summarised in Figures 4.10 and 4.11. As can be seen in Figure 4.10 there are two sites where in situ chalk art appears: at Flagstones, Dorset (four examples) and North Marden, Sussex (three examples). While these are mostly linear, two examples at Flagstones are circular/spiral in design. All sites are dated to the early-mid Neolithic, with no site exhibiting non-portable chalk blocks or art occurring into the late Neolithic. In terms of specific designs, cup marks are not present on in situ markings but appear on decorated blocks, with the most common design being a circular or semicircular design or perforation (Figure 4.11). Linear decoration and cup marks only occur as decoration on two blocks each. In non-portable architectural terms, three chalk block burials are evidenced, two in Sussex and one in Dorset. This type of burial implies a temporality in their deposition as fresh chalk would have been required to pack around the burial and parts of the ditches would necessarily have to be exposed prior to the chalk being reached. Hence, these burials occur at a particular stage in the construction of the monuments when the surface and sub-soils have been removed and yet prior to further deposition taking place.

Chalk art and chalk blocks present at contemporary Neolithic sites have many similarities to those at flint mines. In general terms the practice of inscribing in situ art, the creation and decorating of chalk blocks, the use of unmarked chalk blocks for architectural features and their subsequent deliberate deposition can be substantiated at both flint mines and other early-mid Neolithic sites in Dorset and Sussex. There are also design and depositional similarities which will be highlighted in the discussion below.

Site Name	Site Type	In situ – Linear Decoration	In situ - Cup Mark	In situ - Circular Design	Decorated Blocks	Chalk block burials
North Marden, Sussex	Long Barrow	●			●	
The Trundle, Sussex	Causewayed Enclosure				●	●
Whitehawk, Sussex	Causewayed Enclosure				●	●
Maiden Castle, Dorset	Causewayed Enclosure				●	
Flagstones, Dorset	Causewayed Enclosure	●		●		
Monkton Up Wimborne, Dorset	Pit Circle with Shaft				●	●
TOTAL		2	0	1	5	3

FIGURE 4.10 TABLE OF ART AND DECORATED BLOCKS WITHIN NEOLITHIC MONUMENTS CONTEMPORARY WITH THE FLINT MINES

Site Name	Site Type	Block with Linear Decoration	Block with Cup Mark	Block with Circular or Semi-Circular Design/Perforation
North Marden, Sussex	Long Barrow	●	●	●
The Trundle, Sussex	Causewayed Enclosure	●		●
Whitehawk, Sussex	Causewayed Enclosure			●
Maiden Castle, Dorset	Causewayed Enclosure			●
Monkton Up Wimborne, Dorset	Pit Circle with Shaft		●	●
TOTAL		2	2	5

FIGURE 4.11 TABLE OF THE TYPES OF DECORATION ON DEPOSITED CHALK BLOCKS

4.6 Understanding Chalk Art and Non-Portable Artefacts in the Neolithic

It has been demonstrated that there are chronological and design similarities in non-portable chalk art and in situ art in the British Neolithic and this section seeks to discuss in more detail how these occur as a phenomena. In doing so, I will return to the concepts outlined in 4.3 in conducting this analysis: Form, Style and Context. Non-portable chalk art and blocks were categorised for analysis in 4.3 as following:

- Carved or marked chalk blocks above 20cm in size.

- Chalk art - marked chalk in situ within the architecture of monuments on the natural chalk wall.

- Non-marked chalk blocks in terms of their architectural/contextual placement.

However, while form was a necessary step for analytical purposes, once defined it relates interpretively more closely with context; in archaeological terms relating which forms are commonly found within which contexts aids interpretation. Hence in order to interpret chalk art and blocks I will discuss similarities in their depositional contexts and style/decoration.

Context

The use of chalk blocks as internal architecture in the construction of hearths (Barber *et al.* 1999: 64), platforms and structures such as the 'cave' at Cissbury suggest both a functional and symbolic use. The inclusion of unmarked and marked chalk blocks in association with human remains has been noted at Cissbury mine and Whitehawk and the Trundle causewayed enclosures with deliberate placement of chalk blocks around the bodies. Another chalk block burial is also seen with the interment of four people within the Monkton Up Wimborne pit circle (Green 2000: 78). Chalk blocks appear to have been used to separate and signify space, at times associated with human remains, with art enhancing certain locations.

Thomas has discussed this delineation as being representative of chalk as a substance forming part of a social understanding of it separating space, which also had meaning within mortuary contexts (1999a, 1999b). He has proposed the spatial reorganisation of significant places thus:

> The construction of monuments in earlier Neolithic Britain introduced discontinuity into the landscape by establishing boundaries around secluded and differentiated places. This was achieved by rearranging the materials which were present locally, at once drawing attention to ubiquitous substances and rendering them unfamiliar (1999a: 52).

By viewing chalk blocks as a ubiquitous substance rendered unfamiliar in this manner allows us to examine contexts with more clarity. In this way, we may be able to determine that mine sites and ditched enclosures on chalklands have nested scales of meaning; separating the landscape through the use of labour and chalk, with chalk in turn being socially significant as a material of delineation. Moreover carved chalk artefacts can also occur with burials and cremations at the flint mines and contemporary sites which will be discussed in Chapter 5, hence this meaning may also extend to portable artefacts in chalk (Thomas 1999b).

Chalk blocks are therefore used in distinct ways: as a method of separating one feature from another in spatial terms; as a means of separating dead bodies from the wider context therefore creating a context within a context, and furthermore as a substance which is culturally appropriate for the burial of *these particular persons*. The Cissbury burial is that of a man; at Whitehawk, that of a woman and baby (possibly a pregnant woman); the Trundle both a woman and a child; at Monkton Up Wimborne, one woman and three children, and therefore it is not simply a division of appropriateness dependant on biological sex or physical age.

These spaces may simply have been used for the burial of people who died during aggregation at these sites. The social norm may have been to inter recently dead people within ditches, within the chalk, when it was exposed. Yet one would expect that over the course of the building of such monuments more people may have died and be evidenced in deposits. Furthermore, these human remains are not older people, but often women and/or children (Thorpe 1984). Death may have been caused deliberately. As the burials are socially sanctioned within these spaces, it is not unreasonable to investigate if the deliberate deaths of these people were also socially sanctioned and hence represent a form of sacrifice. It is rather unlikely, especially in respect to the Monkton Up Wimborne burials that four people died of natural causes in such a short space of time. While a virulent disease may have caused such an outcome, one would expect others to have also been affected. Also, interpreting the burials as diseased suggested that the chalk blocks may have been thought to contain or segregate the illness and hence a purifying substance. Moreover, the Cissbury Shaft VI burial (which will be discussed further in Chapter 6) appears to be a composite body of two persons, and near simultaneous death by natural causes or accident would also be unlikely. I suggest that deliberate socially sanctioned murder as an interpretation should be considered when investigating burials such as these.

However, it seems that whichever interpretation we apply to these burials, the chalk blocks will signify segregation of space in some way. Perhaps further study on other examples will enlighten this further. The practice at flint mines and other monuments appears to be fairly consistent within the early-mid Neolithic. In terms of chronology, the Monkton Up Wimborne burial is dated to c. 3300 cal BC (Green 2000: 78) whereas the burial at Shaft 27 at Cissbury has been dated to 3640-3360 cal BC (Barber *et al.* 1999: 81-2).

Turning to decorated chalk blocks, their placement in Shaft 21 at Harrow Hill is suggestive of planned depositional practice comprising of oppositional placement within the bottom 1m of the shaft. The continuation of structured deposits in this context is secure in that it cannot have been subject to a later re-cut, and was therefore contemporary with the mining and backfilling. It has been suggested that the in situ markings around gallery entrances may have been 'intended to impart information about those galleries to anyone entering the shaft' (Barber *et al.*: 1999: 65), but this argument cannot account for the marked blocks higher in the shaft, or at the Monkton Up Wimborne shaft where the chalk block occurs at around 1m from the base of the shaft and there are no galleries. If we accept that the separation of certain chalk blocks around burials is for the delineation of space, perhaps the marked chalk blocks are also socially functioning in this respect. The concentration at the base of Shaft 21 at Harrow Hill may highlight the central space at the base of the shaft, rather than providing information about the galleries. The decorated chalk blocks at Monkton Up Wimborne, being similar in form to the other blocks, imply a continuation of this practice outside the flint mines, where galleries are not present or referenced.

Pit 2 at Grimes Graves contained two examples of chalk art, the 'Tally Marks' and the 'Sundial' (Clarke 1915: 73-75). I have already discussed that this appears to be unusual for the shafts at Grimes Graves, as is the large chalk block in Pit 1 referred to as 'Grime's Tombstone'. No monuments local to Grimes Graves have been reported to have exhibited chalk art or blocks. The size of Grimes Graves as a Neolithic/Early Bronze Age monument in this locality is unparalleled and while we can compare its size with contemporary mid-late Neolithic monuments (such as Durrington Walls or Mount Pleasant) these are not geographically local. Hence, interpretively Grimes Graves in Norfolk appears to be isolated yet with similarities to earlier traditions at mines in Sussex.

Context Summary

This separation and delineation of space appears to be a theme which influences the placement of both chalk art and decorated and undecorated chalk blocks. The flint mines express this three dimensionally at times, having large enclosed spaces which suggest the base of the shaft is relevant and up to 1m in the fill especially significant in some way. With respect to chalk art, in the two examples studied of inter-related shafts chalk art appears to occur with more frequency, with evidence of longer term use and reuse of the space. If we view all the shafts with galleries as possibly being inter-related, it is possible that the art occurs within particular formats where perhaps entrances and exits to mining shafts complexes are controlled and manipulated over time. Chalk blocks in architectural features or as decorated forms are rarely discovered singly, but rather together or in placement with each other, as at The Trundle and Whitehawk. The marked chalk blocks at the Cissbury Cave Pit appear to relate to the earlier depositions at the base of the fill, while also highlighting the unusual architecture at the top of the shaft. Once we interpret the blocks in a relational format rather than as discrete depositions we can begin to see this evidence within a wider social context.

The separation of hearths through chalk blocks is reminiscent of the mortuary ritual of separating the body in death from the wider context. Hence, the conceptual significance of rings of chalk blocks may indicate a similarity in social construction of death and the understanding of hearths. Furthermore, the consistency of internal architecture within mines could reflect a practice of building with chalk blocks on the surface at a variety of sites which no longer survives archaeologically. Mercer (1980) has suggested that blocks may have been used in this way at Hambledon Hill. The size of blocks suggests that they have been extracted from the lower levels of the chalk as surface chalk deposits are likely to be too friable for subsequent modification and may be of too small a size. Therefore, the extraction of certain chalk blocks was *predetermined*, dependant on social requirement, whether for burial, decoration or a combination of the two. In this way, chalk extraction was as much a deliberate, focussed, social activity and requirement, as the extraction of flint.

These differences in depositional character between causewayed enclosures and mines have also similarity in practice; the separating and nesting of deposits within chalk blocks allow the separation of deposits within this culturally separating material. While unmodified and at times modified blocks have this character, carved chalk artefacts also suggest an integrated and relational aspect to chalk material which will be discussed in Chapter 5.

Style: Skeuomorphism

From the flint mines there are few examples of blocks which may be functional or skeuomorphic in any respect and arguments of skeumorphism for the later Neolithic abstract designs with reference to portable forms have been largely rejected by Thomas (1996: 156-8). However some chalk blocks from non flint mine sites could give some indications of this practice, reflecting other things in other substances. For example, The Trundle decorated chalk block is reminiscent of an ammonite yet at a huge size. This exaggeration is clearly intentional and the execution of the design unique. This represents a once living animal, though other examples may reference other Neolithic artefacts.

Some perforated blocks have been referred to as 'loom weights' (at Maiden Castle and Cissbury) although there were only four where suspension was noted from Tindall's Shaft at Cissbury (Willett 1875) and regrettably as these are lost, could not be re-examined. While these may have been used in functional terms, others may represent wooden weights or blocks which do not survive in deposits. Blocks such as another from The Trundle having a funnel to one side (Bedwin and Aldsworth 1981) may also suggest function (with perhaps the sheen on the funnel indicating evidence of use) or be representative of another artefact in a different substance. The large cup mark in the chalk block from the base in the shaft at Monkton Up Wimborne could represent a socket for a post (Green 2000: 82) or alternatively perhaps a vessel for pounding or grinding substances, akin to a pestle and mortar. It seems prudent that with the lack of definitive evidence of function for these blocks in themselves, to suggest that these blocks are more likely to be symbolic representations of artefacts which may be real or mythological. Hence, while contemporaneous functional artefacts made out of other degradable materials, such as wood have perished, our only clues to them lie within the representations of them in chalk. Conversely, chalk may be seen as a symbolic substance for the creation of the representation of mythological artefacts for use in ritual and/or in deposition. Whether the artefacts represent skeuomorphic representations or mythological ones, we should not forget they form real artefacts in chalk and hence are likely to have had multiple scales of meaning.

Style: Design Comparisons

In 4.2 I detailed the functional interpretive understandings previously applied to chalk art within mining contexts and that this approach has not been taken with more the recent findings of chalk art. As noted by Barber *et al.* (1999: 60-61, 65-67), and demonstrated above, shaft wall markings and incised blocks are often found at the entrance to galleries at the base of the shafts or up to 1m from the base; the decorated blocks from causewayed enclosures occurring either at the base of ditches or close to them with a similar pattern at Monkton Up Wimborne.

At two contemporary Neolithic monuments Flagstones, Dorset and North Marden, Sussex, chalk art has been argued as being similar to rock art design traditions (Drewett 1986; Woodward 1988; Healy 1997). It has further been suggested that the Cave Pit art is similar to later Grooved Ware decoration yet comparisons to rock art have not been offered (Barber *et al.* 1999: 65-66). These comparisons have been made through linear and circular markings being visually similar to those found within Grooved Ware, specifically the use of spirals, hence the structure of the argument in accepting these as rock art comparable designs is based on subjective parallels. This is adequate for the purpose of expressing chalk markings as genuine and within chronological norms for the period, however, it does not move interpretation forward.

In terms of chalk art, the designs represented in the mines are mostly linear scratches. They are present during the early to mid Neolithic at the flint mines of Cissbury, Harrow Hill and probably Church Hill in addition to the Flagstones enclosure and North Marden oval barrow. Linear scratches also form part of recognised rock art and appear on rock art at Loughcrew, Co. Meath, Baurnadomeeny, Co Tipperary, Scrahanard, Co. Cork and Knocknashee Co, Sligo in Ireland (Shee Twohig 1981: figures 234, 278-280). Similar designs are also seen at Skara Brae in various locations, (*ibid.*: figures 289-290). The chevron patterns and the 'chessboard' design of the Harrow Hill piece (Graffiti 6) are perhaps the earliest examples of the more complex designs (or at least ones which have survived excavation). This shaft is dated to 3780-3540 cal BC and is therefore the earliest known art date in England (Barber *et al.* 1999: 81-2). The Cissbury date of 3640-3360 cal BC for Shaft 27 (*ibid.*) provides a supporting date for art in this shaft complex, as do the very broad range dates from Harrow Hill which at the minimum show probability of the art prior to 3300 cal BC and possibly even slightly earlier for Shaft 13, even as early as 3900 cal BC (*ibid.*; McNabb *et al.* 1996: 21).

Turning to designs on decorated blocks, there have been similarities noted between chalk decoration and rock art, one of the most apparent being the chalk block from Monkton Up Wimborne (Green 2000). The pecking decoration on the chalk on block found 1m from the base of the shaft is reminiscent of the application of rock art designs on stone, and such a hole on a piece of rock art would be termed a 'deep cup' (Beckensall 1999: 13). There are two examples of similar rock art: stone blocks from a cairn at Weetwood in Northumberland, excavated by Beckensall (1999: 143-146) and a larger single decorated stone block from Dean in Cumbria (*ibid.*: 35). Many of the blocks from the Weetwood cairn have multiple designs, yet some also exhibit single 'deep cups', as the Monkton Up Wimborne chalk block. The second example again contains more motifs but gives the impression of similarity in design to the Monkton Up Wimborne block.

However caution must be exercised in simple comparisons of this nature in two respects: chronology and regional distribution. Rock art is largely a Later Neolithic/Early Bronze Age tradition and occurs mainly in the north of England, Scotland and its islands, and Ireland (Beckensall 1999, Bradley 1997). As has been demonstrated, chalk art and decorated blocks occur in the chalklands of Sussex, Dorset, Wessex and Norfolk. While the dating of rock art cannot be achieved through direct dating, the context of much rock art is within mortuary contexts or as isolated examples in the landscape. Furthermore the investigation of rock art has a different interpretive history in which designs are suggested as being similar to designs on Grooved Ware and this has been documented by many (Bradley and Chapman 1984; Richards and Thomas 1984: 192-3; Bradley 1997: 64; Brindley 1999a).

This relating of design has led to a level of dependence in research where pottery chronologies are more securely dated. Chronology has begun to be examined following the direct dating of deposits around rock art at Newgrange in Ireland suggesting that the motifs were depicted c. 3000 cal BC (Brindley 1999a: 135). This is seen as an Intermediary Style in terms of a chronology of designs offered by O'Sullivan (1986). Yet the earliest Grooved Ware in Ireland is also dated to *c.*3000 cal BC (Brindley 1999b: 30-1) hence rock art at the Intermediary Style is seen as contemporary with Grooved Ware designs in Ireland. It appears that Brindley is arguing two proposals: that rock art perhaps predates Grooved Ware, and that there is a contemporaneity with rock art being depicted through the later Plastic Style (argued by O'Sullivan) and later Grooved Ware designs.

The dates could be comparable in Britain. While Bradley (1997: 65) suggests there are some indications for early British rock art at *c.*3000 BC, or open-air rock art possibly emerging around 3300 BC, he also argues that this type of art is likely to have commenced at the start of the Neolithic, possibly being a continuation from the Mesolithic at least in some parts of the country (*ibid.*: 58-9, 92-3). Yet while Bradley argues that the lack of dates in an early period and the reuse of stone providing later dates could all mask an earlier origin of rock art, it is not proven. However the two radiocarbon dates that exist for shafts with chalk art predate 3300 cal BC, being 3780-3540 cal BC for Harrow Hill Shaft 21 and 3640-3360 cal BC for Cissbury Shaft 27 (Barber *et al.* 1999: 81-2). Therefore, chronologically the flint mines with art predate Grooved Ware by at least 400-500 years, and possibly as much as 800 years (Brindley 1999b; Thomas 1999a: 118) and rock art even at 3300 cal BC. In terms of art in general, during the early Neolithic pottery took the form of undecorated fine bowls (Thomas

1999a: 98). Hence, designs seen on chalk blocks or art as linear scrapes, chevrons and chessboard designs were relevant for application on chalk in southern Britain, prior to markings being adopted as a social practice for pottery and most probably other types of rock.

At this juncture, we have two major interpretive differences compounded from the start of this section. We still have contradictory dating evidence for rock art and chalk art, with chalk art almost exclusively being prior to 3300 BC (and possibly as early as 4000 - 3800 cal BC) and rock art almost fully dated to after 3300 BC and secondly, the geographical distribution of chalk art and rock art are mostly exclusionary, there are no sites where both occur together or sequentially under traditional methodology. Under this approach it seems likely that the markings on pottery, chalk and stone are symbolically comparable yet occur at different times, in different geographical locations in the Neolithic. However, this consensus on rock art is not wholly correct. A decorated rock was recently reported as being uncovered by a ploughing farmer thirty years ago at the southern henge at Knowlton, similar in design to decorated stones reported from Bronze Age barrows in the area, excavated in the nineteenth century (Lewis *et al*.: 2000). These designs are described as a rare Grooved Ware design of concentric circles (found on a few instances of local pottery), but due to the lack of context the Knowlton stone cannot be dated to the Neolithic. Despite this it seems that these regional distributions of rock art are awry, with Dorset being excluded in the Bronze Age.

Yet, if we move away from design comparables to pottery and arguments of the origin of practices perhaps other comments can be made. Only linear designs are present at Grimes Graves in Pit 2, when Grooved Ware pottery occurs in other shaft contexts at the same site. While the similarities to the Sussex mine art are therefore apparent, the scratches depicted in this way appear to be culturally significant and separate from cross-hatches and other designs present in Grooved Ware. There are no spirals designs, or pecking or stab marks. Hence, at Grime's Grave in particular, the social significance of the linear scratches is separate to that of Grooved Ware design, in terms of both design and portability. To summarise, it seems that linear scratches are referenced in static or non-portable media at Grimes Graves and reflect earlier Neolithic chalk art traditions from Sussex rather than appearing as an equal substitute for Grooved Ware design either in terms of social practice or in terms of style. Furthermore, Grooved Ware designs are not appearing as in situ art at Grimes Graves.

Therefore while chalk art may have comparables in rock art, with the dates suggesting that chalk art may precede rock art, I believe we should examine chalk art as an entity in itself. The chronology and regional distribution separates it from early Grooved Ware and yet both are arguably a part of early Neolithic abstract design. The evidence from Grimes Graves seems to differentiate this tradition from pottery and portability. While they have a common heritage, the use of chalk art was restricted to certain areas in certain regions. Chalk art seems to be a specific manifestation of an early-mid Neolithic tradition which is of an abstract nature. It is designed as non-portable and hence its meaning is partly constituted through its context: in mines and ditches and on chalk blocks. The application of this art adds a particular meaning to existing contexts, enhancing the significance of certain areas in a specific way.

This understanding of context and art placement refers back to earlier discussions of chambered tombs and art, where rock art has been argued to appear at liminal or transitional areas (Thomas 1990). There are no chambered tombs in Sussex and the few long mounds present appear to be chamber-less earthen mounds (Russell 2002). The flint mines however create internal spaces that could be said to reflect the type of architecture seen in chambered tombs. Both shaft complexes studied, the Cave Pit at Cissbury and Shaft 13/21 at Harrow Hill, exhibit intricate nested spaces which may have had different access routes from different shafts throughout their use. Hence entrances and exits may have been inverted or altered through the generations as the galleries were adapted. The lack of any other architecture of this kind regionally could imply that these underground spaces, created through extractive activity, socially functioned in a similar way to chambered tombs or long barrows, without the emphasis on human remains evidenced at many of these sites. Adopting the use of art in this way can enhance our interpretations on the use of monumentality in Sussex. Integrating art and architecture can be a key concept to understanding monuments themselves and yet for one chambered tomb in particular this has not been attempted, the West Kennet long barrow.

Bridging the Gap: Rock Art in Wessex

In the early-mid Neolithic in Wessex, chalk art occurs as a contextual design tradition in flint mines and contemporary monuments. I have already shown that rock art studies are limited in not including Dorset and also that their studies are heavily linked to pottery studies which may not always be a productive way forward. In the traditional way of interpreting rock art by reference to specific Grooved Ware designs, no other Neolithic art is present in Wessex as no spirals, zigzags or pecking marks have been noted as present on stone in any of these areas. However designs on non portable stones do exist, and in at the West Kennet long barrow have been incorporated into monumental architecture.

Polissoirs are stones which have been utilised for the grinding and polishing of axes. This repeated action on their surface creates pits (or 'cups') and grooves (or parallel lines) embedded in their surfaces. Returning to arguments concerning the functionality of artefacts in Chapter 3, these stones are only excluded from interpretations of rock art because they have a functional explanation for their form. This functional explanation requires that in the cases

FIGURE 4.12 PHOTOGRAPH OF THE FYFIELD DOWN POLISSOIR (PHOTOGRAPH AUTHOR)

FIGURE 4.13 PHOTOGRAPHS OF POLISSOIRS AT LEWES MUSEUM, LM1 ABOVE, LM2 BELOW (PHOTOGRAPHS AUTHOR; © LEWES MUSEUM)

of these *recognisable* markings, they are not designed but emerge as a consequence of functional use. Hence, where rock art has symbolic connotations, polissoirs are simply a reflection of past functional activity. Figure 4.12 illustrates polissoirs from Wessex (Fyfield Down, Overton near Avebury) and Figure 4.13 two from Lewes Museum in Sussex (LM1 and LM2). The Fyfield Down polissoir design is almost identical to that of LM1. While this discussion may suggest that polissoirs should be take perhaps more seriously as artefacts, (and/or contexts) the monumental aspect of them is apparent at West Kennet. The study of this monument in particular can bring greater clarity to this argument due to the recent conclusions of its construction dating to before 3670 – 3635 cal BC (Bayliss *et al.* 2007).

Polissoirs are integral in the architecture of the West Kennet long barrow with several being present in various locations within the stone chambers (Piggott 1962: 19-21). All are placed in locations where they could no longer function as polishing stones, being in a vertical or upwardly angled position which would give no opportunity for pressure to be placed upon an axe being polished. The largest polissoir with the most striking grooves is on the left hand side of the monument as you enter (Figure 4.14). On close examination, it is quite rough internally and instead of the two grooves having been produced through axe grinding, they may be an exaggerated carving to represent axe polishing grooves. They do not appear to be natural. Following the passage (or gallery), further polissoirs occur between the South West Chamber and the West Chamber, and in the rear West Chamber. If we examine the placement of these markings in a comparable way to examination of rock art in Ireland (e.g. Thomas 1990) we can come to some similar conclusions. The art appears at liminal boundaries of the monument, between chambers, and at the entrance which indicate they have been placed with attention to practice within the monument. Notable examples cluster on the southern aspect of the monument. Furthermore, as the date of construction is likely to be before 3635 cal BC (Bayliss *et al.* 2007), the polissoirs had to have been in use prior to this date, quite possibly for many years for the depth of markings to be made.

This could indicate several aspects for enhancing the meaning of West Kennet. Firstly, if we accept polissoirs represent a form of art, their locations within the monument reflect highlighted transitional areas. Furthermore, that they are polissoirs suggests that axe polishing is being referenced as an activity and yet the stones themselves could no longer be used for that purpose within the monument. They are clearly stones which have been socially significant for many years and are used at key junctures within the construction of the monument which was used for the deposition, disarticulation and sorting of the dead. I would argue that this suggests that prior to the construction of the long barrow, the polishing of axes may have been an integral part of mortuary activity. It may have been taking place as bodies were being excarnated, most likely in areas very local to the monument (though the retrieval of polissoirs from further distances should not be discounted). This situates axe polishing within a prescribed social activity only performed at distinct temporal events. Perhaps only the kin of the decreased would have the authority to grind their axe(s) at this time, a repetitive activity carried out by the mourners (perhaps in turn) over several days, grinding their grief?

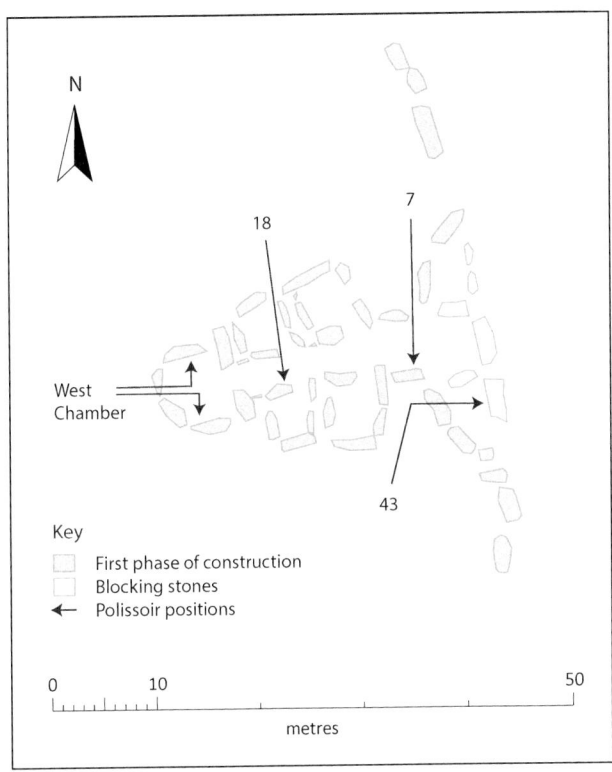

FIGURE 4.14 LOCATION OF POLISSOIRS AT WEST KENNET LONG BARROW (AFTER PIGGOTT 1962; APPROXIMATE SCALE)

The construction of this long barrow both prevented that past activity and yet referenced it, as if to legitimise this new internment practice. The polissoirs could be reached and touched, yet not used. The end chamber, or West Chamber with several polissoirs, contained the body parts of at least 4 male individuals and one child (Bayliss *et al.* 2007: 87), whereas the South West Chamber contained the most number of individuals of both sexes and all ages over 12. The long barrow as a whole is representative of a normal demographic and suggestions there may be the deposition of specific individuals based on age or gender groups is unsubstantiated.

This long barrow is only in use for a short period of time (perhaps as little as 10 years) before the site was abandoned for just over a century (or as much as 300 years) and then filling of the chambers began in a secondary phase. These deposits consisted of discrete groups of mostly disarticulated or partly articulated human remains in chalk rubble, mixed charcoal, pottery and animal bone fragments and continued over a much longer period of time, perhaps as much as 800 years (*ibid.*: 94-5). Therefore, the enduring significance of this monument is extraordinary given its short initial phase of activity. I would argue that the continued significance of it for the deposition of disarticulated human remains is due to the enduring significance of the polissoirs integral in the monument, which themselves referenced practice prior to the monuments construction. By interring recently excarnated human remains with the ancestors in the long barrow, the ancestors that are referenced through the polissoirs but are not contained within the long barrow,

are also socially present. Axes polished in this way are biographical artefacts, embodied with cultural references to past human lives.

Theoretically I propose that instead of viewing polissoirs as functional, we examine them as art, which within this book is also artefact. Hence polissoirs are both art and artefact, signifying context. This argument has attempted to expand our concept of early Neolithic art and suggest that polissoirs could be seen as rock art, functioning as active social media in their own right and not simply a reflection of past functional activity. Hence considering this example and what it could suggest for the integration of axes in mortuary activity at the beginning of the Neolithic in Britain, perhaps we can accept that polissoirs form a type of southern British rock art, where other designs are depicted in chalk rather than stone.

Returning to flint mines, another type of marking is noted in some shafts, the mark of polished or chipped axes on the walls in various places, sometimes in groups or singly (Greenwell 1870; Clarke 1915: 59, 129-133). In Pit 1 Gallery 12, up to twenty of these marks were noted (Clarke 1915: 59). Similar marks were located 1m from the base of the Monkton Up Wimborne shaft at the same level at the highly decorated chalk block (Green 2000). If we take interpretively the same approach to the polished or chipped axe marks as to the polissoirs discussed earlier we may register these marks as significant and deliberate at places which may have been of social importance. Furthermore axe marks may also be referencing axes in a similar way to the polissoirs above.

In summary, polissoirs are art, artefact, and signify context. They contribute to the discipline theoretically in this way prior to referencing axes or axe polishing. Yet, once they are considered artefacts we can include these interpretations of them. I have argued that the use of polissoirs in monuments references axes, axe polishing and my also suggest extraction, forest clearance and exchange links. Their theoretical re-categorisation gives us a greater interpretive breadth from which we can enhance our interpretations of the Neolithic. Additionally, field finds of polissoirs should also be considered as rock art sites and their distribution mapped in similar ways. Perhaps polissoirs are on routeways or liminal landscape boundaries as argued for other types of rock art (Bradley 1997). Throughout this section I have argued a number of interpretations of chalk art, non-portable blocks, monumentality and rock art. I will attempt to provide some cohesion to these below.

4.7 Conclusion

In this chapter I have discussed the location and form of chalk art as both in situ markings and non-portable blocks. I have argued that the decoration and placement of chalk blocks is socially significant following themes of spatial separation expressed through both mortuary practice and architecture. Concepts of chalk as a material being a symbolic and representational media have been introduced, a theme which will be discussed further through the study of portable chalk artefacts (Chapter 5). These themes have been demonstrated as occurring both at flint mine sites and those of contemporary monuments (causewayed enclosures and long barrows) thereby integrating the study of the materiality of chalk into wider Neolithic discourses.

Moreover, deposition and non-portable art within the mines gives indications as to how chalk as a substance was deliberately exploited to create flint mines. The mines were the product of the intentional creation of space underground, undertaken in specific ways within cultural norms, in a similar way to standing, surface architecture. Hence, agency and intentionality feature more cohesively than interpretations of their architecture when viewed as a by-product of extraction activity. The subtlety emphasised here is that extraction is no less an architectural creation than the application of materials to build a structure or monument. Flint mines are monuments; no more, no less, yet in a much more designed fashion than argued previously (e.g. Barber *et al.* 1999; Russell 2000, 2001). Their similarity to chambered tombs has been mentioned. Integrating the perceptions of different forms of monumentality in the Neolithic is crucial, and the practice of chalk block burials and chalk art occurring at different contemporary sites indicative of this.

However, many decorated chalk blocks occur without burials and the ubiquitous nature of unmarked blocks means that their depositional placement cannot always be studied. Thomas (1999b: 13) argues that incised chalk is 'associated with transitions between personal space and communal space, so early Neolithic mortuary practice often involved a transition from a fleshed whole person to a disarticulated "communal" mass of bones'. While this correlates well with mortuary evidence in the mines, many mines with art do not contain burials or human remains. The incising and creation of chalk artefacts may underlie many meanings; changing and emphasising different significations in different depositional contexts (*ibid.*).

Differences do occur at flint mine sites and other monuments however. In relation to form, the chalk blocks from flint mines appear to display less complexity of design overall. Many markings are simply linear scrapes or scratches whereas those at these other monuments appear to have had more time spent in their creation. This should not however impact on the depositional placement or importance of these artefacts/contexts. Indeed, it is more likely that the differences in decoration are concerned with the social appropriateness of certain motifs and designs at different locales or could indicate differences in chronology as I have discussed with regard to Grimes Graves. At Grimes Graves the practices in terms of chalk art seem to reflect and reference earlier practices in Sussex and Wessex, and this theme will be also explored further throughout this study in Chapters 5 and 6. It is likely that the linear scratches occur as an early Neolithic motif which later become largely out of use. Why that may the case is uncertain: are they using different strategies and practices where this art is no longer relevant? Or does the art represent some cosmology which has been rejected? How conscious is this chronological shift?

Nonetheless, the similarity of certain chalk block designs to that of rock art should be acknowledged. While interpretively we may only be able to be secure of the fact that the similarity of design within different mediums and geographical scale is suggestive of continuing practice, the continuing practice in itself is significant. Stone, like chalk, has been extracted and quarried, and within the northern monuments serves to define cultural space within the landscape, albeit in the case of mines, a subterranean landscape. I have argued that in addition to chalk as being incorporated into mortuary activity, it is significant in an analogous way to rock art in mortuary contexts. While this may suggest that chalk art is a chronologically earlier activity to rock art, I have suggested that the inclusion of polissoirs as rock art may have been relevant in the past and valid for further interpretations. Similarities occur across the Neolithic in depictions, style and form and we do not have to attempt to project these into a linear, hierarchical progression of one style leading chronologically to another. Chalk as a substance may encompass many cultural meanings expressed through form as well as deposition and these will be discussed further in Chapter 5.

Chapter 5

Portable Chalk Artefacts

5.1 Introduction

The separation of flint mines from other discourses within Neolithic Britain is challenged in this research through an analysis of artefacts recovered from them. This is completed with reference to contemporary Neolithic sites, in close regional proximity to the mines, where possible. It has been argued that this interpretive separation is visible both in viewing the flint mines sites as being functionally different and their deposits in some way unusual, when compared to other sites (Chapter 2, Chapter 3). While the previous chapter studied non-portable chalk art and artefacts, the next category for analysis is portable chalk artefacts within similar contexts. The challenge of integrating these previously unconsidered artefacts into traditional discourses within the discipline, and with reference to appropriate theoretical frameworks of study, was outlined in Chapter 3. In that chapter I discussed how historically chalk artefacts appear to have been part of a dichotomous perception in the discipline of non-functional /functional artefacts, with different interpretive analogous structures as a result.

It has been proposed that rather than viewing some artefacts as providing more information than others about a past society in this non-functional/functional way, we instead examine them through their materiality and depositional relationships. The methodology argued is that structured deposition, as seen in recent work in the Neolithic by both Pollard (1995) and Thomas (1996, 1999b) provides analytical tools to aid interpretation by breaking down the context/artefact separation through phenomenology. Recognising artefacts is a key initial step and is outlined as my methodology for the chapter in 5.3. Artefact categorisation and typology have been at the core of archaeology since it began and took many decades to form; this study should be seen as contributing to this process with chalk artefacts, rather than any providing any definitive conclusion. Once this is complete, typological discussion begins the analysis of the parameters of chalk artefacts (5.4, 5.5) and allows chronological factors and regional comparisons to broaden this study (5.5, 5.6), before conclusions are drawn in 5.7.

When viewed as an artefact class in this manner, chalk artefacts embody their importance through the detail and execution of form or design on many pieces. The more chalk artefacts one views, the more of an understanding can be gleaned. The sourcing of chalk to particular areas is geologically impossible, yet while no chalk artefacts are present in non-chalk geological deposits, the exchange of items across the chalklands should not be wholly discounted. As understanding and interpretation are the ultimate goals of this study, effort has been expended in portraying both the range and variety of artefacts within this chronological and typological framework.

The aims of this study are to integrate the flint mines into traditional discourses in the Neolithic; this chapter adds to this integration through proposing that the deposition of portable chalk artefacts in mine sites is reflective of analogous practices seen in contemporary sites. Furthermore I propose how chalk artefact forms can both retain their cohesion or be subject to manipulation, through regional variation in the creation of the form of a chalk artefact, in different substances. These themes will also be explored in Chapter 6. However, this needs to be situated against understandings of chalk artefacts which have been developed over more than a century, and its history is detailed below.

5.2 Emerging Understandings: A History of Portable Chalk Artefacts

Cups were the first category of chalk artefact to be recognised following Greenwell's excavations at Grimes Graves (1870). Parallels were soon being published from excavations at Cissbury (Willett 1875; Lane Fox 1876). Harrison's research and subsequent papers between 1877 and 1878 provided useful details of portable chalk artefacts and chalk art markings found there. It appears a substantial number of plaques were studied by him having been discovered at Cissbury, yet sadly few are illustrated and none seem to have survived (they were left outside Ballard's mill, Findon; Harrison 1877a).

During early twentieth century excavations at the mine sites of Blackpatch and Harrow Hill, more marked chalk and portable artefacts came to light and duly appeared in reports. Pull's excavations at Blackpatch produced numerous chalk charms, small often circular or oddly-shaped pieces of chalk with shallow stab marks made over them (1932: 108-9). He assumes, due to their deposition in burial contexts at this site and having discounted a functional use, that 'certain magical properties were attached to them' (*ibid.*: 108). Cups and marked chalk were excavated at The Trundle by the Curwen's in the 1920s (Curwen 1929; 1931), and at Whitehawk (Curwen 1934). The presence of chalk cups found at datable Neolithic sites and also at mine sites was one of the arguments used to date the flint mines to the Neolithic period rather than the Palaeolithic, but any further interpretation of them was not offered (Clark and Piggott 1933: 172, 178; Chapter 2). Windmill Hill causewayed enclosure also exhibited a range of chalk artefacts and although the report was not published until the 1960s (Smith 1965a), some details of chalk artefacts from this site had emerged earlier through other publications (Clark and Piggott 1933: 172; Childe 1940: 39-40; Piggott 1954). In this later book, Piggott discusses perforated chalk blocks, weights and all types of smaller chalk artefacts such as phalli, discs, cups and balls. He suggests the phalli are of fertility significance (*ibid.*: 46, 86). The possible chalk figurines found at Maiden Castle and Windmill Hill he also argued were ritual, perhaps parallels of clay continental ones (at Fort Harrouard and La Grotte Nicolas, *ibid.*).

During Bradley's analysis of Maumbury Rings he claimed that the discovery of phalli on Neolithic sites is 'almost ubiquitous' (1975: 25), yet they were rarely discussed in the discipline. Some more finely executed plaques excavated in the 1980s and 1990s, in addition to the discovery of larger chalk artefacts and in situ art (as at Flagstones, The Trundle and North Marden, Chapter 4) retained a small academic level of interest. For example, the Chalk Plaque Pit on the King Barrow Ridge near Stonehenge produced two of the better known decorated plaque examples (Harding 1988). The rather fragile Butterfield Down plaque was found geographically nearby but was regrettably unstratified (Salisbury Museum reference W359, CD930111). Varndell undertook some fine analysis on Grimes Graves chalk artefacts (1991) and has also examined other chalk artefacts such as the possibly Iron Age in date Killam plaque (1999).

While this study has effectively ignored Bronze Age chalk, more examples are seen in later prehistory with a greater variety of forms shown the Grimes Graves assemblage (Varndell 1991). At Grimes Graves, an Iron Age burial with a chalk plaque was excavated by Mercer in what appears to be a later insertion into the shaft fill of Pit 1 (Mercer 1981a: 16, PL VII). The chalk plaque which was placed at the hip of the female individual is approximately 9cm by 6cm and is etched with a chessboard design of squares. I encountered two further decorated chalk artefacts from Caburn (a hillfort in Sussex) at Lewes Museum, one of which may be a decorated spindle whorl (M. Giles, pers. comm.). Durrington Walls also has evidence of chalk artefacts within an Iron Age pit (Stone *et al.* 1954). The Killam plaque was within an Iron Age context yet has decoration consistent with the Neolithic (Varndell 1999). Varndell argued this may situate it as a Neolithic artefact however the number uncovered during the course of this research, and with recent research in Iron Age studies, indicates there may be more examples of this practice than previously acknowledged (M. Giles, pers. comm.). It seems that chalk as a substance for the creation of portable artefacts together with particular styles of decoration could have persisted in prehistoric cultural practice, or interest in it reawakened, over millennia.

Chalk artefacts in more recent discussions have been seen as part of the Neolithic cultural assemblage and hence are interpretively instructive as a group. Thomas (1996: 150) refers to them as being closely associated with Grooved Ware, which many of the later artefacts are (e.g. at Mount Pleasant). When interpreting the meaning of chalk motifs, Thomas situates them within the tradition of later Neolithic 'complex artefacts' (*ibid.*). These include motifs such as lozenges, spirals and lattices giving 'a concrete manifestation of a series of networks of significance' (*ibid.*: 159). Similarly, Pollard (1995: 148-9) has included them in later Neolithic structured deposition, and though acknowledging the presence of carved chalk artefacts in both early and late Neolithic contexts does not attempt a specific interpretation of them. It could be argued that in many senses the designs on various portable chalk artefacts have gained significance simply through their resemblance to these later Grooved Ware design traditions. As discussed in Chapter 3, it appears that the symbolic nature of portable chalk artefacts has been acknowledged simply because chalk itself is too soft and friable to be seen as a functional substance. Negotiating this functional /non-functional interpretive dichotomy is necessary for interpretation and I outline my methodology below.

5.3 Structuring Typology: Adding Categorisation

There are three aspects to organising chalk artefacts in a typology which allows for categorisation of artefact class: artefact recognition, typology and chronology. These aspects are hermeneutically created through an ongoing interpretive process as they directly relate to each other. For example, as there is no method of directly dating chalk artefacts, in chronological terms only relative impressions can be gained. Hence chronological indications can either be provided by associated dateable artefacts or a relative age can be provided through dating similar forms in the same way.

This process begins with artefact recognition. This has already been ascertained by the excavator whether the artefacts are in published reports or in museums. Collections of chalk artefacts have been formed primarily as a result of a few particular individuals from the earliest period of Neolithic studies and are therefore only a sample of what may have been encountered at many Neolithic sites. It is possible that many chalk artefacts excavated were not seen as artefacts at the time and subsequently discarded. The chalk artefacts encountered during my research are therefore the result of this initial recognition, though this is not at a consistent level and assemblages from some sites appear large in comparison to others. It is probable that in many cases this is a result of excavation bias. Some artefacts appeared in museum archives which had not been mentioned in reports. It seems some pieces were seen by excavators as possibly being artefacts, but without reference to other chalk artefact types they judged them as not convincing enough to publish.

Hence I have assigned particular artefacts to certain categories based initially on general form, or morphological similarities to others. I have attempted clarity in the typology, constructing it in reference to existing nomenclature with interpretive language used in identification. I believe that if we attempt to categorise form at a more indistinct level we quickly lose any advantage gained through typology. For example, if chalk balls were discussed as simply 'spherical', it may cause confusion when referring to published excavation reports where they are referred to as 'balls' and also present problems where other artefacts exhibit roundness (for example, cylinders). The balance strived for is a categorisation and typology which allows easy recognition, further interpretation and analysis. All recognised artefacts have been included, as have recognisable fragments which are clearly representative of their typological place. Some of these include artefacts which have not been published but have been recognised through reference to other similar forms.

Geologically, chalk is a type of rock and artefacts or decoration created from it are produced through reductive technologies in a similar way to flint. This means that the raw material is reduced in specific ways to create the form or decoration required. Chalk artefacts should be viewed as similar to flint or stone as an artefact class where fragments are present in the archaeological record, in addition to whole artefacts. However within this study it has not been possible to examine these fully. Fragments which may be included in other typological structures (for example in flint as 'debitage' or 'waste flakes') cannot be accommodated here as full assemblages are not present, but they should be acknowledged as being part of the archaeological record and any future excavation work in fairly dry contexts such as the galleries of flint mines, should attempt to include them.

In this research I have divided chalk artefacts into two areas of study: portable and non-portable artefacts. I define portability as under 20cm in size at any point, as this roughly determines the ability to hold a chalk artefact in one hand and hence suggest its portability. Differences in the use of portable and non-portable material culture have been discussed (Bradley 1997; Kopytoff 1989; Root 1983; Chapter Four) and been argued to reflect the likely ways in which in these artefacts may be materially active. This will be assessed in relation to chalk artefacts and art in concluding both this chapter and the book.

5.4. Chalk Artefact Typology and Categorisation

The inheritance of chalk artefact nomenclature, in a similar way to other areas of the discipline, contains a microcosm of history. The use of terms such as 'cup', or 'bun-shape', is only helpful for general descriptive comments on form (an Edwardian 'bun' was entirely different in shape and size to the more modern 'buns' we associate with American muffins in the twenty-first century). Our challenge is therefore twofold: to include existing nomenclature when appropriate and yet allow new terminology where necessitous.

Typology

In terms of seeing chalk artefacts as *artefacts*, only Varndell has attempted to draw together over one hundred years of descriptive and analogous approaches to them and challenge a proportion of these issues of nomenclature, to create a typology (1991). Varndell's typology of chalk artefacts (*ibid*.: 94) divides them into categories I have expressed in Figure 5.1. As she states, many chalk artefacts are amorphous and her suggestions for categories are divided by broad morphological similarities. Her typology has been based solely on the Grimes Graves material and therefore the chronological implications of chalk forms at the later Neolithic to Bronze Age are more clearly defined. In this respect, it is an ideal starting point for determining which artefact types may be more or less prevalent at this period, in this region.

There are however some limitations with Varndell's work. The strengths gained in a regional and chronologically bounded analysis are also constrained by this. While we can gain a reasonable picture of Late Neolithic and Bronze Age chalk artefacts in East Anglia, it is only at one site and local comparable sites simply do not exist. Furthermore Grimes Graves is chronologically later than many of the other sites and artefacts studied in this research and a considerable number of the chalk artefacts studied there are firmly Bronze Age (*ibid*.: 120). With over 350 chalk artefacts being retrieved from all the excavations at Grimes Graves and studied by Varndell, only 37 are of certain Neolithic date (*ibid*.: 94). Hence, Grimes Grave chalk artefacts are only mid-late Neolithic at best and there are no possible analogous early Neolithic artefacts for comparative purposes in the same assemblage. Moreover, her typology does not allow for differences in artefact size. So, a large block with a perforation is classed (b), the same as a small perforated disc. As large blocks with perforations are likely to have different practical and social functions to those of small perforated discs, categorising them in this way may be argued as unhelpful (5.3). Phallic objects are classed in category (f) Miscellaneous, which does not assist in separating these forms from more amorphous shapes for interpretation. However, Varndell's dedicated work in producing this initial typology should be applauded.

Category	Form	Description
(a) Cups	No further description given	Four subdivisions: 1. Well made and fairly well made receptacles 2. Large blocks with a depression 3. Smaller lumps bearing a depression and irregular shape 4. Small lumps with small depression often made by boring
(b) Perforated objects	Any piece fully perforated, small or large, regular or irregular in shape	Piercings often made by boring opposing faces
(c) Objects with incomplete perforations	No further description given	
(d) Balls		1. Spherical to ovoid in shape, some carefully rounded 2. Rough, smooth or pitted surface, some bearing marks of a flint blade
(e) Work Surfaces	Large chunks or smaller fragments of chalk blocks where one surface has been worn by rubbing and/or scoring. Four subdivisions	1. Smooth - further divided into four categories: *(i) convex, (ii) concave, (iii) flat/indeterminate, and (iv) fragments* 2. Coarse 3. Broad and/or deep grooves in one direction 4. Smooth surfaces subsequently marked by further activity
(f) Miscellaneous	A catch-all category but including 3 specified types	1. Oddities (including phalli) 2. Carvings in the round 3. Blocks bearing deeply grooved lines with deliberate but abstract configurations
(g) Blocks with pick-marks	No further description given	
(h) Finds from Pit 15	No further description necessary	

FIGURE 5.1 TABLE SUMMARISING VARNDELL'S (1991:100-3) SUGGESTED TYPOLOGY FOR CHALK OBJECTS

My own typology of chalk artefacts follows in Figure 5.2 and seeks to address these issues in part. As discussed previously, artefact size may influence artefact use and therefore should be accommodated within the typology. Hence I argue for a division based on portable and non-portable artefacts initially, followed by further subdivisions. Much of Varndell's work has been adopted, specifically the term of 'Work Surfaces' to describe a particular type of artefact not seen at mine sites other than Grimes Graves. My typology has been based more broadly on those artefacts which occur at other Neolithic and Bronze Age sites studied here.

The tension between nomenclature, typology and chronology is part of the defining relationship between the recognition of both context and artefact which was discussed at length in Chapter 3. In order to both recognise categories of artefacts (and hence contexts) and interpret them, we require the language and structure with which to discuss them. While broad morphological characteristics define the character of an artefact, subtleties of execution and form can indicate chronological and perhaps regional variability. One could easily compare this approach to bronze axe typologies, or the subtleties of flint axe form or any number of typological studies. Categorisation and typology should be seen as the starting point from which further discussion can take place.

Applying Categorisation

As Varndell has categorised and analysed the chalk artefacts from all the excavations at Grimes Graves (1991) it is necessary to review her findings and typology and re-categorise the artefacts to be consistent with the new typology offered. Of the 359 objects she studied, only 37 have a Neolithic date with 63 being of uncertain date. The remaining 259 are argued to be Bronze Age (*ibid.*: 120). Varndell's analysis was not conducted to provide chronological boundaries and hence it has been necessary to reanalyse her data to have separate out the certain

Category	Form	Further Description	Size
(1) Axes	Rounded triangular form	Can be chipped or polished in appearance	Under 15cm in length
(2) Balls	Spherical or partly artefacts	Circular but often have a flat side (or base)	Under 10cm in diameter
(3) Beads	Small triangular or rounded pieces	Fully pierced	Under 3cm in diameter
(4) Charms	Smooth and decorated lump	Various shapes usually fully decorated with a flint blade	Under 10cm in length
(5) Cups	Round depression inset in rounded object	May have lugs, depression can be scraped or pitted	Under 10cm
(6) Cylinders	Smoothed chalk cylinders	Often broken at both ends and finely made, can have one or more flattened sides	Under 15cm in length
(7) Discs	Rounded in plan but flat, can be either fully, partially or non-perforated	Includes pendants	Under 10 cm in width
(8) Drums	Large cylindrical artefacts with inset raised top and flattened base	Can be decorated, evidence of flint blade	Under 20cm in height or width
(9) Phalli	As human male penis	May or may not exhibit prepuce	Under 30cm in length
(10) Plaques	Flattish or squared sided, decorated block	At least one straight side, evidence of planned design	Under 20cm in length or width
(11) Work surfaces	Flat block often with surface depression which is more often linear than circular	Pitted or scraped use evidence	Over 10cm, under 20cm

FIGURE 5.2 TABLE SUMMARISING THE REVISED CHALK TYPOLOGY

Neolithic artefacts from the Bronze Age. Furthermore as I did not have access to the British Museum excavated collections, only illustrated artefacts are re-examined and re-categorised. Figure 5.3 shows the categories each illustrated artefact appears in Varndell's work, with Figure 5.4 portraying how this alters under the typological scheme I offer. The artefacts studied here are those from Greenwell's Pit, Area A, Shaft X, Pits 1, 2, 4 and 12, Floors 4 and 46 and an unusual object from Greenwell's shaft D (*ibid.*).

The results of using my typology can be summarised as follows:

- Three artefacts are labelled Phallic rather than Miscellaneous (C229, C299a and C321).

- Three become plaques – C327, C328 from the Miscellaneous category and C215 from the Work Surfaces category (albeit all rather rough but all exhibit evidence of planned design on a least one face).

- One perforated object - C93 - becomes a Disc.

- Two artefacts become cylinders rather than Miscellaneous - C301 and C288 (one with a flattish side and a finished and broken horn-shaped artefact).

- I have included the peg-like chalk protrusion (C321) as included in the phallic category, following similarities to the wooden God-Dolly's phallus from Bell's Track (Coles 1968: 256).

This re-categorisation of the Grimes Graves material allows these artefacts to be treated in a similar interpretive fashion to the other chalk artefacts studied. In addition it opens interpretive avenues which were previously closed, primarily in allowing greater definition and discussion of the artefacts concerned. For example, the separation of phallic artefacts from a miscellaneous category provides scope to examine the number and role of these artefacts within Neolithic contexts. Plaques as a category also benefit from a greater inclusion of numbers which will assist in

Mining and Materiality

Location	B - Perforated objects	C - Incomplete perforations	E – Work Surfaces	F - Misc
Pit 1			**C215**	
Pit 2				**C301** C302
Pit 4				
Pit 12				
Area A		**C119**		
Shaft X	**C93**			**C288** C289
Greenwell's Pit				**C299**
Greenwell's Shaft D				**C299a**
Floor 4				
Floor 46				**C320 C321**
Sieveking Tr 3				C326 **C327 C328**
Number Illustrated	1	1	1	8
TOTAL	1	1	1	11

FIGURE 5.3 TABLE OF VARNDELL'S (1991) CATEGORIES, WITH THOSE ALTERED WITHIN FIGURE 5.4 IN BOLD

Location	Cylinders	Discs	Phalli	Plaques	Work Surfaces
Pit 1				C215	
Pit 2	C301				
Pit 4					
Pit 12					
Area A		C119			
Shaft X	C288	C93			
Greenwell's Pit			C299		
Greenwell's Shaft D			C299a		
Floor 4					
Floor 46			C321		C320
Sieveking Tr 3				C327 C328	
TOTAL	2	2	3	3	1

FIGURE 5.4 TABLE OF RECATEGORISED ARTEFACTS FOLLOWING FIGURE 5.2

Category	Blackpatch	Church Hill	Cissbury	Harrow Hill	Easton Down	Long Down	Stoke Down	Grimes Graves	TOTAL
(1) Axes	1		1						2
(2) Balls	1	3	+	1		1		7	13
(4) Charms	13+	8	5+					2	28+
(5) Cups			5					6	1
(6) Cylinders	3							2	5
(7) Discs		2		1			1	3	7
(9) Phalli								3	3
(10) Plaques		4	2	1				3	10
(11) Work surfaces								1	1
TOTAL	18+	17	13+	3	0	1	1	27	80+

+ indicates more artefacts probable, but not quantifiable

FIGURE 5.5 TABLE SUMMARISING THE NUMBERS OF CHALK ARTEFACTS IN THE MINES

determining the scale, execution of design and use of these forms in deposits. Including a smaller disc as a portable artefact rather than simply as a perforated object equally allows us to examine the possible individual number and use of certain forms. Furthermore, by acknowledging that the categories of balls and cups are currently adequate within the typology means it is unnecessary to revisit these few chalk artefact forms in deposits which have already been subject to recognition in publication.

Having completed this reassessment it is now possible to examine chalk artefacts from other mining sites and include them into the typology. Some additional artefacts will be discussed from Grimes Graves that were not included in Varndell's analysis. Artefacts will also be discussed which have subsequently been lost, to provide as full a picture as published records.

5.5 Including Portable Chalk Artefacts from Mines with Comparable Forms

Figure 5.5 following provides a summary of the types of chalk artefact present at each mine site, based on my typology outlined above. This is the first time this data has been drawn together and is based on published sources, unpublished sources and information derived directly from artefacts held at museums as detailed in Chapter 3. While this should be seen as comprehensive, some omissions are inevitable due to the scattered nature of the excavation records. With specific regard to both Grimes Graves (Kendall 1920) and Long Down (Salisbury 1961), chalk artefacts were recovered and yet unpublished. Chalk artefacts recovered from Pull's excavations have also suffered in two ways: their locations were not always mentioned in excavation records and furthermore, they have been re-boxed and labelled in subsequent years. Some of this re-organisation has resulted in artefacts with a similar decoration being held together, particularly some chalk artefacts being possibly erroneously attributed to Church Hill. As this suspicion cannot be answered with any certainty given the available evidence, I have included these chalk artefacts as originating from Church Hill. While this is in many senses unsatisfactory it cannot be reconciled further.

Description of Categories

Chalk Axes

Chalk axes can appear in chipped or polished forms. There is only one secure example from mining contexts, from Blackpatch Shaft 1 which is representative of a chipped axe (Pye 1968, Figure 5.6). Fragments of what appear to be perhaps part of a polished chalk axe are in the Rosehill collection at Lewes Museum and attributed to Cissbury and it can only be assumed that they were found during the 1870s excavations of which Rosehill was a part. Despite an amount of research and attempts to discover further detail both from Rosehill's descendants (the 13th Earl of Northesk) and Christies (the auction house responsible for their sale) it has proved fruitless. It seems likely they originate from Tindall's shaft alongside the other chalk artefacts noted as appearing, or alternatively towards the top of the Cave Pit when marked blocks are noted, yet these conjectures are by no means secure. Equally, they could have originated from anywhere on this site. In non-mining contexts there are three other recorded examples. A chipped chalk axe form from Stonehenge has been rather disputed as representing an axe, perhaps simply due to few parallels (N. Thomas 1952: 462). Only two polished chalk axes forms have been retrieved, both from Woodhenge (Cunnington 1929: 112, Pl 22).

Chalk Balls

Morphologically these are circular, yet often have one flat side (or base), hence any general ball-like form has been included. In contrast with charms, these are always undecorated and form one of the most ubiquitous chalk forms of the Neolithic. They are consistently under c.8cm in diameter although in general terms are mostly c.4cm in diameter. Those at Grimes Graves (accessed at Norwich City Museum from the pre-war excavations) were larger than other examples seen at Windmill Hill or other Neolithic sites, being towards the higher end of the scale where many are c. 5-8cm in diameter. From the mines they are noted at Blackpatch, (Shaft 1 Gallery 1) and Church Hill (Shaft 1, Layer 5 and Floor 4). At Harrow Hill, a bun-shaped artefact is noted from Shaft 21 (Curwen and Curwen 1926: 125) and at Long Down a 'chalk egg' from Floor 2 (from a noted illustration at Chichester Museum). Harrison (1877a) mentions rounded chalk objects from the Number 2 Escarpment shaft at Cissbury and while these may be charms I feel in probability he would mention any markings and they should therefore be classed as balls. At Grimes Graves they occur at Pit 2 (two balls), Pit 12 (two balls) and Area A (three balls) (Varndell 1991).

Chalk Beads

No chalk beads occur from any Neolithic context studied here. They occur in two sites, at the Arreton Down barrow on the Isle of Wight from the probable primary burial (Alexander, Ozanne and Ozanne 1960: 275-6) and one was also excavated from the Neolithic midden at Durrington Walls during recent excavations (M. Parker-Pearson pers. comm.).

Chalk Charms

The overall shape of chalk charms varies (from oval, to circular, to cylindrical, to rounded triangular) yet in terms of decoration they are often distinguished through their complete covering in dragged flint blade marks. The decoration applied may also be feathered or gouged. Chalk charms seem to be present at only Blackpatch and Cissbury. Pull's excavations at Blackpatch produced a large amount of them: 10 chalk charms from barrow contexts, 10 from Shaft 6, one with a cremation from Shaft 7 and an un-quantified number from 'hut' sites (Pull 1932:108-9). Pull's excavation of Cissbury Shaft 27 produced four chalk charms (Figure 5.7) from the burial context (Topping 2005). Also deposited at Worthing Museum from Pull's excavations are 8 small, squared and scratched chalk blocks suggesting a different type of decoration with a flint blade. This type of decoration is 'feathered', creating deeper and defined recesses in the chalk akin to linear scratches. Regrettably no depositional placement records exist for any of these though they appeared within a Church Hill box. I have categorised them as charms due

FIGURE 5.6 PHOTOGRAPH OF BLACKPATCH CHALK AXE (PHOTOGRAPH AUTHOR; © WORTHING MUSEUM AND ART GALLERY)

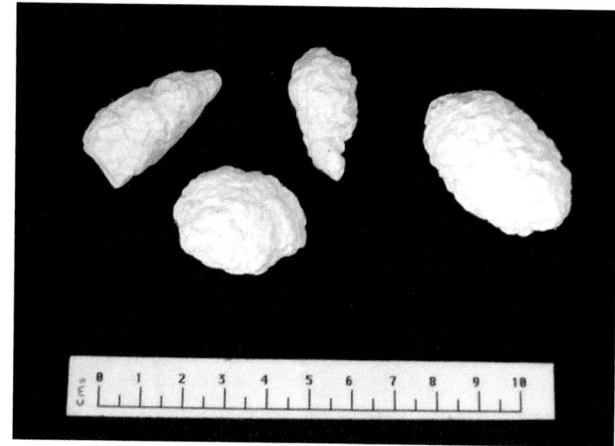

FIGURE 5.7 PHOTOGRAPH OF CISSBURY SHAFT 27 BURIAL CHARMS (PHOTOGRAPH AUTHOR; © WORTHING MUSEUM AND ART GALLERY)

to their comprehensive decoration though their form could be argued as having similarities to Plaques having squared sides. They may represent a regional variation of plaques or be a chronological forerunner to this type of artefact.

Chalk Cups

Cups form the first category of chalk artefacts acknowledged by Greenwell in 1870. They are rarely larger than 10cm in diameter and consist of a depression within a small chalk block. The cavity has in almost all circumstances likely to have been made by a flint blade, where evidence of scraping by a sharp edge which creates tiny furrows can be seen, though some appear smoothed. Other examples have slightly pitted interiors. Eleven appear from flint mine contexts, from only two mine sites (five from Cissbury and six from Grimes Graves). From Cissbury one chalk cup was excavated from 30 feet (9.1m) down in the Large Pit (66 feet [20m] in diameter) which was examined by Lane Fox in the 1880s. It was never fully excavated, being abandoned at a depth of 42 feet (12.8m), (Lane Fox 1876: 380-82). Also at Cissbury four cups were noted to have been found from Tindall's Pit yet none are present in the museum archives either at Worthing or

Lewes Museums (Willett 1875). Four cups also originated from Greenwell's Pit at Grimes Graves. Three cups were whole, two were described as being under two and a half inches in diameter (6.3cm) with the third being larger; the fourth was only a fragment (Greenwell 1870: 430). One cup and the fragment were excavated in the shaft fill at 26 feet (7.9m), the other two being found in galleries at their termini. The cup from the second gallery was placed on a ledge, and that from the side gallery branching from the first gallery was placed on the floor. The other three cups are one each from Pit 4, Shaft X and Floor 4 (Varndell 1991).

Chalk Cylinders

These are smoothed cylindrical pieces of chalk often c. 8-10 cm in length with either one or both ends fractured, as if broken. It is possible some of these were phallic artefacts and have been damaged either pre- or post-depositionally, although they may represent a separate artefact class entirely. They only occur at Blackpatch and Grimes Graves. At Blackpatch, Shafts 1 and 7 and Barrow 7 each contained one cylinder, Figure 5.8 (Pull 1932: 108). From Grimes Graves two are noted by Varndell (1991), one from Pit 2 and one from Shaft X. However Greenwell (1870) discusses other chalk cylinders found during his excavation. Three pieces of chalk suggested as being representative of the human body were found at 31 feet (9.5m), the base of the shaft being at 39 feet, (11.9m), (*ibid.*: 423). One of the artefacts was the phallus (discussed below), the other two being cylindrical artefacts Greenwell (*ibid.*: 430) argued could form part of an arm (10 inches length by 14 inches circumference - 25cm by 36 cm), and the other part of a finger (1.5 inches by 2.5 inches – 4cm by 6.5cm). These cylindrical objects showed evidence of a flint blade on their surface and were broken at both ends.

Chalk Discs/Pendants

These are often rounded in plan but flat and can be fully or partially perforated. This category includes chalk rings (partial or complete) and any other artefacts which may be pendants. The piercing of chalk has been seen in several pieces and this appears to have been achieved in various ways. One of the common methods has been extraction with a flint blade through a scraping motion; in other pieces more of a circular drilling action seems to have created the hole. There is very little evidence of suspension by a cord or twine as corresponding use-wear is not present.

Six examples originate from four flint mines, occurring at Church Hill, Harrow Hill, Stoke Down and Grimes Graves. The two from Church Hill were excavated from Floor 4, one being perforated (a half-ring, Figure 5.9) and the other un-perforated. The one example from Harrow Hill originated from Shaft 7 and is a piece of chalk exhibiting a natural hole, which has been elaborated through the creation of another hole, making two complete holes through the piece. At Stoke Down the disc occurred

FIGURE 5.8 PHOTOGRAPHS OF CHALK CYLINDERS FROM BLACKPATCH (PHOTOGRAPH AUTHOR; © WORTHING MUSEUM AND ART GALLERY)

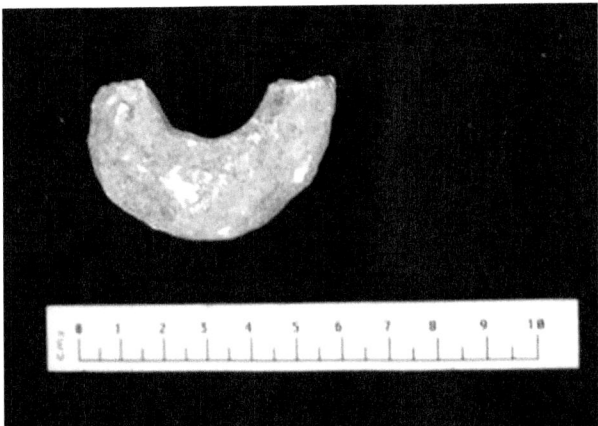

FIGURE 5.9 PHOTOGRAPH OF CHURCH HILL CHALK DISC (PHOTOGRAPH AUTHOR; © WORTHING MUSEUM AND ART GALLERY)

at the surface of Shaft 2 (Wade 1922), while a disc was found 18 feet (5.5m) in the shaft fill of Greenwell's Pit at Grimes Graves (1870).

The last chalk pendant artefact from Grimes Graves is unique. The pendant appears to have been suspended from a twine or rope and shows hairline fractures around this point. The inside is like a chalk cup, being scraped with a flint blade and may have been used as perhaps a container for grinding powders or herbs. The provenance is slightly vague though it is attributed to a working floor through an excavation by Kendall (Norwich City Museum). Kendall conducted his excavation under the remit of the Prehistoric Society of East Anglia in 1920 and dug thirteen floors (Kendall 1920). Some chalk marked blocks are mentioned though this artefact is not and the possibility remains it is Bronze Age.

Chalk Drums

The best known chalk artefacts ever recovered from a prehistoric context in Britain are the Folkton Drums which were excavated from a barrow in east Yorkshire (Longworth and Kinnes 1985: 115-18). These three decorated drums vary in size from approximately 9 to 12cm in height. Regrettably no radiocarbon dates have been produced from their context. Morphologically they are cylindrical artefacts with an inset raised top and flattened base. An unpublished example of a chalk drum (Figure 5.10) was on display in the former Chichester Museum in 2005 and studied by the present author, having been excavated in 1993 from within a Neolithic pit complex at Lavant, West Sussex. No other finds from this site were accessed at this time and its provenance was provided by museum staff and James Kenny, the excavator and current County Archaeologist for West Sussex (pers. comm.). There are no drums recorded from flint mine contexts.

No specific decoration is present on the Lavant Drum which may be unfinished, based on comparison with the Folkton Drums. Some flint blade marks are apparent and two parallel incised lines can be seen, yet there is not any suggestion of the motifs present on the Folkton Drums which have been argued to be part of a Neolithic design tradition seen in Grooved Ware, passage grave art and other forms of material culture (Wainwright and Longworth 1971: 246, Thomas 1996: 156). While there are only two deposits to analyse, chalk drums as a category could be said to occur either in decorated or undecorated forms.

Chalk Phalli

Again one of the older categories of chalk artefact noted from Neolithic contexts, they are under 30cm in length (usually much smaller) and represent the human male penis in form where the prepuce may or may not be present. Three are noted from Grimes Graves, one from the base of Greenwell's Pit, one from Greenwell's Shaft D and one from Floor 46.

No other chalk phalli are found at mine sites although they appear in other Neolithic and Bronze Age contexts.

FIGURE 5.10 PHOTOGRAPH OF THE LAVANT DRUM (PHOTOGRAPH AUTHOR; © THE NOVIUM [A SERVICE PROVIDED BY CHICHESTER DISTRICT COUNCIL]. ALL RIGHTS RESERVED)

The more famous examples are from Maumbury Rings (Bradley 1975) and Mount Pleasant (Wainwright 1979). However, one of note is the chalk phallus No. 15 from Windmill Hill (Smith 1965a). While phallic this is also cylindrical and yet rather flattened, suggesting that it may have been adapted from another artefact to create a phallic artefact. Therefore, the phallic reference may be secondary to another meaning of use of this particular piece.

Chalk Plaques

These are flattish and/or squared sided and decorated blocks under 20cm on any side. They vary in terms of the execution and style of their design, most are marked by a flint blade though others may have had rounded bone or wooden tools to create wider markings. Decoration may also include chevrons and lozenges, or linear or radiating lines. They seem to be present in all types of Neolithic contexts, from early-late in the period. Occasionally their surfaces are raised in some form.

In total six are noted from mine sites. One occurs at Shaft 21 Harrow Hill, the context of which is uncertain as it does not appear to correlate well with the description given (Curwen and Curwen 1926: 121-125). Three small unstratified artefacts from Church Hill are attributed to this category as they appear to be fragments of plaques, small, squared yet not whole. A variety of marked chalk is noted by Harrison (1877a) occurring from several pits at Cissbury: Tindall's Pit, the Number 2 Escarpment shaft and the top layers of what later became known as the Cave Pit, none of which survive in the archives of Lewes or Worthing Museums. A plaque is discussed being found by Guiles the workman, though it was damaged during excavation (Harrison 1877a). The block from Tindall's Pit is described as having figures which resembles 'those found on rocks and early stone monuments in Scotland, amongst other places, in the Isle of Eday' (*ibid.*: 267). The Isle of Eday markings exhibit spirals consistent with Grooved Ware motifs (Simpson 1867). Harrison goes on to describe it further:

> as 7 inches long by 5 inches wide was, as I have already said, covered with lines, many of which crossed each other, whilst others radiated from small pits, and some continued in a straight course quite across the chalk. A different pattern, composed of curved lines, occupied the sides (1877a: 267).

From this description, in form this appears to be similar to the Church Hill plaque, attributed by Pye (1968) to Shaft 6 at 2m depth. This plaque is rectangular and while does not have the design as described above, it has a feathered half-circular flint blade design with different curved lines of the sides. Furthermore, it appears to have been coated in a slip of reddish material which is most likely ochre (Figures 5.11 and 5.12). Despite these two fine plaques (and the possible plaques from Church Hill which I have categorised charms here) the lack of the retention of any others means that any cohesive statistical data cannot be offered for mine sites. However, plaques as a category have been better documented from later excavations and hence representations as a whole across the Neolithic provide a useful comparison to the mining sites. Plaques found in other excavated sites were discussed in 5.2.

Chalk Work Surfaces

These are flattish blocks often with a surface depression which is more often linear than circular with evidence of pitting or scraping use wear. In size they are usually over 10cm and under 20cm. They occur at Grimes Graves in the Early Bronze Age though one example from Floor 46 is Neolithic. Interpretively there is difficulty in separating the less well executed plaques from work surfaces though it appears the main characteristic of the work surfaces is that they exhibit use wear rather than decoration. Indeed, in terms of affinities in morphology they seem more akin to querns or small polissoirs, and could be representative of them. For example the work surfaces C172 and C175 at Grimes Graves are similar in form to the polissoir and saddle quern fragments and rubbers at Etton (Pryor 1998: 257-8 and Figures 2 and 7). Furthermore, some of the work surfaces Varndell illustrates (C216 and C282) could be argued as rather elongated cups. Of all the categories given this appears to be the least satisfactory however as the main body of this artefact group occurs in the Early Bronze Age a detailed review is out of the scope of this study. It is possible though that work surfaces are a chronologically later form of plaques and/or cups.

Discussion

I have discussed how there are certain omissions from the categories represented in the flint mines. There are no beads or drums and, in general terms, few numbers of chalk artefacts at all with the one exception of chalk charms. By a considerable margin the most common chalk artefact form is chalk charms. More chalk artefact forms appear at Grimes Graves, though this could be argued to represent the later chronology of this site in addition to a possibly different excavation strategy. Blackpatch exhibits the second highest number of chalk artefacts which could be argued, as Grimes Graves, to be largely the result of the Late Neolithic/Early Bronze Age activity at the site. The charms present with the Cissbury Shaft 27 skeleton, which has a shaft date of 3640-3360 cal BC (Barber *et al.* 1999: 82) indicate that this practice of burial or cremation accompanied with modified chalk artefacts was an early to mid-Neolithic tradition in this area which seems to have continued into the Late Neolithic/Early Bronze Age. However the lack of charms or burials at Harrow Hill suggests that these four sites may have had an element of differing uses for Neolithic society. Due to the lack of detailed chronological information, further analysis can only be completed through reference to deposits in contemporary monuments.

FIGURE 5.11 PHOTOGRAPHS OF CHURCH HILL PLAQUE SURFACE (LEFT) AND BASE (RIGHT) (PHOTOGRAPH AUTHOR; © WORTHING MUSEUM AND ART GALLERY)

FIGURE 5.12 PHOTOGRAPHS OF CHURCH HILL PLAQUE SIDES WHERE OCHRE SLIP CAN BE SEEN (PHOTOGRAPH AUTHOR; © WORTHING MUSEUM AND ART GALLERY)

5.6 Chalk Artefact Forms in Regional Context

While the previous section examined the proposed chalk artefact categories in mines and other monuments, regional analyses can provide greater definition to interpreting artefacts with respect to distribution and chronology. As discussed in the history of chalk artefact research (5.3), portable chalk artefacts have been found at various Neolithic sites. This section provides a chronological summary of chalk artefacts from the mining sites in Figures 5.13 and 5.14 with evidence of chalk artefacts from other Neolithic sites in Sussex, Wessex and Dorset, represented in Figures 5.15- 5.18. The tables contain information gained from excavation reports, secondary accounts and those artefacts encountered during the study visits I completed.

The process of classifying and creating a typology of any artefact type is complex. Artefacts manufactured within a substance do so within social restraints; there are tensions of what the substance can be used for in addition to the social understanding of what it should be used for. The approach taken in this study was to assimilate and understand types of chalk form and then allow these to determine the categories. This process begins with the material itself. As with the Grimes Graves chalk material which had been subject to a typological scheme by Varndell (1991), the re-categorisation conducted in this book could only be satisfactorily completed when viewing the illustrations of those artefacts as the archive was unavailable. Re-categorising chalk material which had not been viewed or illustrated was felt inappropriate considering the often poor recording or description of material and variations encountered in excavation archives. Figures 5.15- 5.17 therefore portray the probable range of artefacts available at each site where the archive had not been viewed, giving an indication of presence and absence of forms, with figures to the side of the potential numbers in each category which are then represented within Figures 5.19 and 5.20.

These tables incorporate those chalk artefacts which appear as part of a chalk assemblage at a site (rather than single instances) and include decorated chalk non-portable artefacts. As stated in the summary of chalk artefacts in mining contexts, charms are the most common artefact yet as they are not represented outside the Sussex mining sites are not included here. This analysis suggests that while certain forms are more prevalent at certain times, a

Flint Mine sites EARLY PHASE	Chalk Discs/Pendants	Chalk Axes	Chalk Cups	Chalk Phalli	Chalk Plaques	Decorated Chalk Blocks/Art
Cissbury, Sussex			●		●	●
Church Hill, Sussex	●					●
Harrow Hill, Sussex	●				●	●

FIGURE 5.13 TABLE OF MINING SITES WITH EARLY-MID NEOLITHIC CHALK ARTEFACTS

Flint Mine sites LATER PHASE	Chalk Discs/Pendants	Chalk Axes	Chalk Cups	Chalk Phalli	Chalk Plaques	Decorated Chalk Blocks/Art
Cissbury, Sussex					●	●
Blackpatch, Sussex		●				
Church Hill, Sussex					●	●
Harrow Hill, Sussex		●				●
Grimes Graves, Norfolk	●		●	●	●	●

FIGURE 5.14 TABLE OF MINING SITES WITH MID-LATE NEOLITHIC CHALK ARTEFACTS

Causewayed Enclosures	Chalk Discs/Pendants	Chalk Axes	Chalk Cups	Chalk Phalli	Chalk Plaques	Decorated Chalk Blocks/Art
The Trundle, Sussex			● (3)	Bone		●
Whitehawk, Sussex			● (3)			●
Windmill Hill, Wessex	● (4)		● (10)	● (2)		
Knap Hill, Wessex			● (1)			
Maiden Castle, Dorset						●
Flagstones, Dorset						●
Monkton Up Wimborne Shaft, Dorset	●				●	●

FIGURE 5.15 TABLE OF CHALK ARTEFACTS IN CONTEMPORARY EARLY-MID NEOLITHIC MONUMENTS WITH QUANTITIES INDICATED IN BRACKETS WHERE KNOWN

Long Barrows	Chalk Discs/Pendants	Chalk Axes	Chalk Cups	Chalk Phalli	Chalk Plaques	Decorated Chalk Blocks/Art
North Marden, Sussex	● (1)				● (1)	●
Thickthorn Down, Wessex	● (2)		● (1)	● (2)	● (8)	
Horslip, Wessex					● (1)	

FIGURE 5.16 TABLE OF CHALK ARTEFACTS IN CONTEMPORARY EARLY NEOLITHIC LONG BARROWS WITH QUANTITIES INDICATED IN BRACKETS WHERE KNOWN

LN/EBA/BA Monuments	Chalk Discs/Pendants	Chalk Axes	Chalk Cups	Chalk Phalli	Chalk Plaques	Decorated Chalk Blocks/Art
Stonehenge, Wessex	• (3)	• (1)	• (1)	• (1)	• (1)	
Woodhenge, Wessex	• (1)	• (2)	• (2)		• (1)	
Durrington Walls, Wessex		• (1)	• (1)		• (2)	
Wilsford Barrow, Wessex			• (1)			
Tarrant Monkton Henge, Dorset					• (1)	
Maumbury Rings, Dorset			• (1)	• (1)		
Mount Pleasant, Dorset	• (1)		• (1)	• (3)	• (1)	• (2)
Itford Hill, Sussex				• (1)		

FIGURE 5.17 TABLE OF CHALK ARTEFACTS IN CONTEMPORARY LATE NEOLITHIC TO EARLY BRONZE AGE MONUMENTS WITH QUANTITIES INDICATED IN BRACKETS WHERE KNOWN

	Axes	Balls	Beads	Charms	Cups	Cylinders	Discs	Drums	Chalk Phalli	Plaques	Work Surfaces
Early-Mid Neo		•		•	•	•	•		•	•	
Late Neo/BA	•	•	•	•	•	•	•	•	•	•	•

FIGURE 5.18 TABLE ILLUSTRATING A CHRONOLOGY OF CHALK ARTEFACTS IN NEOLITHIC BRITAIN

tentative chronology of portable chalk artefact forms can be offered (Figure 5.18).

Figures 5.19 and 5.20 may give an indication of some of the more frequently occurring forms of portable chalk artefact from southern British Neolithic monuments. The detail has been obtained from published records of those sites referred to in Figures 5.15 to 5.17, where such records are available. It should be noted that as many of the archives of these sites have not been viewed, their existing categorisation has necessarily been accepted and applied within the typology offered in this book. Where descriptions have provided no distinguishing features or where there is sufficient ambiguity, artefacts have been excluded.

These chalk artefacts forms occur throughout the Neolithic and into the Bronze Age in Wessex, Sussex and Dorset with no exceptional exclusion noted. The presence of them at flint mines is consistent with other monument types. With regard to the early Neolithic monuments, long barrows have few of these portable chalk artefacts yet they occur in greater numbers at causewayed enclosures, though the comparative size of sites and percentage of the sites excavated may also have an impact on the amount of artefacts retrieved (there being a greater area of ditch to excavate at causewayed enclosures than at long barrows for example). As they are not excluded from any site of this period it could be suggested that chalk artefacts were seen as culturally appropriate for all types of monumental site during the early-mid Neolithic in these regions, though perhaps activities at causewayed enclosures required greater numbers of them. Recent dates suggesting that use of long barrows may have been restricted to only a few centuries may also indicate that continued use of causewayed enclosures may have increased the deposition of portable chalk artefacts (Bayliss *et al.* 2007).

There is a trend to view the later Neolithic and Bronze Age as having greater numbers of chalk artefacts and an enhanced typological range, which is justified through Table 5.11 with four more categories being seen in the Late

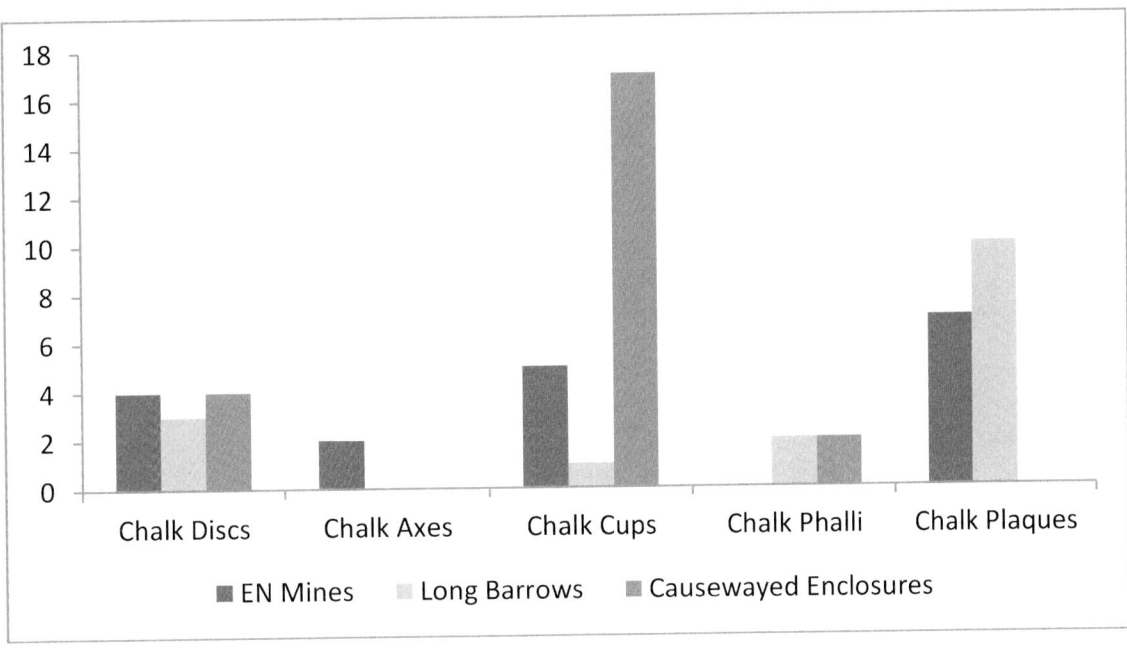

FIGURE 5.19 CHART COMPARING CHALK ARTEFACT TYPES AT DIFFERENT EARLY NEOLITHIC MONUMENTS

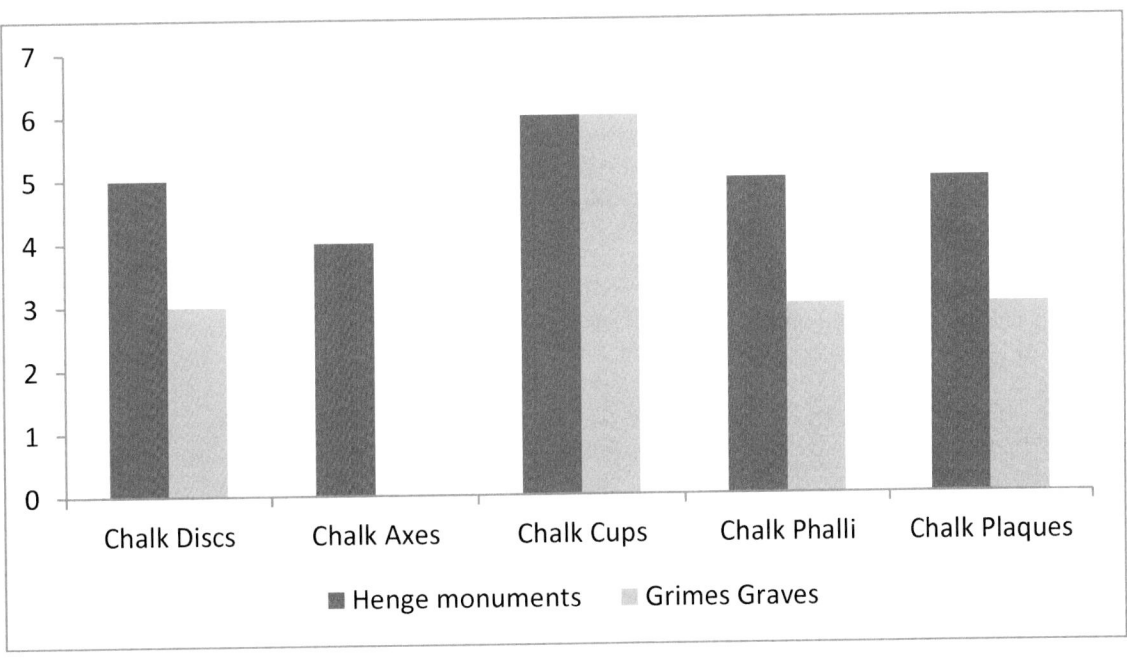

FIGURE 5.20 CHART COMPARING CHALK ARTEFACT TYPES BETWEEN LATER NEOLITHIC MONUMENTS

Neolithic and Early Bronze Age. However I would suggest that this is also likely to be proportionately representative within deposits. In other words, the chalk artefacts occurring in earlier contexts within earlier monuments are within an assemblage which is generally relatively small in comparison to later ones. Perhaps in that regard chalk artefacts are not less important at earlier periods but rather are subject to elaboration and increasing use (and/ or deposition) as are other types of material culture during this later period.

5.7 Understanding Portable Chalk Artefacts

There are several aspects to exploring an understanding of chalk artefact forms which relate to practical issues of production and use and interpreting metaphorical understandings of chalk. These concepts could be argued to have indications of temporality: how the material is gathered, how the artefacts are formed, use-wear and affinities with other artefacts.

The acquisition of chalk in the correct size for production of a specific artefact will have played an important role in the planning and execution of the piece, but many of the chalk artefacts seen here have not required a particularly large piece of raw chalk rock. Indeed, a considerable number of the artefacts could have been created from quarried material as a by-product of digging the shafts (or ditches in contemporary monuments). If we focus on this thought, in these terms we can view chalk as a substance which, for the production of artefacts of this size, was only being acquired only during these processes. Chalk does not occur as a surface material and has to be extracted: it will not be encountered otherwise. These artefacts are therefore likely to symbolise at least part of this process in their production; they are intimately connected through their materiality with the creation of banks, ditches, pits and monuments.

With reference to specific artefacts, chalk phalli and plaques are two forms which occur at early and later sites, in increasing numbers over time. In both cases this seems to coincide with increased execution of detail in certain examples which is not consistently displayed. For phalli, the Grimes Graves phallus tip (C229a) and the Maumbury Rings phallus are particularly representative of the human form and yet the later Itford Hill phallus rather rough. Chalk plaques are often elaborate in the later Neolithic to Bronze Age, with the Chalk Plaque Pit, Durrington Walls and Tarrant Monkton examples being finely detailed in both the form of the piece itself and decoration. However this is not to negate the probable earlier pieces which show greater detail in either this category (Church Hill) or on non-portable pieces (as at The Trundle, Chapter 4).

Hence while generally there can be greater or lesser detail or time expended in the production of many chalk artefacts there is little evidence to suggest any progression in either technology or social motivation to create more 'perfect' artefacts over time. I would suggest instead that the production of chalk artefacts appears temporally relevant for their immediate social purpose. By this, I mean that the numbers and variation in execution of detail in these artefacts suggests they were manufactured for particular social reasons close to the time they were required. There is not enough conformity in any piece to indicate prescribed social constraints in their production in size or detail but rather that general forms, forms recognisable to Neolithic persons, needed to be adhered to. The creation of highly structured plaques and phallic forms may suggest in certain circumstances an increase in the use of these artefacts for enhanced or exaggerated visual impact in certain social relations or ritual activity. Their decoration may have taken longer in immediate production terms to signify something in addition to simply form. The deposition of less decorated plaques may not suggest a lack of care but rather that the manipulation of form may have been of adequate purpose in itself for certain social circumstances. Furthermore, almost all examples appear to have little use-wear evidence (though the fractures on the Grimes Graves suspended pendant/cup indicate use). The clean chalk forms, many appearing freshly carved, also suggest that they may have either been manufactured for immediate use in social activities and/or deposition, or deliberately re-worked for cleaning purposes prior to deposition.

Many artefacts are whole or may have been broken as part of post-depositional processes (e.g. the Maumbury Rings phallus, Bradley 1975). Yet some excavated chalk artefacts appear to have been broken prior to their deposition. The retention of any broken chalk artefacts from excavations is likely to be less than other classes of better studied artefact and there are potentially many more examples which have not reached the archives. The practice of deliberately breaking artefacts and their subsequent dispersal in creating and reinforcing social relations has been discussed with regard to the European Neolithic and Copper Ages by John Chapman (2000). He argues that by fragmenting material culture, the artefact and its meaning is duplicated and hence can perform in more social relationships than a single whole artefact. The parts of artefact hence both represent the whole and part; they continue to be linked to the other fragments of the original artefact while still functioning on their own as a process of enchainment. It could be suggested that similar social relations are being manifested with the deposition of some chalk artefacts. Pieces of these artefacts were deposited but others may have been curated or passed to other persons as a way of creating enchained relations of geneaology and exchange (*ibid.*: 45). Hence part of the chalk artefact is placed in a deposit while potentially still being active within the society creating a process of enchainment between the deposit and the continuing societal function. With more study, chalk artefacts could be argued as having been present in the types of fragmentation and exchange schemes that may have been evident in other artefact types such as polished stone axe fragments or pottery sherds. For example, conjoining Grooved Ware sherds within different re-cut pits at the Southern Circle at Durrington Walls, Wiltshire were noted on excavation (Wainwright and Longworth 1971: 111, 133, 139, 141, 147).

The manipulation of substances and artefacts seems relevant for understanding portable chalk artefacts which appear to be illustrated through variations in both substance and decoration. For example, while chalk plaques are always decorated and consistent in form, at Etton a fired clay artefact was excavated from a Neolithic context (Pryor 1998: 270) which may represent a clay plaque. It was finely finished and unlike any other artefacts of this nature and date (*ibid.*), and could be imitating an undecorated chalk plaque. Furthermore a clay phallus was also recovered at Etton, which appears to unique in the British Neolithic (*ibid.*). We can see different types of manipulation evidenced here. With regard to the clay phallus, it has been created in a similar form to chalk phalli differing only through the choice of substance in its creation: the form is continuing and constitutes a cultural norm. In respect of the clay plaque, the imitation of a similar form to a chalk plaque indicates a cultural understanding of the form of plaques which appears to have been manipulated in this region (East Anglia). With the Etton clay plaque two forms of manipulation have taken place: the altering of substance and the lack of decoration. This discrepancy in decoration is also seen with chalk drums where the Folkton Drums appear as decorated forms, however the Lavant Drum is undecorated. I believe these variations suggest two factors: that form represents one meaning and decoration another, and that regional variation supports or inhibits this additional decoration to form. Hence, the form itself has inherent meaning which may be enhanced or altered or detracted from dependant on the application of design or change of substance, and these are manifested in regional variations. That certain forms seem contained and rarely exhibit variations seems also worthy of note: for example chalk balls. These forms may therefore not be socially sanctioned as artefacts which should be manipulated through decoration. While acknowledging that, the difference in size between chalk balls at Grimes Graves and other sites has already been mentioned, hence while the form itself may be constrained, the size of the form perhaps could be manipulated. Moreover the size difference may represent a chronological shift to increase size during the later Neolithic and early Bronze Age.

It is also of interest that some chalk axes represent chipped forms, and others polished. In the previous chapter I argued that axe polishing may be part of mortuary ritual and metaphorical for the human body's transformation from whole and fleshed, to the revealing of bone during excarnation and decay. With this suggestion, chalk axes could also be said to be representation of the body during this process. The Woodhenge examples perhaps indicate a later Neolithic reference to this polishing rather than the chipping of axes (excarnation completed, where axes have a greater social significance embedded within them), when alternatively perhaps the chipped examples from Stonehenge and Blackpatch signify the start of that journey, a readiness of chipped axes for the start of the transformation of the dead. This concurs with suggestions that Stonehenge may be an area or domain of the Neolithic dead (Parker Pearson and Ramilisonina 1998, Parker Pearson *et al.* 2007). In this way, suggestions that some chalk work surfaces may represent quern stones or small polissoirs could become part of this argument, weaving into the fabric of the later Neolithic portable artefact repertoire. Even in North Wales this may be referenced in the mid-Neolithic at c. 3200 cal BC with a cremation burial in Henge A at Llandegai being interred with a portable axe polishing stone from a Pembrokeshire source (Houlder 1968: 218). It has not been ascertained that this originates from the Preseli mountains where the bluestones at Stonehenge were quarried, yet the affinity with this same region could indicate a social referencing consistent with the proposal outlined. Chalk axes and chalk polishing stones do not occur together, yet nor do flint axes and polishing stones. Their form is relational and contained.

Once the form of an axe is referenced, or any other artefact, they form part of the network of wider meanings of substance. Moreover, engaging with the human body in a corporeal rather than just in a metaphorical sense provides different insights. Use-wear in terms of the scrapings in chalk cups or working surfaces may have been made while applying chalk in different ways on the body itself, as seen ethnographically in the Suma Tribe in Ethiopia, Africa.

Hence while skeuomorphism is a relevant concept, it should not be seen as simple re-representation. The portable chalk artefacts may reflect other types of form, but retain significance in their chalk form. They continue to embody the significance of the artefacts represented and yet embody additional significance through the form represented in their new substance. While chalk artefacts form the most cohesive body of non-functional artefacts for study in this way, other substances and artefacts are reviewed in Chapter 6, in a similar way enhancing these interpretations more fully.

5.8 Conclusion

This chapter has sought to bring cohesion to the study of portable chalk artefacts in the British Neolithic, establishing them as an artefact class. The reviewing of both typology and chronological issues through investigating a wide ranging number of contemporary sites has elucidated the more subtle aspects to them. I have described how portable chalk artefacts can be examined through qualifying reoccurring forms into a typology and have conducted a degree of analysis in their deposition across some Neolithic and Bronze Age sites in southern Britain. In a similar way to that of some non-portable chalk artefacts (Chapter 4), skeuomorphism is a likely factor in the representation of certain shapes. Portable chalk artefacts should therefore be seen in a wider scheme of reference to other artefact and substance types.

In terms of chalk artefact forms, many are consistent for hundreds of years and there are indications of complex skeuomorphic manipulation. This can be argued as being most productively viewed through Thomas's *bricolage* where artefacts and substances can be manipulated within themselves in a variety of ways (1996). With the sole exclusion of chalk charms, the flint mines do not exhibit greater numbers of chalk artefact, or more peculiar forms than those at other sites. Indeed, the types of chalk artefacts found in mines are entirely consistent with other contemporary monuments. In addition, the variation in both chalk artefacts and their form across different substances categories imply a degree of sanctioned manipulation with many artefact forms. Hence the meaning of chalk artefacts is situated within the wider meaning of substances. Following evidence from Chapter 4, the inclusion of Sussex into wider discourses of Neolithic Wessex is again argued on the similarities and use of portable chalk artefacts. Hence flint mines can aid the interpretation of chalk artefacts and other previously unconsidered artefacts through this comparative analysis. The following chapter will examine non-chalk artefacts in flint mine deposits to aid this process further.

Chapter 6

Natural Objects to Cultural Artefacts

6.1 Introduction

This chapter considers deposited objects such as antler and bone tools, fossils, iron pyrites, faunal remains and human remains within flint mine shafts and galleries, reinterpreting them as cultural artefacts. Furthermore, once re-categorised as artefacts their deliberate and structured deposition is considered though various examples. Consequently, within the book as a whole, this chapter explores with perhaps the greatest emphasis the relationship between three interpretive factors: specific types of deposit as singular entities, their cumulative relationship within a depositional event, and meaning. As discussed in Chapter 3, the recognition and interpretation of archaeological deposits has previously focussed on what is perceived as significant to our enquiries, and commonly these have been economic or functional concerns. Any material which may be viewed as not critical to this process has often been excluded from wider discourses, a view which has been challenged through studies of structured deposition. Antler picks, carved chalk, quartz stone and fossils have begun to become incorporated into structured depositional arguments about deposition, illustrating the complex and deliberate actions of Neolithic persons at specific depositional events (Pollard 1995; Thomas 1996; 1999a).

Structured deposits discussed by both Thomas and Pollard occur in monuments which exhibit shallower deposits than those contained at mine sites. These deposits in pits, causewayed enclosure ditches or henge monuments are often seen as occurring, and perhaps being influenced by, repeated re-cutting episodes. Therefore while we can assign specific relationships in structured deposition as being temporally significant and deliberate, the fact these sites have been reoccupied or subject to later activity allows for some uncertainty in chronology. Moreover, while the presence of some natural objects within deposits may have been significant during the Neolithic, many can occur naturally within the subsoil and so there can remain a degree of uncertainty as to their deliberate inclusion, an important issue I intend to address here. At their lower levels, flint mine shaft fills and galleries represent completely closed deposits and hence such practices within flint mines can be argued as less likely to have been subject to any interference after their initial deposition. This study concentrates on deposits at mid-lower levels of shaft fill and within galleries in order to avoid possible re-cuts as discussed in Chapter 2.

I interpret these deposits as being evidenced as structured in various ways. For example, some artefacts are positioned in particular ways which may be interpreted as aesthetic; some deposits may be in combination with others, or the cumulative deposits within a particular shaft may indicate prolonged attention was given to structuring deposits in certain contexts. The deliberate placement of artefacts within galleries and specific deposits studied here signify temporal expressions on their last action, hence the relationship of certain artefacts to each is unlikely to be accidental. Furthermore, the relationship between structured deposits adjacent to each other, or in opposition, can be explored as can the discrete deposits at a temporal distance (for example in different levels of a shaft fill). The premise of this approach is the same as those studies already completed - it is merely the closed nature of the architecture which is different.

Due to the various different excavators and variations in excavation records, there is a wide discrepancy in the amount of detail available for each site. For example, very little analysis was completed by specialists on animal or human bone from Pull's excavations and therefore this information is simply unavailable for many of the Sussex shafts. Furthermore, deposits at Grimes Graves are well documented and also well published, hence examples of deposition here have at times already been discussed. A focus has been retained on the less well published, earlier sites to aid interpretations of early Neolithic mining and provide a background to interpret the later activity. Therefore case studies of particular shafts and/or galleries are discussed where enough evidence exists to indicate structured deposition.

The scale of analysis fluctuates due to the differences in deposition. For example, some artefacts are so unusual that their immediate depositional relationship is all that is necessary for discussion, yet other shafts show complex fills which require greater discussion in order to render a valid interpretation. This study should not be seen as a comprehensive list of every deposit at each site which would be beyond the scope of this work. Hence, after considering how human and animal remains have previously been seen (6.2), a discussion on expanding contexts to include different objects as artefacts follows with a description of depositional categories (6.3). Specific deposits are analysed and discussed (6.4, 6.5) with aesthetic deposits separately in 6.6. Phallic artefacts and sexual forms are considered in 6.7 due to their form being created in many different substances and the chapter concludes in 6.8.

6.2. Reconsidering Animal and Human Remains

As discussed in Chapter 3, human and animals remains have previously often only been considered in functional and/or economic ways. This is situated within the history both of the Neolithic and the discipline more widely. The transition to the Neolithic in Britain has been historically defined as both a chronological boundary and a change in economy from hunting and gathering to farming. While there is no evidence for either sedentism or agriculture on a large scale in southern Britain at the start of the Neolithic (Thomas 1999a: 7-23), there is a heavy emphasis on the study of the archaeological remains of domesticated species such as cattle (*Bos taurus*) or pig (*Sus scrofa*) in terms of herd management strategies, or economy (e.g. Entwistle and Grant 1989; Albarella and Serjeantson 2002). Initially the excavation of large amounts of cattle and pig remains at sites such as Durrington Walls and Windmill Hill related these new domesticated species as animals with ritualistic emphases in the Neolithic, being used in mass consumption or feasting (Richards and Thomas 1984; Whittle *et al.* 1999). More recently the conception of cattle as both domestic and ritually important animals has been advanced with the suggestion that the presence of cattle skulls and bones in relation to human burial indicates an affinity in the Neolithic of categorising cattle herds with human groups (Ray and Thomas 2003).

Human remains in the Neolithic are subject to a 'strategy of representation' through mortuary ritual (Thomas 1999a: 130), being manipulated within various practices, which at different times and locations are more archaeologically visible than others. They have been processed through organised disarticulation at many Neolithic chambered tombs and long barrows (e.g Haddenham, Fussell's Lodge, Nutbane and West Kennett) where bodies appear to have been left to break down within the structures themselves and subsequently reorganised. The disarticulated remains can then be subject to secondary burial (*ibid.*: 136). Excarnation in the open air is suggested for many causewayed enclosures, such as Hambledon Hill (Mercer 1980), but it should be acknowledged that human remains appear in varying quantities in most Neolithic excavations. The monumentality of Neolithic middens and their potential as either territorial markers (Renfrew 1976), or as parallels with chambered tombs which can infer or invoke possible ancestral belief (Cummings and Whittle 2004) has been discussed (Chapter 2), yet the intimate management and continuing physical engagement with them is rarely referred to (but see Pollard 2005).

New studies interpretively combining animal and human evidence have turned to analysing human remains in order to discover the eating patterns of the living in the Neolithic (Schulting and Richards 2000). This type of analysis can only differentiate between marine and terrestrial foods, and the evidence appears to point to an abrupt decline in the consumption of marine foods at the start of the Neolithic. This has constructed a circular argument in favour of the consumption of domesticates in the Neolithic. We study domesticates, and hence when indications in isotopes suggest a meat diet we infer they ate domesticates rather than wild species, yet it is acknowledged that the types of faunal assemblages found on Neolithic sites are probably unrepresentative of everyday living (Thomas 1999a: 27).

This chapter seeks to examine human and animal remains with a different focus. Rather than prioritise these bones as more important that other types of deposition, they are seen alongside the other artefacts such as fossils or nodules. Under this phenomenological approach each part of the deposit can reflect and enhance aspects of past understandings in a structured and meaningful way. All the deposits were deliberately brought together. The interplay between individual elements within certain deposits was significant, their interpretation complex. This is illustrated both in the combination of artefacts within structured deposits and aesthetically the way they are deposited. An overview of each type of natural deposit is given below with examples from other Neolithic British deposits.

6.3 Expanding Contexts: Creating Artefacts

This section seeks to discuss what types of previously unconsidered objects should be reclassified as artefacts and have their deposition acknowledged as relevant for structured depositional analyses. Following Brück's discussion on rationality (1999) and Hodder's on context and artefact being relational (1999; Chapter 3), this explores both these concepts: that artefacts can be unrecognisable to a modern western view and that, once recognised, the rationality of their deposition need not be determined as motivated by ritual only. Whether or not these practices or artefacts make sense to us is irrelevant, yet we should recognise that they did make sense during the Neolithic.

In this way, artefacts which appear in deposits are considered to be meaningful and hence their interpretation begins with their deposition. Yet, considering individual deposits could lead to interpretive fragmentation and therefore categorisation is important. As this research is a study in materiality approached through phenomenology, I have arranged artefacts in terms of the human engagement required in acquiring them, or in other words, according to the ways in which they have been created as artefacts from natural sources. While this may not have been a Neolithic way of understanding them, I believe it allows us to move beyond a modern Western understanding. I have divided these categories into three: Excavated Artefacts, Transformed Artefacts and Retrieved Artefacts.

Excavated Artefacts

Included in this category are flint nodules, iron pyrites and fossils. These contexts appear in depositional relationships with other artefacts in the flint mines and contemporary monuments; however, detailed consideration of how they become artefacts has not been attempted before. The natural forms are all excavated from chalk. They appear naturally within chalk and need to be extracted from the chalk and cleaned of chalk in order to be used within deposits. In previous studies fossils have been referred to as 'encountered' objects and not artefacts, a premise I challenged in Chapter 3. In terms of excavation, these artefacts are not made as cultural artefacts in their form, but rather are socially constructed through their excavation and critically, the decision to keep and use them in deposits. Although not physically made, they are culturally constructed into artefacts, and hence *are* artefacts.

Transformed Artefacts

Certain artefacts present in deposits are only recovered on the death of a body, be it animal or human. Bone shovels or fragments of human bone cannot be used as tools or as active parts of a deposition until there has been a transformation from a living entity to a dead entity, which may have been a result of deliberate action or natural causes. This initial transformation from living to dead is often only the beginning with evidence of manipulation or post-mortem activities often being present on the bone. While we have previously only examined cattle as a food and feasting animal, using ox bone shovels required bone material produced from the carcass and may have also have been a factor in determining when a particular beast was killed. In addition to this, other uses and products from an ox carcass include the presence of skulls and hooves at Neolithic sites which Ray and Thomas (2003) suggested may have involved hides being used to cover particular mortuary structures or bodies. The question that we must consider though is how these tools conceptually relate to each other through use; was there an intention to combine 'domesticated' and 'wild' species within a particular tool kit of pick and shovel? How did this create meaning? Or are these simply products of everyday life without structured meaning in themselves but constitute meaning through their use? The remains we excavate provide clues as to what may have been expressed or highlighted in the vicinity through the deposition of animal remains. A further transformation can be seen when the bone artefact is constructed for a tool. The bone shovel is a tool frequently found in Neolithic mine deposits and at other monuments, comprising a shoulder blade of an ox which has been modified for the insertion of a wooden handle. The shovel can only be used once the animal is dead, the carcass processed and the bone dried out. Another type of transformed artefact was antler cut from the carcass of a deer rather than antler shed from a living deer. At times these are used as tools yet they can also be deposited without modification. Whether these artefacts are used as tools or not is another category of analysis, or avenue of description, yet the existence of them in archaeological contexts renders them artefacts. One activity evidenced in Neolithic deposits is animal or human bone which has been subject to decay in a midden (or similar environment) and/or curation prior to deposition, therefore providing another avenue of description in interpretation. Bone deposits, fresh and articulated or degraded from exposure and/or middens have different specific histories and their inclusion within deposits may emphasise different factors within the deposits (Pollard 2001, 2005).

Retrieved Artefacts

This category describes those contexts which occur as discard and in this study is represented by shed antler. The antler taken and modified (or unmodified) and then placed in archaeological contexts renders them artefacts as they cannot occur naturally within deposits through a result of the action of deer alone. Antler picks (quite often unused) can be deposited in the mines at gallery entrances on top of rubble. This led to many excavators commenting that it appeared miners had left suddenly due to the threat of an imminent roof collapse yet these are most likely to constitute ritual deposits (Topping 2005: 78-9). While this mostly concerns red deer, the remains of roe deer are also recovered from deposits at flint mine sites. However, the antler of a roe deer does not grow to the size or shape of that of the red deer and hence its antler are not used as tools. Red deer antler were therefore the usual material used for picks whereas in almost all circumstances roe deer remains consist of the occasional bone, suggesting it was killed and consumed. Outside flint mine contexts, other retrieved artefacts could include hazelnuts, twigs, mosses, grasses or other materials which have been gathered.

Summary

The categories above argue that these forms when present in deposition cannot occur without deliberate human action and therefore should be classed as artefacts, following arguments in Chapter 3 that artefacts construct contexts as contexts construct artefacts (Hodder 1999). Moreover, the complexities involved in their creation as artefacts prior to deposition require consideration in viewing them as artefacts, whether they were excavated, retrieved or subject to transformation. The following section discusses individual cases within the mines and examines specific artefacts.

6.4 Excavated Artefacts

Flint Nodules

At flint mines there is evidence of deliberate deposits of nodules in particular places within both shafts and galleries. In flint mine shafts they can occur in artificially created 'seams', mirroring the natural deposits, spanning the breadth of the shaft (as at Church Hill Shaft 7, Russell 2001: 117) and also occurring as 'platforms' or other architectural features (as at Shaft V Cissbury, Chapter 4; Pit 15 Grimes Graves, Varndell 1991). Certain nodules because of their size or shape can also be contained in structured deposits. One third of the way down the backfill of Shaft 7 at Blackpatch, a cremation burial was discovered in between clean chalk layers (Pull 1932: 57-8). Within the oval layer of charcoal and burnt remains were a few burnt flints, and deposited with them a chipped axe, a flint knife, a scraper and a worked chalk charm. Two thirds of the way down the same shaft a working floor was encountered 9m in circumference and 10cm in depth. This was covered by a large quantity of animal bone (principally cattle ribs), and to the northern edge of the flint spread was a large pile of flint nodules (Russell 2001: 43). Pull interprets this as the nodules being 'abandoned' possibly after a collapse of backfill into the shaft (Russell 2001: 44), though Russell argues it may be the deliberate deposition of unutilised floorstone.

The possibility of working flint in an area within a flint mine shaft during a break in its backfill has to be considered as viable, though practically this would involve many stages. For example it might have followed this course: when work was completed in the shaft and galleries, a third of the shaft was filled and then piles of nodules returned to the shaft from the surface. These are then mostly worked creating the spread of debris with some nodules left untouched. Pull (Russell 2001: 43) interprets the animal bone as being the remains of meals taken by the workers during this activity. It is also possible that this deposit is a return of surface workings to the shaft in this particular formation, mixed with midden material.

Single nodules can also occur of interest. A 'Great Nodule' in one of the western galleries of Shaft 27 at Cissbury was noted by Pull as a feature, though no other details survive (Russell 2001: 182). At the end of the second gallery of Greenwell's Pit, Grimes Graves, a flint nodule resembling the head of a cat was placed which appeared to have been used as a hammer (Greenwell 1870: 430). While this is not illustrated, a similar example came to my attention excavated from the Black Patch Bronze Age settlement excavation of 2005 and is shown in Figure 6.1. We cannot say that this was recognised as this particular species, yet the resemblance to a skull of a small animal could have been recognised. Also at Grimes Grave in Pit 2, gallery 10, pottery was found just inside the gallery resting on a piece of tabular flint (Clarke 1915: 75). Pit 2 also contained art which was discussed in Chapter 4.

Flint nodules as architectural features have been noted at monuments such as Boles Barrow (Wiltshire) where the mortuary area was floored with a compact spread of flint nodules (Kinnes 1992: 25) and at Fussell's Lodge (Wiltshire) where an ox skull was sealed by a stack of flint nodules between the entrance and human bone group B

FIGURE 6.1 PHOTOGRAPH OF FLINT NODULE RESEMBLING A CAT SKULL, BLACKPATCH 2005 (PHOTOGRAPH AUTHOR)

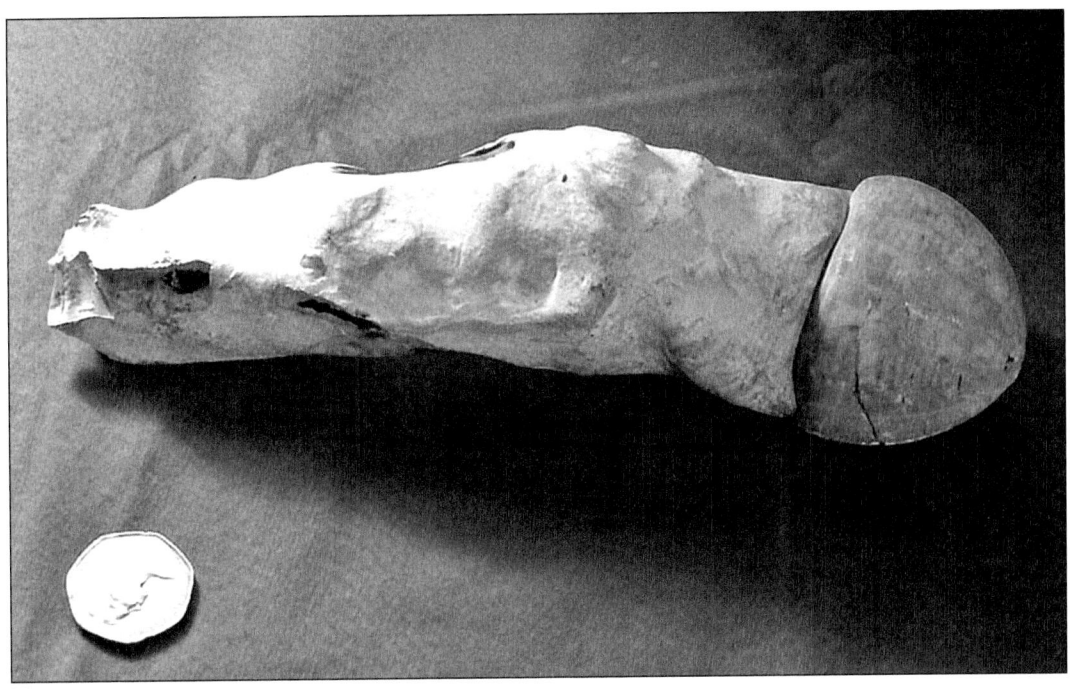

FIGURE 6.2 PHOTOGRAPH OF CISSBURY SHAFT 27 FLINT/FOSSIL PHALLUS (NOW LOST; PHOTOGRAPH COURTESY OF DAVID FIELD)

(Grigson 1966: 65). A flint nodule with an attached fused fossil resembling a human phallus was found during the excavation of the galleries surrounding Shaft 27 at Cissbury and is illustrated in Figure 6.2 (Russell 2001: 186). A phallic flint nodule was also excavated from Dwelling Pit 11 at Easton Down (Stone 1935). At Grimes Graves a flint arrangement of a flint nodule and two flint balls, seemingly to imitate male genitalia more comprehensively was found at the base of Shaft 15 by Armstrong in 1939 (Varndell 1991; Barber et al. 1999: 64).

Parallels are noted elsewhere in the Neolithic. During excavations conducted at Durrington Walls in 2004, a pit was discovered now referred to as the 'sex pit' (Parker Pearson et al. 2006). In this pit a flint nodule, in the shape of a phallus, was discovered alongside two flint balls (Figure 6.3) in the pit fill, close to a pelvis-shaped flint which was set into the wall of the pit and covered with a large block of flint. Excavations in 2005 uncovered another two flint nodules also in the shape of phalli (one of them came from the western part of the Southern Circle). The flint phallus from the 'sex pit' has been modified. Most of its surface modifications are of geological origin (Andy Farrant, Mark Wood and Peter Hopson pers. comm.) and the flint nodule uncovered in its natural state could be said to be more representative of a male penis than any other discovered to date. It is possible that this double groove represents the female vulvae and clitoris. It was then deposited with two flint balls, seemingly to represent testes, within a pit whose lining included the flint nodule shaped as a pelvis.

FIGURE 6.3 PHOTOGRAPH OF PHALLIC GROUPING FROM DURRINGTON WALLS (PHOTOGRAPH MIKE PARKER PEARSON)

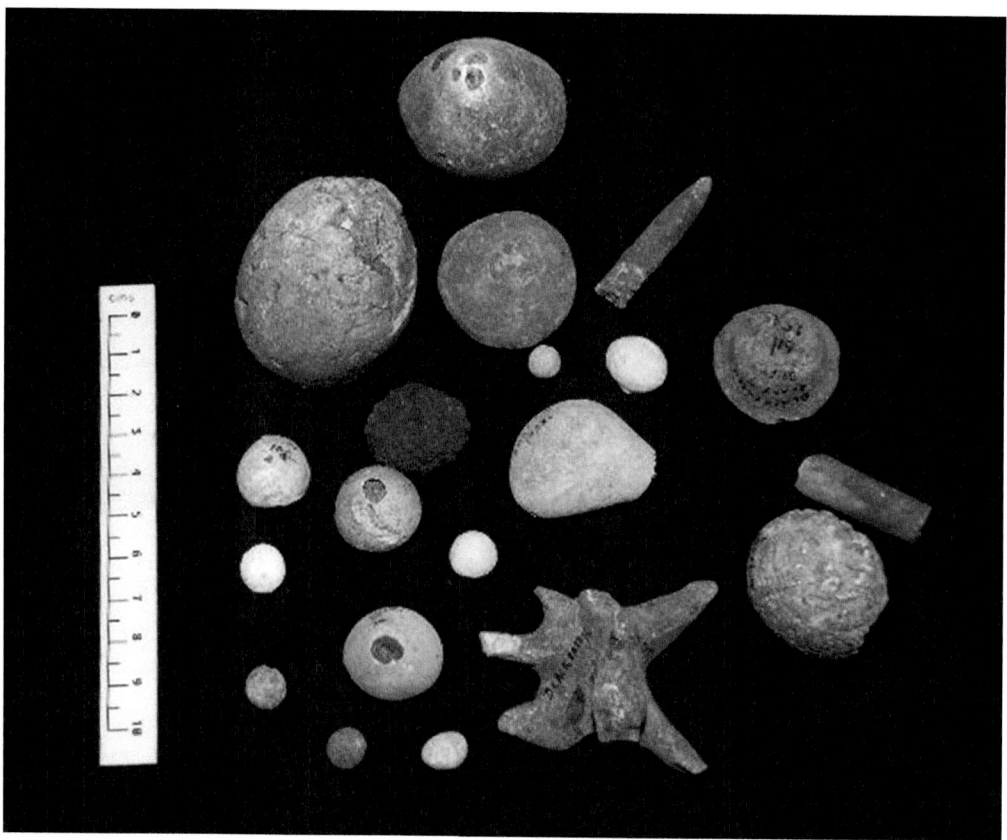

FIGURE 6.4 PHOTOGRAPH OF ASSORTED FOSSILS FROM PULL'S EXCAVATIONS (PHOTOGRAPH AUTHOR; © WORTHING MUSEUM AND ART GALLERY)

Fossils and Shells

A deposit of fossil shell is noted from Blackpatch Shaft 2, to the south of gallery III (Russell 2001: 37-8). There are groups of fossilised shell in the collection (Figures 6.4, 6.5) and it is likely some of these are the items Pull was referring to in Shaft 2. Unfortunately he has not detailed the number of species and the number of shells present in this deposit and as many occur in the collection it may suggest more have been uncovered throughout these excavations and have been grouped together. The placement of fossil shell appears to have only occurred at Blackpatch, with none being noted at other mine sites and though this may represent excavation bias, Pull would almost certainly have noted examples from the other mines he excavated such as Cissbury and Church Hill. While fossils and shells do have deliberate placement, some instances may be accidental. At Stoke Down, Shaft 3 contained a hearth which included shells of *Helix nemoralis* (Wade 1922: 89-91). This type of large land snail is edible but as the shells are not noted as being burnt it is likely that they accumulated there naturally and collection bias was most likely to be the cause of this seemingly placed deposit (Michael Allen pers. comm.). The *Helix nemoralis* found with the Cissbury Shaft VI burial are also probably an accidental inclusion rather than deliberate deposition.

Fossils of marine species occur naturally within chalk deposits and have been noted during excavation at other Neolithic and Bronze Age sites. At the West Kennet long barrow, shell beads were excavated from the north east and south east chambers (Piggott 1962: 53). Three marine shell species appear at Maiden Castle with one shell having been drilled for a bead (Kennard in Wheeler 1943: 372). Marine shells are also noted at Woodlands, Durrington Walls, Ratfyn and Woodhenge though it is suggested they may have been collected for use as tempering in pottery production (Wainwright & Longworth 1971: 265). During the 1984 excavation at Liff's Low round barrow in the Peak District a Jurassic fish tooth was found (Barnatt & Collis 1996: 117). Nearly one hundred chalk fossil sea urchins were uncovered from a double burial of a woman and child on Dunstable Downs in Bedfordshire (Grinsell 1953: 274).

While numbers are not given, a substantial quantity of fossils was excavated from a passage tomb at Ballycarty in south-west Ireland (Wyse-Jackson and Connolly 2002: 139-143). These seem to have been brought to the tomb mostly from a surface collection of the local limestone outcrops and would have only required a small effort to extract, although one fossil exhibits broken surfaces which may indicate more of a determined extraction from the rock (*ibid.*: 142). A fossil or worked stone deposit was

FIGURE 6.5 PHOTOGRAPH OF FOSSILS FROM PULL'S EXCAVATIONS (PHOTOGRAPH AUTHOR; © WORTHING MUSEUM AND ART GALLERY)

made at Etton with a fragment of human skull (Pryor 1998: 269), which may be indicative of similar practice.

Iron Pyrites

No specific studies have been completed on the presence of iron pyrites at Neolithic sites in the UK and therefore in common with fossils and chalk artefacts its possible significance to Neolithic persons by depositional behaviour remains unexamined and unquantifiable. Iron pyrites are present within the chalk subsoil of southern England and occur frequently alongside fossils and flint. Yet the natural occurrence and cultural deposition of iron pyrites are two discrete entities, one factual and one socially significant. It is tempting to try to assimilate a cultural meaning to iron pyrites with that of flint, when we know it occurs with flint and was used functionally with flint to create fire. However wider issues are important. Iron pyrites is also referred to as 'fools gold' as visually it is shiny and metallic. It is a crystallized substance and hence its appearance within a pre-metallic society would have been unusual.

A group of four lumps of iron pyrites were found in at a depth of 20 feet (6.1m) in the shaft fill of Shaft VI at Cissbury, approximately 1m from the shaft floor at the entrance to a gallery. This shaft also contained the burial of a man at 16 feet (4.88m) below the surface (Harrison 1878: 432; Rolleston 1879: 380). These pyrites were deposited half a metre from a nest of flakes numbering approximately 300-400. A further example of the deposit of iron pyrites is also discussed in relation to an aesthetic deposit (6.5). Deposits of iron pyrites are not noted from many other prehistoric contexts, however in 2006 a lump of iron pyrites in the shape of a phallus with attached testes was excavated from a house floor at Durrington Walls, within its abandonment layer and associated with Grooved Ware. It is small at approximately 6cm in length and is unlike many phalli in its size and also in that the prepuce is present; it looks very much like the relaxed genitalia of a young or baby boy.

Excavated Artefacts Summary

Flint nodules, iron pyrites and fossils appear to have been subject to deliberate deposition in the flint mines which is consistent with depositional activity at other Neolithic sites as discussed. The detail present in excavation reports for this evidence is often rather vague and in many cases largely absent. Apart from the presence of flint nodules in a shaft fill, all the fossils, iron pyrites and flint nodules occur at the base of shafts or in galleries, consistent with other forms of deposition in the mines. As discussed, all these artefacts have been extracted from the chalk and been subject to deposition as a deliberate strategy. In some cases, flint nodules have represented phallic forms and these seem to be subject to deposits in what may be seen as congruent with Neolithic practices. The use of fossils in the Neolithic has been discussed in the discipline more frequently than flint nodules or iron pyrites, no doubt largely due to the amounts encountered in different excavations. In addition, many of these contexts are mortuary contexts where we as archaeologists are perhaps more willing to interpret odd deposits as deliberate and indicative of ritual.

The use of fossils in other contexts has been interpretively described by Richard Bradley (2000). Bradley (2000: 91) argues that the inclusion of fossil shell into pottery vessels as tempering may have been as these were recognised as being the remains of once living creatures, in a similar way to the use of bone tempering noted at Hazleton North. While his main concern is with the use of oolite stone incorporated into monuments (which also has fossil impressions embedded into it) expressing connections with both places of origin and the past, I would rather examine the integration of these within concepts of materiality as discussed in Chapter 3. As a collection strategy, the extraction of fossils from chalk would have had to be completed with some care due to the easy fracture of the material. The use of fossilised shells as deposits may have invoked watery environments (river, estuary or sea) whether fossil or fresh (*ibid.*). This connection with water creates wider associations of depositional relationships which may be concerned with axe deposits in rivers, mortuary practices, rites of passage more generally or as a food source. Paradoxically, and perhaps as important in expressing opposition, they may as fossils have also evoked associations with the earth, the past and both physical and temporal distance through their deliberate extraction. Regretfully the use of flint nodules are iron pyrites have not been subject to similar analysis and hence the possible interpretation of them in these deposited contexts still subject to conjecture.

6.5 Transformed Artefacts

Animals: Bone Tools

Bone tools form a category of artefact which is often seen as a functional use of material which would otherwise be useless and discarded. The transformational aspects of the material or collection strategies are not considered: for example, we do not interpret the killing of cattle for the purpose of creating bone shovels, rather just a use of an already dead animal. Only ox scapulae as bone shovels occur within shaft fills and galleries at the Sussex and Wessex mines, whilst bone (as opposed to antler) picks seem to only have occurred at Grimes Graves. Excavations at Grimes Graves included two pits (Pits III and IV) which were noted as being different to other shafts at the site (Armstrong 1932). These pits were shallower (being no deeper than 12 feet 6 inches [3.8m] to the base) and contained unusual 'hand picks' made of bone. These were mostly ox bones which had been trimmed and sharpened for the insertion of a flint flake to assist in extracting chalk (*ibid.*: 121). These pits also showed apparent 'steps' cut into the sides of the shaft for easier access. Similar pits to these, including deposits of bone picks were excavated in 1928, Pits VIII and X (Armstrong 1932: 59). It was largely thought by Armstrong that these bone picks were a chronological variation of extraction method, as he had argued there were earlier and later shafts (Chapter 2). Specific antler deposits were noted at the conjoining Shafts 6 and 7, Church Hill (Russell 2001: 121). At the base of Shaft 6 at the entrance to one of the galleries on top of a pile of rubble almost to the ceiling of the gallery was placed one antler pick, a broken bone shovel and two flint knives (*ibid.*: 110). On the entranceway between Shafts 6 and 7 a two handled antler pick was placed, and at the furthest eastern edge of each shaft gallery system were more antler and bone tools (*ibid.*: 115). Pull (*ibid.*: 116) also comments on the large number of bone tools and antler picks that were present in the fill of Shaft 7, including antler mallets.

Retrieval or Transformation: The Case of Antler

Antler picks occur in deposits from both slain and shed origins. Pull (1932: 104) notes that the antler used at Blackpatch was in the main from shed sources, although at Cissbury the opposite was true for the early excavations. He suggests there is a paucity of antler tools at Blackpatch in comparison with Cissbury and Grimes Graves and furthermore, of the antler tools found at Blackpatch many picks had been re-sharpened, were broken or had been heavily used (*ibid.*: 106-8). While one red deer antler was discovered in gallery III of Shaft 2 he does not specify the exact locations of other examples and it is likely they proved too fragmentary for further discussion (Russell 2001: 38). Curiously, a roe deer antler from a slain source was found in the Large Pit at Cissbury (M). This pit was not excavated to its base and the location of remains unrecorded (Rolleston 1877: 23)

At Shaft IV at Cissbury an antler hammer from a slain deer was placed over the entrance of the gallery to this shaft (access having been gained to the base via the gallery system from the Cave Pit, Shaft II) (Harrison 1878: 417). Several antlers which do not appear to have been used as tools were found in two of the galleries at the base of Shaft VI, the shaft where the burial surrounded with chalk blocks was excavated and close to chalk art of which no details survive (Harrison 1878: 432). These are described as having several tines still attached and therefore have not been modified at all. Antler picks appear with regularity at Grimes Graves in shaft fills and in specific deposits and placements in galleries. They were discovered in the lower layers (7 and 8) of Pit 1 excavated in 1914 and several deposited as a group over the entrance to gallery 8 (Clarke 1915: 50-1).

Few studies have focussed on the origins of the antler used, that is whether the antler has been shed or obtained from slain animals, although Clutton-Brock's comparative analysis of antler from Grimes Graves and Durrington

Walls is comprehensive. Clutton-Brock's (1984: 25) data suggest that of the antler found at Grimes Graves 77.13% is shed with 22.87% from slain deer whereas at Durrington Walls 85.66% is shed and 14.34% from slain deer. Her analysis also shows that the antler at Grimes Graves is larger in circumference than those at Durrington Walls and furthermore the slain antler significantly larger at Grimes Graves than the slain antler from Durrington Walls. While it is likely that the deer in Norfolk would have a wider ranging habitat than that of Wiltshire (where at this period agriculture and land clearance is more widespread) and so the deer in Norfolk may have been simply larger in general (Legge 1981:102), this does not account entirely for the difference. Indeed, if there were an abundance of red deer in Norfolk, slain antler may not have been necessary due to the vast amounts shed, therefore we should expect a greater proportion of slain antler in Wiltshire. Legge's (*ibid.*: 100) study of antler at Grimes Graves following Mercer's excavation yields slightly different results to that of Clutton-Brock's as 90% of the antler studied by him was shed. Slain or shed antler have different collection strategies and these two regions exhibit evidence which could be contradictory. The slaying of very large red deer to produce antler which were significantly larger than those from the Wiltshire region suggests that hunting red deer for antler to be used may have been a particular social strategy incorporated in mining activity. Conversely, the much smaller proportion of slain antler at Durrington Walls may indicate more of an emphasis on collecting shed antler.

Two interpretations can be argued here. Firstly, recovering shed antler or detaching the antler from the skull after hunting and killing the deer would have been entirely different cultural social practices and secondly, they would have occurred in different seasons (antler is shed in February/March and only regrow to full size between September and February). Hence, not only does slain antler and shed antler have specific collection strategies it is also seasonally, and so temporally, distinct. To gain the greatest antler size, a deer must be killed between September and prior to shedding in February/March. Red deer shed their antler in the same place each year and, once shed, can eat the antler. Hence the deer must be closely observed during this period of time in order to ensure adequate collection can take place. As at Grimes Graves and Durrington Walls at least 75% of the antler are from collecting shed antler, a considerable number of people would need to be involved in this process. Furthermore, the above studies by Legge and Clutton-Brock have examined both left and right handed antler, as there is evidence that different sides of the antler branches are more appropriate for left and right handed human individuals. The statistics appear to suggest this is the case. Therefore, we could infer that particular individuals collect their own antler prior to mining or digging monuments, collecting only the right or left handed branch (and perhaps several of them to use).

When examining the deposition of antler, I suggest that we need to examine antler in these categories, shed or slain, as socially different. A shed antler has a different biographical heritage than that of a slain antler and I would argue that associations within a structured depositional framework would have had different emphases. Slain antler should be categorised alongside animal bone as a transformed artefact whereas shed antler are a retrieved artefact. Perhaps antler deposition was more of a personal statement, signifying a particular person's contribution to the season's work. Where antler are not deposited in mine shafts or galleries or in ditch deposits, where are they placed? Do they contribute to midden deposits? However we examine the individual deposits, antler collection by either method situates this activity prior to construction or extraction, possibly being tied to particular individuals and a seasonal event. The forethought and planning prior to events such as digging can therefore be situated as more formal and considered than previously imagined.

Animal Remains

Animal remains occur in flint mine shafts in discrete deposits at Cissbury in shaft fills, with few examples found in gallery contexts or fills at other sites. Two shafts will be discussed here from Cissbury: Shaft 27 and Tindall's Pit. The fill of Shaft 27 has been analysed by Topping (2005) who suggests that the various depositions of animal bone and flint are indicative of extraction rites of renewal, cleansing and offerings. A human body was excavated from this shaft and is discussed in 6.5.4. Unfortunately, due to the lack of a comprehensive faunal report we remain ignorant of many details of the evidence of the species or condition of the material. Remains of a nearly whole ox was present two thirds of the way down the shaft, with remains of small animals found both at upper levels in the shaft and below this ox deposition (Russell 2001:181). While the description of nearly a whole ox implies it was articulated, this is in fact not the case. The vertebrae appear articulated, similar to those vertebrae found in the Skeleton Shaft (Shaft H). However, Pull states that many of the long bones of the ox are broken for marrow and below them are further deposits of both ox and pig bone and molluscs which may suggest midden material (*ibid.*).

Tindall's Pit at Cissbury was excavated in January 1874 (Willett 1875: 341). Unfortunately Tindall died before making a report of his findings and there is only information available from his contemporaries following his comments before he died (Willett 1875; Lane Fox 1876; Clarke 1915). The shaft appears to have had no galleries radiating from the base of the pit at 39 feet (11.9m) (Lane Fox 1876: 377; Harrison 1877a: 268). The shape of the pit was like a 'large funnel' the width reducing to 5 or 6 feet at its base (1.5m or 1.8m) with the base of the shaft containing a basin-shaped hollow Harrison suggests as being for water to accumulate (*ibid.*). The profile of this shaft is therefore unique.

Animal remains were the predominant deposition in this shaft and finds were only reported from the lower 13 feet (3.96m). Tindall found pieces of broken antler and single tines of red deer, mostly from slain deer in addition to flint implements which are not described in any detail (Willett 1875: 341, 346). At 8.54m two 'fine and perfect' skulls of ox were deposited and a few feet beneath these bones of this animal species, the skull and some bones of a wild boar and bones of red deer, otter, badger and roe deer (*ibid.*; Harrison 1877a: 267). Dog is also noted as being present though its location is not noted (Lane Fox 1876: 390). An unusual tool was excavated, made from antler pierced for the insertion of a stone, though it has not been illustrated and therefore cannot be described further (Willett 1875: 341). Clarke reports that five blade bone shovels of ox, pig, deer antler from slain animals, and single tines (again from the lower 24 feet) were also excavated here (1915: 31).

Human Remains

Human remains are subject to different depositional strategies at the flint mines. Whole bodies in addition to single bones are deposited in different ways and some examples of these will be described below. As they have been recorded from excavation in much greater detail, a greater level of description and analysis can take place when discussing their remains.

The first burial found at Cissbury was in the Skeleton Shaft (also known as Shaft H, or No 1 Escarp Shaft). It was interpreted as the body was of a female approximately 25 years of age and excavated during 1875 (Lane Fox 1876). The position of her skeleton has been reported as being inverted, her head below her body in the centre of Shaft H, 2 feet 6 inches (0.76m) above the floor of the shaft (*ibid.*). This head down deposition is unique and previously unknown in Neolithic deposits. Around her body were animal remains namely goat, roe deer, *Bos primigenius* but mostly pig, the bones of which had evidence of marrow extraction. Rolleston suggests through their fragmentary nature they were likely to be a result of midden material, though four near complete vertebrae of the domestic pig are also present (Rolleston 1877: 26-7) suggesting they were deposited fleshed. A few bones of toad, shrew mice, field mice and teeth of a fox cub were also present which perhaps suggest above ground activity, or may have fallen into the shaft. The shaft itself was comparatively small and shallow, being only 4 feet 6 inches in diameter (1.38m) and its depth 6 feet 3 inches (1.9m) from the base of the later Iron Age ditch (Lane Fox 1876: 376). However, Rolleston (1877: 31) reports that the shaft depth is 14 feet (4.26m), which may have been from the ground surface. Apart from the animal bone found with the body, no other deposits were found.

There are some concerns about the positioning of this skeleton. The head, whilst under the body, was discovered initially through the base of the shaft, by Lane Fox coming across it through galleries linking it to shaft E. Through removing rubble slumped into the gallery entrance from the base of the shaft, he discovered animal bone and on continuing to rummage, the human jaw bone fell out. The skull appeared to be jammed in an upright position between two pieces of chalk rubble above it (Lane Fox 1876: 375). This description suggests that the skull is vertical in the shaft with the jaw down and the crown of the skull facing upwards. The rest of the skeleton was found above the skull when the shaft was subsequently excavated from the surface down. Rolleston (1877: 31) relates that a heel bone from the skeleton was found on a ledge at the side of the shaft, 1 foot 7 inches (0.48m) higher than the skull. With the limited width of the shaft (1.38m) compared to the woman's suggested height of 4 feet 9 inches, 1.45m, (*ibid.*: 32), it is likely she is slanted head down only to a degree where her feet are less than 50cm above her body. Furthermore, Rolleston states the distance between the crown of her head and her heel bone was also only 1 foot 7 inches (0.48m), (*ibid.*: 30). This suggests the body was tightly compacted or in a crouched position rather than inverted.

Two possible explanations can be offered for the odd placement of the skull: that firstly the body was head first in the shaft and the subsequent settling of the fill allowed the skull to become partially detached and move into this position; or secondly that the head was removed from the body and placed underneath the body. The body was sexed by Rolleston as female, although the skull is of an unusually large size for a female and exceeds the maximum measurements known for male skulls at the time, it is more likely the skull is from a Neolithic male and hence this deposit represents a composite body (Andrew Chamberlain pers. comm).

A second skeleton was also found during Lane Fox's excavations, in the following year and is entirely different in character to the possible composite body in Shaft H. This contracted burial of a male in Shaft VI was surrounded by blocks of chalk and also large unworked flints. A worked flint 'hatchet' was found by the body's knees and eight edible snail shells of *Helix nemoralis* and a fire marked pebble were placed with the body before it was covered in chalk blocks (Rolleston 1879: 378). Rolleston notes from examination of the skeleton that as a child the man suffered with hemiplegia, a condition which can be congenital or acquired through injury. It is caused by damage to the brain and commonly effects either the right side of the body, or the left depending on which side of the brain has been effected (the right side of the brain controlling the left side of the body and vice versa). In this skeleton the long bones of the left arm are considerably shorter than those on the right, however as hemiplegia affects one side of the body it should affect both limbs on one side of the body and not only one limb. It is possible this is another composite body.

A third body was excavated from Shaft 27 at Cissbury. This shaft was excavated by Pull in 1953, the body of a female skeleton being found deposited on a pile of rubble at the entrance to gallery 1 (Russell 2001: 183). This is a complete body though accidental death was suspected and cannot be ruled out, due to the poor condition of the skull which may have been broken by falling rubble. It is more likely that this burial was deliberate, being accompanied by a number of chalk charms (2, 3 or 4 depending on the account given, these were discussed in more depth in Chapter 5). Similar to other formal deposits of human remains, this shaft fill is complex and the gallery systems extensive. It contained deposits of flakes, antler tools, a 'great nodule' and chalk art (*ibid.*; discussed further in Chapter 4).

A human skull, without its jaw bone, was in the possession of Rosehill passed to him following Tindall's death with other excavated material, with a note it had originated at Cissbury (Harrison 1878: 388). While not certain, it is assumed it was found during the latter stages of excavation at Tindall's Pit. Rosehill and Tindall had worked on the excavation of this shaft together, Rosehill being absent in the later stages and returning after Tindall's death. A rare find such as this would have caused dialogue between them if it had been recovered prior to the shaft's excavation, hence it is logical to assume it was excavated from the lower levels of the shaft. The lack of jawbone indicates it is likely to have been deposited unfleshed and hence may be a curated artefact. Both Willett and Lane Fox argue that this pit is likely to be older than those at Grimes Graves due to the greater presence of wild and not domesticated species (Lane Fox 1876: 384; Willett 1875: 346).

An incomplete adult male skull was recovered from halfway down the shaft of Pit 1 at Grimes Graves in layer 5, together with chips and flakes of floorstone, just above layer 6 which had several fine tools and 'pockets' of flint chippings (Clarke 1915: 48-9). The base of this shaft had evidence of three fireplaces although no burning of the chalk is mentioned so they are likely to be charcoal deposits rather than in situ fires (*ibid.*: 52). The rib of a red deer was also found at the lower levels. One bone pick excavated from the shallow Pits III and IV at Grimes Graves was made from a human femur (Armstrong 1926: 121). A single human tibia was excavated from very close to or on the floor of Shaft 6 at Church Hill (Russell 2001: 121).

Transformed Artefacts: Summary

Lane Fox (1876: 378), noted following the Cissbury excavations that animal remains are rare within the shafts and galleries, except for the Skeleton Shaft and, as discussed above, they were prominent in Tindall's shaft. This is seen in other flint mines where animal remains tend to be subject to specific deposition rather than occurring randomly. Regretfully the deposition of animal remains in Shaft 27 cannot indicate many interpretive aspects to them due to the paucity of excavation details. However the presence of nearly a whole ox indicates perhaps an event where the animal was mostly consumed and then discarded. The marrow-splitting reported by Pull does not necessarily suggest a feasting scenario where large parts of the animal were deliberately wasted as a social strategy of conspicuous consumption argued for some Neolithic deposits (Richards and Thomas 1984; Thomas 1999a;

Whittle *et al.* 1999). It is unfortunate we are not aware of the different animal species also deposited in this shaft though it should be noted that the ox is separated from the other material, which in turn is separate from the human burial (discussed below).

The placement of animal deposits in Tindall's shaft shows definition. It is fairly certain no remains were whole skeletons as that would have been noted and therefore some processing had been completed on the carcasses of these animals. This indicates they were either food remains or perhaps utilised for other reasons, such as skinning for furs or hides. The two perfect ox skulls which are depositionally separated from the remains of wild animals in the same shaft suggest that there was a measure of deliberation in this. It may suggest that the skulls themselves of the ox were important or curated, or their juxtaposition with the wild animal remains may be being referenced in a wild : domesticated division. The ox skulls represent a small part of the dead beasts and the remainder of their bodies were subject to deposition elsewhere. Architecturally, the base of the shaft having a basin-shaped hollow is suggestive of differential use to other shafts where this feature is not present. Small hollows can be present at the base of flint mine shafts where the base of the ladder has been placed repeatedly in the same position and as a result the footfall of the person alighting from the ladder is continually in the same place. This is seen at the open shafts of Greenwell's Pit and Shaft 2 at Grimes Graves and therefore may not be a deliberate architectural feature but rather use-wear.

With regard to humans, there are several ways in which human remains have been deposited. Human remains appear to be deposited only in shafts where there are multiple and complex depositions, or architecture, and do not occur as singular deposits in an otherwise artefact free backfill. This is evidenced at all shafts described where human remains are present. Furthermore, there appears to be a particular emphasis on the importance of heads, or skulls. Whilst these are complementary concepts their treatment in a fleshed or unfleshed state is different and so indicates a difference in social categorisation during the Neolithic. The possible composite burial of the male skull and female body at Cissbury Shaft H indicates that the male skull was probably fleshed, having the jawbone present. While it is not mentioned that all cervical vertebrae were present on excavation, clearly enough were present for the excavator to deduce it was a complete rather than composite burial. The female body must also have been at least mostly fleshed and articulated.

The single skulls excavated at Grimes Graves and Tindall's Pit at Cissbury without accompanying jawbone is suggestive of de-fleshing (probably as a result of excarnation) and perhaps curation prior to deposition. In Tindall's Pit, the lower levels containing bones of wild and not domesticated species imply hunting prior to deposition. The four skulls present, one human, two of ox and one of wild boar without the full complement of bones are suggestive of both curation (even if for a short time) and specific re-deposition of the skulls. In the case of the two cattle skulls this occurs at a higher level and therefore at both a physical and temporal distance to the other deposits. The remains of broken antlers and tines at a higher level which were the product of kills rather than shed antler is indicative of depositional continuity in the remains. Therefore all bone remains in this shaft seem to represent curation prior to deposition and suggest they may have been deliberately killed through hunting. The presence of the ox and human skulls therefore may suggest a contrast with the hunting, a similarity of these individuals with hunting methods, or another type of social manipulation.

The incomplete skull at Grimes Graves displays a slightly different emphasis as this was at some height within the shaft fill, indicating a temporal and physical distance from the shaft floor. The evidence of three hearths was found at the base which may alternatively represent deposits of charcoal. The importance of the head within the Neolithic is seen at other locations. For example, at Easton Down there is the burial of a male skull within a barrow together with a large piece of flint, though this may be Early Bronze Age (Stone 1935). The cervical vertebrae found within the mound indicate it was also deposited fleshed.

The inclusion of middened material within shaft deposits or in direct association with human remains merits further discussion. The bones present and seemingly enmeshed with the female/male composite body in the Skeleton Shaft at Cissbury imply as noted by the excavators that they were deposited together. However, the articulated vertebrae present suggest a quantity of fresh meat was also deposited with this composite burial and we could perhaps begin to reconstruct events immediately prior to this deposit. If the male skull was indeed fleshed, then both participants in the composite burial must have died within a few days prior to the deposit, or at least was certainly not subject to curation after excarnation. The near complete vertebrae sets of four domestic pigs by (Rolleston 1877: 27) suggest a feasting incorporating at least four pigs, though feasting may have been conducted over a period of days or weeks and the shaft left open after the body and skull were deposited. A fully grown domestic pig will feed over a hundred people but clearly a younger animal may only feed 20% of that amount and at least one vertebrae was from a pig of only around five months (*ibid.*: 28). However it is unlikely that this number of articulated vertebrae indicate a feast for under a hundred people. While the burial of human remains with midden material is similar to human deposits at causewayed enclosures, the presence of the articulated vertebrae is similar to closing deposits of ox vertebrae found at Durrington Walls in the hearths of abandoned houses or at the top of pits (Mike Parker Pearson, pers. comm.). The possible midden material in this shaft is composed of mostly non-domestic species, and while there are many bones of pig present, most are bones are from non-domesticates such as the auroch, suggesting both hunting and husbandry were carried out. The specificity of faunal and human deposition from such material suggests that the Neolithic middens were highly structured.

While we acknowledge more widely that animal and human remains are structured deposits and that across the Neolithic as a whole, placements are specific and deliberate, the acquisition of such material as animal bone for deposition is accepted without question. Disarticulated animal remains would occur through time in a midden environment but the retrieval of particular species for deposition for particular social reasons must indicate structured practice at the midden site. While above ground Neolithic middens are rare within the UK (West Kennet Avenue, and underneath the G55 barrow at Avebury and the West Overton G6b round barrow) Mesolithic middens are noted as being structured as in western Scotland (Mellars 1987) and the midden sites at Norsminde and Bjørnsholm in Denmark (Andersen 1989; 1991). While these are predominantly known as shell middens, Norsminde used between the late Mesolithic and into the Neolithic contained evidence of five fireplaces and fragmentary human remains (Andersen 1989). At Bjørnsholm many more fireplaces were encountered with animal bones scatters around them (Andersen 1991: 79). In Wiltshire, the midden spread near the West Kennet Avenue covered c.100m x 40m and consisted of huge deposits of flint debitage and tools and around 600 sherds of pottery (Pollard 2005; Smith 1965b: 210-216). The absence of bone in many working floors does not necessarily indicate they are not middens; middens in which bone over the centuries has been lost. An amount of animal bone was present in Long Down Floor 2 (Salisbury 1961). Deposition in the mines seems to indicate the ability of persons to retrieve midden material for this purpose and it could be argued working floors may represent the remains of temporary, sporadic middens which were nevertheless structured.

6.6 Aesthetic Deposits: Two Examples

Aesthetic deposits include those depositions which by their cumulative nature appear to imply meaning in their structure. Hence in addition to aspects of their materiality which might be indicated through deposition (as discussed in Chapter 3) their relational context requires both further description and analysis. Two cases are particularly noteworthy.

The first example is from Greenwell's Pit at Grimes Graves the skull of a phalarope (*Phalaropus sp.*), a wading bird, was excavated from a gallery lying between a pair of antler picks, the tines of which faced inwards with a ground stone axe at the base of the picks (Barber *et al.* 1999: 66). This deposit was at the end of the gallery where three recesses had been hollowed out of the chalk (Greenwell 1870: 427). The picks were different being one for a left-handed individual and one for a right-handed person and could be said to 'frame' the skull and point to the centre of the gallery. It has been suggested that this may represent a kinship affiliation (Barber *et al.* 1999: 67). A complete dog skeleton was excavated from another gallery associated with this shaft, buried within chalk waste which may have represented a deliberate niche (*ibid.*).

The second occurs at gallery B of the Cissbury Cave Pit which is described as being a triple cave rather than a gallery, with chalk markings and graffiti at its entrance (Harrison 1877b: 415; Chapter 4). The centre cell was only 1ft 6 inches (46cm) in height and within the flint seam on the south wall of the cell, a mass of iron pyrites projected from the wall into the cell. They were loose but gathered together, kept in place solely by way of gravity and resembled a 'distorted reptile' (*ibid.*). Twelve flints remained in situ within the seam on either side of this deposit, mostly with clean exposed fractures. The presence of this unusual deposit in this gallery could have been highlighted through the art at the entrance to the gallery from the shaft. The iron pyrites were present within the seam, yet loose indicating they had been placed within the seam among the flints. The flints have been deliberately kept in place to 'frame' the iron pyrites enhancing the character of the deposition. The height of this gallery was very restricted and access would have been difficult.

The Grimes Graves deposit including the wading bird skull has been argued as being representative of a Neolithic/Early Bronze Age clan affiliation with that bird species (Barber *et al.* 1999: 66). This is the only bird skull excavated from the English mines and its uniqueness should be acknowledged. However, this acknowledgement also counters against this argument, as if this bird were associated with a clan more may be found deposited in special contexts. As a wading bird, and so associated with water, it has wider Late Neolithic/Early Bronze Age parallels. At Durrington Walls remains of two water bird species were excavated (Mallard and Cormorant; Harcourt in Wainwright & Longworth 1971: 346). Bones of a Crane and Greylag Goose were found at Mount Pleasant (Harcourt in Wainwright 1979: 218). The two antler picks seemingly framing the skull suggest that this is probably the intention – to both highlight the skull and 'bound' it in some way within that context. The inclusion of a flint axe with this deposit is reintroducing a created artefact from the natural material of the mine, combining it with the skull and antler.

The iron pyrites at Cissbury are suggestive of a different type of deposition. The location within a cave-type gallery, in a complex system of galleries suggests that in common with rock art within chambered tombs, their access and knowledge of their location may have been restricted (Thomas 1999a: 223-4). In terms of deposition, this type of aesthetic group may be termed a 'context-specific material statement' (*ibid.*: 224), where the pyrites have been placed in a particular context in a particular way in order to evoke a certain meaning. While the description of a 'reptile' is clearly subjective, no large reptiles are native to the UK and therefore that cultural frame of reference would not be present in the Neolithic. This particular statement may have represented a mythological being which may have been an animal, or representative of symbolic nature of iron pyrites escaping from the flint seam without aid. Was the flint seen as an active substance or the iron pyrites? The suggestion of mythology to explain both deposits and art has had some attention in discussing domesticated animals (Whittle 2003: 101-6) and clearly moving this argument into mythological beasts could be seen as too subjective. However, following Weiner's approach (discussed by Whittle 2003), the probable metaphorical associations and contrasting interpretations even with recognisable animals, do not result in easily read conclusions.

The contextual associations of antler are difficult to ascertain from excavation records due to the ubiquitous nature of antler picks and hence often a lack of detailed recording. Antler picks are often only mentioned as occurring in fills or on the floors of galleries (e.g. Shaft 27 at Cissbury, Russell 2001: 182; Mercer 1981: 23, 26, 100) and details of all deposits within layers are lacking for the Pull excavations. Many of the antler represent tools but examples occur which are unused, as an antler from a killed deer at Shaft 1, Church Hill (Pull in Russell 2001: 91). Animal bone is deposited as a discrete deposit of possible midden material at Cissbury but this is not reflected in the other Sussex mines (e.g. Russell 2001; Stone 1933b) or Grimes Graves with the majority of faunal remains occurring in the Middle Bronze Age middens (Legge 1992: 16). Whether this represents site differentiation at Cissbury or the chance excavation of such shafts here and not elsewhere is difficult to ascertain. Contextually, it appears that in general terms antler pick deposits do not occur associated with animal bone except when in relation to cattle scapula shovels, such as at Shaft 6, Church Hill (Russell 2001: 110).

A further exception to this is the phalarope skull and double antler pick deposit in Greenwell's Pit at Grimes Graves discussed above. There is only one recorded placement of fossil shell within the mines which is within its own discrete deposit in the Blackpatch Shaft 2 gallery (6.4). A carved chalk charm was found within the same gallery but at 3m from the fossils (Russell 2001: 37-38) any direct association is rather tenuous. Fossils are associated with the later barrow internments at Blackpatch and occur in the archive though regretfully without provenance. Some may have originated from Church Hill but this cannot be proved; as an amateur geologist, John Pull's retention of fossils from archaeological contexts may have been more enthusiastic than other excavators in Sussex, and hence the non-appearance of fossils at Harrow Hill may be a result of excavation strategies rather than non-deposition. The fossil example noted from Cissbury is the flint phallic fossil, found by Pull and discussed further below (6.7). An analysis of the working floors at the mines sites may offer different associations but the problematic dating of these features and often poor recording would not allow for any degree of chronological sensitivity. While specific artefacts and deposits have been discussed and related to concepts of transformation, retrieval and excavation, there is one class

	Cissbury	Blackpatch	Church Hill	Harrow Hill	Easton Down	Grimes Graves
Fossil	•	•				
Animal Bone Dumps	•					
Animal Bone Isolated Deposits	•	•	•	•	•	•
Antler	•	•	•	•	•	•

FIGURE 6.6 TABLE OF THE DEPOSITS OF FOSSIL, ANTLER AND ANIMAL BONE FROM THE FLINT MINE SHAFTS

Site	Quantity	Substance	From Primary Context	From Secondary Context	Unstratified
Windmill Hill	4	Chalk	1	1	2
The Trundle	1	Bone	1		
Thickthorn Down	2	Chalk	2		
Maumbury Rings	1	Chalk	1		
Etton	1	Pottery	1		
Mount Pleasant	2	Chalk	2		
Magham Down	1	Flint flake			1
Cissbury	1	Flint	1		
Winterbourne Stoke Crossroads long barrow	1	Flint	1		
Itford Hill	1	Chalk	1		
Easton Down	1	Flint	1		
Grimes Graves	2 1	Chalk Flint	2 1		
Durrington Walls	3 1	Flint Iron Pyrites	1 1	2	
TOTAL	**22**		**16**	**3**	**3**

FIGURE 6.7 TABLE OF NEOLITHIC AND BRONZE AGE PHALLI (ADAPTED FROM TEATHER 2007)

of artefact which has escaped full classification within this study due to the variation in substances exhibited in its form: phalli artefacts and other gendered forms. They cannot be excluded from such a synthesis of materials and are subject to discussion below.

6.7 A Special Case: Human Genital Forms and Mutable Substances

While phalli have been found on many Neolithic sites, their numbers are actually few. Yet clearly enough numbers signify that during the Neolithic and Bronze Age, phalli were accepted, although rare artefact which was at times selected for deposition. However, they are one of the few artefacts which display the same form in different substances (Figure 6.7). Yet, an analysis of phalli cannot be based on substance, for if we were to examine flint phalli as separate from chalk phalli, or bone phalli, would it be productive? How can we separate form and material effectively in interpretation? Moreover we cannot interpret them through activities in their manufacture, as this varies with substance. Instead, phallic artefacts need to be examined as a category in themselves, exploring the contexts and deposition of these artefacts.

Once we acknowledge that phalli were artefacts with significance, our challenges could be said to commence with understanding their form. Form is crucial to interpretive recognition, an argument threading through this book. Traditionally, this interpretation directs us towards discussions that collide with our own cultural preconceptions of sex and/or gender relations. When we imagine that the object (phallus) which, in a modern sense, biologically represents men (or a man), so many culturally instinctive reactions of suppression and dominance come immediately to mind that interpretation beyond our experience becomes extremely difficult. In theoretical terms, our immediate preconceptions towards artefacts have been challenged through the later understandings of phenomenology and critical theory. As contemporary archaeologists, we are expected to challenge our own intuitive understandings in favour of reflexive approaches (Hodder 1999); hence it is possible for us to acknowledge that we instinctively recognise certain shapes as being representative of a male penis without forcing our intuitive understandings onto it. This can also be applied to chalk plaques, flint balls, fossils or other artefacts. While we recognise the form, material, or substance that they constitute, their archaeological context aids their interpretation. Form can provide indications as to use, but information from form alone does not provide meaning.

Theoretically, ethnographic approaches to archaeology have emphasised themes of practice with regard to objects. The inalienability of artefacts, the possession of biographies by artefact, and how objects can be representative of persons, or be regarded as persons in their own right have been advocated by many authors (Jones 2002; Tilley 1996; 1999; Thomas 1996; also see Fowler 2004 for comprehensive discussion of personhood). However, while we can easily say that deposited artefacts have importance, and that this importance is socially created, reinforced and manipulated, it matters little what type of artefact it is. As all of the artefacts discussed in this manner are, to our preconceptions, 'ungendered' (such as a pottery sherd), it highlights our lack of experience when examining phalli which seem representative of gender in their form. Yet attempts have been made to gender activities, generally linking men with stone tools and women with potting, using ethnographic arguments (Edmonds 1999: 41; Thomas 1999: 97; Whittle 2003: 11).

Comparisons with other types of phallic imagery can be useful. Bevan (2001: 65-6) argues that, as male sexuality creates our cultural 'norms', an absence of the phallus in ithyphallic representations means female (subservient) whilst its presence is male (dominant). Thus, the attachment of phalli to human representations creates our view as 'male'. Furthermore, she suggests that if biological sex were not important it would not be referenced; hence a lack of sexual attributes in art may express egalitarianism in society. Ethnographically, the phallus itself can appear ritually as discussed by Eliade (1964). The wooden phalli among the Kumandin of the Tomsk are used by three young men during the horse sacrifice (*ibid.*: 79). They wear masks and gallop around the spectators, touching them with the wooden phallus between their legs as part of the ritual to strengthen the men of the group sexually. In this role the phalli enhance the existing male characteristics of the men.

Thus the phallus, as a separate entity, can be said to create gender by influencing the natural gendered characteristics of the person or object it is linked to. This could be argued as being seen in the deposition of the 'sex pit' at Durrington Walls, where the addition of the phallus and flint balls to the pelvic-shaped flint in its slit-shaped pit was to somehow balance male and female biological characteristics within a single depositional event. Other Neolithic artefacts have been excavated where female characteristics are combined with male. The 'God-Dolly' excavated at the Somerset Levels, carved from wood, has both breasts and a peg-like phallus (Coles 1968: 256). A similar peg-like chalk artefact was uncovered at Grimes Graves (Varndell 1991: 149, C321; Chapter 5) which appears to have broken away from a larger piece of chalk. Two figurines discovered at Windmill Hill (C11 and C12) were suggested by Smith (1965a: 130) to represent thighs and lower parts of a torso however, they may also reference a male glans and female vulva. These hermaphroditic objects support an argument for the recognition of balance, conjoining, or equanimity of biological sexual difference. Mesolithic artefacts of this nature also occur, where in Scandinavia modified fossil now reflects a female belly, thighs and vulvae (GlØrstad *et al.* 2004) and in Wales the Nab Head Cave shale phallus was found (Gordon-Williams 1926). Therefore, following Bevan (2001), we could argue that the representation of sexual characteristics was socially relevant but the combination of these in a variety of contexts implies a multiplicity of meanings. Furthermore, portable objects such as these can allow for meanings to be created and also subverted (Thomas 1996: 141-82).

Another crucial factor not yet examined is the mutability of substance when dealing with the form of these artefacts. Phalli are not simply made from one type of substance in Neolithic Britain, but of every type of substance that survives the archaeological record. From the wooden 'God-Dolly' to the bone example from The Trundle, to the clay form from Etton, the many chalk and flint forms over southern Britain, phalli are represented. This renders ethnographically based arguments in favour of particular substances being related to particular biological sexes even less substantial. For if clay is female, what can a phallus represent in this form? Clearly, there may be an element of subverting cultural norms in terms of this form in this substance, yet I do not believe we have enough examples with which to determine this. Furthermore, the three clay artefacts from Etton are noted as being similar to the Grime's Grave Pit 15 ritual deposit, which also echoes that of the 'sex' pit at Durrington Walls discussed earlier, one being phallic and two representing spherical artefacts (Pryor 1998: 270). Therefore we may also be seeing combinations of these forms as a group as particularly symbolic. The spherical artefacts may represent testes or breasts, as they are not connected to the phalli in any of these cases their interpretation as testes is not secure.

While the meaning of a phallus in the Neolithic was almost certainly polyvalent, referring perhaps to power, dominance, the wind, the sea, or life itself: firstly it refers to a penis. In doing so, it refers to men in a sexual respect. This means that sexuality is being referred to with women being part of this structure. Phalli are undoubtedly part of a wider system of referencing sexual organs/sexual activity and relevant societal norms or values in the Neolithic: the wider system simply not being very archaeologically visible. Furthermore we should not ignore the possibility of organic materials being deposited with chalk phalli. The penis's of animals (cattle especially), may have been deposited with, or in reference to, chalk or flint phalli (S. Matthews, pers. comm.). The use of a human tibia as a bone pick from the Pits III and IV at Grimes Graves (Armstrong 1926: 121) may also illustrate a Neolithic understanding of synchronicity between human and cattle remains. During the Neolithic blood lines and the breeding of domesticated animals would have been of increasing importance (Ray and Thomas 2003) and the deposition of cattle penis's with other phallic forms may have been associated with animal husbandry in some way. Similar thoughts were previously voiced by Piggott (1954: 94) when discussing phallic artefacts in relation to the British Neolithic, 'the phallic representations […] would belong better to the magic of stockbreeders than to that of cultivators'. Perhaps that aspect of Neolithic life or cosmology is being particularly present with phallic imagery, yet I would consider such concerns of animal stock as also reflecting on older Mesolithic practices where the breeding of dogs or strategic hunting of deer herds would have been important. Instead of simply seeing phallic imagery as representing a focus on domesticated animals, the importance may have been on retaining a viable balanced community.

6.8 Conclusion

This chapter has attempted to situate my theoretical approach to materiality in the Neolithic flint mines through specific examples of different types of artefact. I have argued two proposals in this chapter: that previously unconsidered natural objects be considered artefacts, and that they occur in structured deposits. Furthermore, I have offered that animal and human bone be also viewed as artefacts rather than simply a forensic view of the dead, and their deposition examined in a similar way to other artefacts. These factors relate to the broader arguments of this study that the deposition of all these artefacts occur in usual depositional parameters at other types of Neolithic site.

In monument building, the extraction of flint, the creation of mounds and digging of ditched enclosures, the engagement of Neolithic people with the chalk bedrock of parts of southern Britain resulted in the discovery of different objects. Flint nodules, iron pyrites and fossils all occur naturally in the chalk, the rock itself having different textures and hardness depending on the depth from which it was excavated. Fossil casts can also be left in the chalk; regular impressions of shell surfaces sometimes appear not unlike the linear designs on some plaques, or Grooved Ware. Some chalk objects especially from Sussex appear to represent fossils themselves (Curwen 1931; Chapter 4). Various depositional schemes seem to have applied. The placed deposits of fossils and phallic flint nodules in mines appear mostly as discrete or singular deposits. The placement of deposits in this discrete manner implies they constitute a full meaning in isolation, they do not need to be 'added' to in order to create significance. All these deposits have a natural origin and are often unmodified, simply re-deposited in significant locations. The locations are as other deposits, at the base of flint mine shafts or within galleries, and it is this factor which perhaps supports the concept of integrated materiality.

The inclusion of human remains in shaft fills or in galleries mostly occurs in those shafts where there was more deposition and more art. Again, the complex of galleries in certain shafts (as the Cave Pit at Cissbury), with chambered areas, appears to reference chambered tombs and possible ritual activity aside from human remains (Chapter 4). Tindall's Pit at Cissbury, with the probable curated skull deposit, did not have galleries. This seems to suggest further complexity in mining sites. Topping has argued that certain shafts may have remained open for secondary activity and this seems probable (2005: 73) and indeed they may have remained like this for several years. It is likely that while Neolithic people saw their world as one, human remains allowed for increased expression in deposition. The combination of fresh meat (especially vertebrae) and midden remains in deposits indicates a complex relationship between immediate feasting prior to deposition and the referencing of past events.

Fossils, chalk objects and other artefacts were subject to specific depositional practices in different contexts in Neolithic Britain (Thomas 1996: 168). Bradley (2000: 121) has suggested that the re-deposition of chalk objects into chalk was culturally appropriate - returned to where it was formed. If we combine these experiences of engagement with the earth and the different, natural shapes encountered – particularly those which appear to have represented the phallus, or other human forms - Neolithic people would have viewed uncovering the soil as an evocative and intense experience. Rather than examining these naturally occurring objects as oddities, they may well have seen themselves as part of a wider integration with the earth at depth. The notions we have of separation from the natural world would not have been present; instead, such objects provided a reinforcement and confirmation of people's rights and presence in the chalklands. Following Bradley (*ibid.*), prehistoric interest in manufactured chalk artefacts (many representing phalli) and fossils may be seen as an elaboration of this connection: the symbolic representation of acting in a way that the earth had done on its own, re-deposition being the feeding back to the earth of an active engagement with a living entity.

These interpretations allow us to broaden and enrich our views of Neolithic people and their active engagement with the earth. It is likely that phallic portable artefacts may have signified human biological sex, and that their application in social situations may, at times, have been contradictory. While we tend to see mid-late Neolithic artefact types as being more elaborate and complex than before, many of the unusual artefacts and phalli were already present on early Neolithic sites such as the Trundle or Thickthorn Down. In this way we should perhaps instead view these later artefacts as continuations of a complex practice which became more visible over time.

Chapter 7

Beyond Extraction

7.1 Introduction

This study has brought flint mines into focus as a class of monument created in the late fifth to third millennium BC in Britain. While the removal of flint took place within them there were other activities, beyond extraction. The aims of this study were to:

- Critique prevailing interpretations of flint mines as economic and ritual resources in the Neolithic by examining how theories of 'otherness' have influenced the understandings of the mines.

- Formulate theoretical frameworks that overcome the function-ritual divide, particularly with reference to concepts of materiality, the inter-relatedness of substances and depositional practice.

- Use the theoretical framework to examine the architectural morphology and depositional histories of flint mines, with special reference to chalk artefacts and art.

- Draw conclusions as to how flint mines and their deposits contribute to understanding substances, artefacts and deposits within the existing cultural repertoire of the southern British Neolithic.

Until recent times, flint mines have suffered from almost a complete lack of cohesive publications and assumptions of them as purely industrial sites. Hence this study suggested both an integrated approach to chalk artefacts, fossils and other deposits, and a reinterpretation of flint mines as a class of Neolithic monument, concluding with additional theories as to their use and placement in Neolithic society. Furthermore, these insights have resulted in a new way of examining traditional discourses of the period, in particular the role of substances and approaches to art in Neolithic society.

7.2 This Study

Functional approaches to the flint mines were discussed in Chapter 3 as a part of a wider interpretive problem that has also influenced the perception of artefacts. This was explained in reference to the origin of the discipline and how initial artefact categories were constructed. These were argued to have been formed through ethnographic analogies, which assisted in defining which objects may have had a human functional (and so archaeological) origin, as opposed to being simply geological (Trigger 1989: 47, 52, 92). It has been argued how this functionality also underpinned later artefact categorisation and site interpretation, and at times was incorporated within structural Marxist approaches.

These views have been challenged in taking an approach to artefacts and substance based on phenomenology and following similar studies by Thomas (1996, 1999a) and Pollard (1995). These studies argue that structured deposition can help interpret the wider meaning of the use of monuments by suggesting where different activities in the monument were manifested in deposition, in relation to others. Furthermore, Thomas suggests that artefacts and substances constitute a *bricolage* in the Neolithic, where combinations of artefacts in deposits can have different meanings depending on their context or associated artefacts. Together with Hodder's (1999) discussion on artefacts and contexts which described how artefacts construct contexts and contexts construct artefacts, the definition and recognition of what an artefact is becomes key to interpretation.

From these arguments, two classes of deposition – those of chalk artefacts (including in situ chalk art), and natural substances such as fossils were included as artefacts. Therefore interpretations were constructed around both their materiality in terms of substance (what they may mean in themselves) and with regard to deposition (what their deposition may signify in monuments, in relation to others). Moreover, all deposits are interpreted as being subject to meaningful deposition. In effect, this work separates only two factors, artefacts and contexts. Everything is either one or the other. These then fit together within a phenomenological approach for interpretation.

Chalk art within mining contexts has provided many avenues for interpretation which were explored in Chapter 4. The art is mostly of a linear abstract nature and corresponds with chalk art seen in the contemporary monuments of Flagstones, Dorset and North Marden, Sussex. It often occurs in the same types of location in mines, most commonly present at the base of shafts at the entrances to galleries. Yet, where galleries conjoin and enough investigation has taken place, they appear to also be located in areas which are away from common entry ways. This suggests that this indicates linear chalk art (also evidenced on chalk blocks) had a currency of meaning within the early-mid Neolithic in mines which extended more widely across Sussex and into Dorset.

From the Late Neolithic, chalk art was found in one shaft at Grimes Graves at the entrance of two galleries. While chalk art has been seen as being related to later Grooved Ware designs, at Grimes Graves where Grooved Ware also appears in mines, the designs are incomparable. It has therefore been argued that linear chalk art appears to contain separate signification to pottery styles and is therefore most productively viewed as a separate tradition. The chalk art at Grimes Graves is comparable with that of the earlier Sussex mines and chalk art at Flagstones and North Marden. The significance of it seems to be enduring. Non portable chalk was also analysed in Chapter 4 as both decorated and undecorated forms. In terms of decoration, linear markings are the most common style and in the case of the Trundle ammonite chalk block, deliberate skeuomorphic designs may be inferred. Moreover many blocks were undecorated and deposited in what appears to have been in symbolic circumstances (Thomas 1999b): in burials or within architectural features. In this respect it has been suggested that they also constituted a context as much as an artefact.

Chapter 5 discussed portable chalk artefacts and also followed regionality and skeuomorphism as themes. Regionality has been examined in relative terms to the decoration and the presence of chalk art and artefact decoration. Yet chalk artefacts themselves have been argued to represent a cohesive group with regular forms, which can be categorised within a typology. This has illustrated that cups, balls, cylinders and other artefact types occurred in many Neolithic contexts in variable numbers. They appear in greater quantities in later deposits but this should be viewed against a background of larger site assemblages of all types of artefact. However, the retention of certain artefact forms to the Late Neolithic/Early Bronze Age is fairly consistent and hence their use in socio-cultural activities was maintained. The few Neolithic chalk axes appear in both chipped and polished forms, and these differences should be noted as cogently as they are in stone and flint axes. Hence a polished chalk axe may be signifying different aspects to meaning than a chipped chalk axe. However, perhaps the greatest addition to understanding chalk artefacts has been through adopting an integrated approach to substances.

In Chapter 6, new archaeological ways of looking at artefacts from natural origins were suggested. These categories of excavated, retrieved and transformed artefacts were argued as coming into being as a result of the theoretical arguments proposed in Chapter 3. It was shown that these biographic histories may have had a cultural understanding which influenced their use and deposition during the Neolithic. In terms of tools, it was suggested that antler picks were formed by both retrieval and transformation. Deer were killed and their antler used, though to a lesser degree than retrieved antler. Ox scapulae can only have been accessed through the death of an ox. There is at least one instance of a human femur being used as a bone pick at Grimes Graves (Armstrong 1926: 121). Therefore human and animal remains can be used in similar ways and deposited together. This similarity in processing and use suggests there was a cultural affinity between human and animal remains; parts of animals can be deposited in the same way as humans. There are some differences however. Complete animal burials are not present at early mine contexts, where human burials are at Cissbury (although some may be composite). No human burials have been excavated from other mine sites from the early period, yet the dating of some of the Blackpatch cremations are uncertain. This may indicate two interpretations: that Cissbury as a mine site was particularly associated with human burial or that Cissbury may represent an excavation bias.

Furthermore, with reference to some artefact forms it has been argued that they are strategically created in differing substances, as phalli appear in chalk, flint, bone and clay forms. While these forms are often skeuomorphic, they also may constitute meaning in their own right and are not a simple reflection of the meaning of the artefact they resemble. Indeed, this mutability of substances and forms was a key process in the Neolithic with which people challenged and reflected on their world (Thomas 1996). Therefore investigating substance is another method by which interpretations have been drawn which reflect more widely on the Mesolithic-Neolithic transition in Britain.

7.3 Expanding Interpretations

Chalk art and artefacts are a cohesive body of material for study in the Neolithic and these results of their study reflect back on our current understandings of the period. In terms of pottery and flint, there are suggestions of a cultural segregation in the use and deposition of these substances at flint mines. The only evidence of early Neolithic pottery at mining sites was discussed in Chapter 5 as being in the upper fill of the Large Pit at Cissbury (Lane Fox 1876) and between probable house slots at Easton Down (Stone 1933b: 232). The date of mining in both Sussex and Wessex situates these mines as contemporary with the early use of pottery across Neolithic Britain, being found within other contemporary monument types such as causewayed enclosures and long barrows. The almost complete lack of pottery here can only be described as unusual. The later Neolithic site of Grimes Graves produced Grooved Ware pottery in deposits (in some cases highly decorated) hence the absence of Neolithic pottery in mining contexts appears to be chronologically variable. This lack of any early Neolithic pottery in mine deposits at the lower levels is argued as deliberate. The exclusion of pottery suggests a cultural prohibition which was almost completely adhered to and may be a result of the substance being seen as culturally inappropriate. In terms of materiality, pottery and clay must have been seen as a particular substance category which somehow defined their exclusion in deposition in these early flint mine contexts. This may have been a result of either new social practices, conceptions of clay/pottery as a polluting substance or simply not being viewed as relevant for the activities conducted at flint mines. The digging and extraction of flint and chalk were in some respects appropriate for the burial and manipulation of the dead, as were processed animal bone and other practices; yet pottery was not.

In Chapter 4 it was proposed that the use of polissoirs at West Kennet long barrow suggested that the grinding of axes during the early Neolithic may have been related to mortuary rituals. Both Thickthorn and Woodford long barrows were constructed over flint extraction pits (Edmonds 1995: 32). During the early Neolithic, very few ground or polished axes are found in mine contexts. Taking these factors into account, flint as a substance and axes in particular may have been associated with mortuary activity from the late Mesolithic and into the Neolithic. The adoption of these early monumental forms may reflect the processed involved in mortuary practice being incorporated into the new ways of engaging with the world. Excluding pottery as a new material encountered at the start of the Neolithic may be concerned with not polluting existing practices during this assimilation and transition. Flint mines, chalk axes and pottery appear to be within a relational scheme of meaning which is referenced in structured deposition.

While flint working is a reductive technology, pottery is additive. For flint, the stone is extracted and revealed while pottery requires the addition of clay, temper and working to create its form. It then requires time to dry, and heat to fire. The processes are long in creating pottery, taking days rather than hours and would be most productive completed in batches of production by a few people. In contrast, unless an axe is ground, flint working would take a much smaller amount of time and is an individual process. Perhaps the reductive technology of flint was seen as a metaphor for the revealing of bone during excarnation in the Neolithic whereas the creation of pottery vessels was seen as simply not complementary for this type of social and physical transformation. The application of fire in pottery production may also have separated flint and clay conceptually: flint fractures when heated where clay becomes stronger. The only other site where pottery exclusion has been noted is Stonehenge (Pollard 1995: 154). This later site is also where a chipped chalk axe was excavated which was suggested may be socially referencing these already ancient mortuary rituals. While chronologically later, Stonehenge is a unique monument in a location which has a history of activity extending back to the Mesolithic and hence continuations of past practices or references to them at this place are more arguable than at other sites of the period.

By the later Neolithic this situation had altered dramatically, with a greater integration of deposited substances as seen at Grimes Graves. Grooved Ware was being placed within mine deposits in addition to ground axes, and ground axe marks, but the pottery deposited is unusually highly decorated and in the case of the two bowls from Mercer's 1971 (1981a: 41-2) excavations, internally decorated. The relationship between pottery and flint had altered immeasurably in the thousand years between the earliest activity at Sussex and Wessex mines and this later Neolithic mining at Grimes Graves. Different monumental forms are contemporary and there are different prevalent social practices.

During the later Neolithic flint and pottery products do not appear to continue to be separated at particular sites, although some suggestions of this are noted from the postholes of the Southern Circle at Durrington Walls (Richards and Thomas 1984). Hence the tension between these two substances may have ceased to be related through site type, but instead be manifested through individual depositional events. Thus, the locales themselves are integrated where the substances are not. However at other sites even at an earlier period there was an integration of pottery in mortuary events with bone tempering noted at Hazleton North (Bradley 2001: 91) and later at Balneaves, Angus (Russell-White *et al*. 1992: 299). This indicates a literal incorporation of human or animal remains and clay, once living entities becoming part of the vessels internal fabric, in effect moulding the clay and human remains together. These practices are therefore subject to regional and chronological variability, continuing to express the temporal nature and bricolage of the British Neolithic.

7.4 Negotiating Presence

This study on materiality at flint mines, examining the deposition and placement of artefacts and substances, has offered new interpretations of these monuments. Mining sites emerge through this as both familiar parts of the Neolithic cultural repertoire of archaeological sites, and the slightly uncomfortable jarring recognition of their difference. Mining and materiality have been shown to have had many facets. Investigating materiality has involved the foregrounding of chalk as an architectural form in addition to an artefactual one. Many substances have been argued as relating to each other within common schemes of reference and I have argued that rather than this simply being a later Neolithic practice, this originates from the late Mesolithic and early Neolithic.

Culturally there does not appear to have been a separate category for natural artefacts and humanly made artefacts in deposition. In the Neolithic, artefacts were simply not categorised in terms of effort expended or the cost of material. Furthermore, the origin of artefacts from the earth may have not been seen as conceptually different to those that were made by humans. At this period all artefacts are, at their heart, made from materials that constitute human beings, other animals, or the earth. Neolithic persons may not have seen that modification was a different social category, but rather the products of animals, or the earth, becoming more useful through modification. This study of creating artefacts implies that during the Neolithic at flint mines there was simply one understanding of inter-relatedness between what we term geology, culture, persons, nature and environment, which did not fully embrace the new practices of pottery production.

At the beginning of this study I proposed that by excluding flint mines from wider discussions of the Mesolithic-Neolithic transition we cannot assess their contribution to this process. Through this study, flint mines are argued as being part of the usual early Neolithic monument types, reflecting complex architecture and symbolic deposition. Their deposits are evidenced as being comparable in nature to contemporary sites with two differences: the frequent presence of chalk art and the lack of pottery. The chalk art perhaps indicates a particular approach to mining which had parallels in ditch digging more widely. Chalk art and artefacts may have been a way of manipulating and acknowledging the land which was being transformed through the Mesolithic-Neolithic transition.

The lack of pottery at mines, the earliest dated Neolithic monuments, and at Stonehenge suggests that the fine bowls of the early Neolithic had some social prohibitions. The acceptance of this form of manipulation of substance, the creation of new ways of holding food or drink and the social processes involved was negotiated within some monuments, but not flint mines. This prohibition was also present at Stonehenge, although at a later date. The communal nature and many processes involved in altering clay to pottery may have taken much longer to be incorporated in the Neolithic than traditional accounts allow. Flint mines suggest that while the Mesolithic practices of flint extraction were altered at the beginning of the Neolithic, at the same time they were protected and enclosed through the bounded sites and architecture of mines. The importance of flint, and its suggested inclusion in mortuary activity, indicates that it is perhaps the transformative nature of flint which needed to be protected from the transformative nature of clay.

Therefore, flint mines allow us to see the Mesolithic-Neolithic transition with subtlety. At this early period, the 'lunar' landscapes of the mines may represent a haven, safe from the changes of the Neolithic where perhaps in terms of temporality, time could be suspended while the practices of the Mesolithic could be reworked and reconstituted alongside the adoption of new experiences.

Bibliography

Albarella, U. and Serjeantson, D. 2002. A passion for pork: meat consumption at the British late Neolithic site of Durrington Walls. In Miracle, P. and Milner, N. (eds) *Consuming Passions and Patterns of Consumption*: 33-49. Oxford: McDonald Institute.

Alexander, J., Ozanne, P. C. and Ozanne, A. 1960. A report on the investigation of a round barrow at Arreton Down, Isle of Wight. *Proceedings of the Prehistoric Society* 26: 263-302.

Ambers, J. 1996. Radiocarbon analyses from the Grimes Graves mines. In Longworth, I. and Varndell, G. (eds) *Excavations at Grimes Graves, Norfolk 1972-76: Mining in the Deeper Mines*: 100-8. London: British Museum Press.

Ammann, F. J. 2005. With a hint of Paris in the mouth: fetishized toothbrushes or the sensuous experience of modernity in late 19th century Bogotá. In Meskell, L. (eds) *Archaeologies of Materiality* : 71-95. Oxford: Blackwell.

Andersen, S. 1989. Norsminde. A *køkkenmødding* with late Mesolithic and early Neolithic occupation. *Journal of Danish Archaeology* 8: 13-40.

Andersen, S. 1991. Bjørnsholm. A stratified *køkkenmødding* on the central Limfjord, north Jutland. *Journal of Danish Archaeology* 10: 59-96.

Armstrong, A. L. 1921. Flint-crust engravings, and associated implements from Grimes Graves, Norfolk. *Proceedings of the Prehistoric Society of East Anglia* 3: 434-43.

Armstrong, A. L. 1922. Further discoveries of engraved flint-crust and associated implements at Grimes Graves. *Proceedings of the Prehistoric Society of East Anglia* 3: 548-58.

Armstrong, A. L. 1924a. Discovery of a new phase of early flint mining at Grimes Graves, Norfolk. Preliminary report. *Proceedings of the Prehistoric Society of East Anglia* 4: 182-93.

Armstrong, A. L. 1924b. Further excavations upon the working floor (Floor 85), Grimes Graves. *Proceedings of the Prehistoric Society of East Anglia* 4: 194-202.

Armstrong, A. L. 1926. The Grimes Graves problem in the light of recent researches. *Proceedings of the Prehistoric Society of East Anglia* 5: 91-136.

Armstrong, A. L. 1932. The Percy Sladen Trust excavations, Grimes Graves, Norfolk. Interim report. *Proceedings of the Prehistoric Society of East Anglia* 7: 57-61.

Armstrong, A. L. 1934. Grimes Graves, Norfolk: report on the excavation of Pit 12. *Proceedings of the Prehistoric Society of East Anglia* 7: 382-94.

Barber, M. 2005. Mining, burial and chronology: the West Sussex flint mines in the late Neolithic and early Bronze Age. In Topping, P. and Lynott, M. (eds) *The Cultural Landscape of Prehistoric Mines*: 94-109. Oxford: Oxbow.

Barber, M., Field, D. and Topping, P. 1999. *The Neolithic Flint Mines of England*. Swindon: English Heritage.

Barnatt, J. and Collis, J. 1996. *Barrows in the Peak District*. Sheffield: J. R. Collis.

Bayliss, A., Whittle, A. W. R, and Wysocki, M. 2007. Talking about my generation: the date of the West Kennet long barrow. *Cambridge Archaeological Journal* 17, Supplement S1: 85-101.

Beckensall, S. 1999. *British Prehistoric Rock Art*. Stroud: Tempus.

Bedwin, O. and Aldsworth, F. G. 1981. Excavations at The Trundle, 1980. *Sussex Archaeological Collections* 119: 208-14.

Bender, B. 1998. *Stonehenge: Making Space*. Oxford: Berg.

Berridge, P. 1994. Cornish axe factories: fact or fiction. In Ashton, N. and David, A. (eds) *Stories in Stone*: 45-56. London: Lithic Studies Society.

Bevan, L. 2001. Gender bias or biased agenda? Identifying phallic imagery, sexual scenes and initiation in rock art. In Bevan. L. (ed.) *Indecent Exposure: Sexuality, Society and the Archaeological Record*: 64-88. Glasgow: The Cruithne Press.

Bibby, G. 1959. *The Testimony of the Spade*. London: Readers Union.

Binford, L. R. 1962. Archaeology as anthropology. *American Antiquity* 28: 217-25.

Bleed, P. 1986. The optimal design of hunting weapons: maintainability or reliability. *American Antiquity* 51: 737-47.

Booth, A. St J., and Stone J. F. S. 1952. A trial flint mine at Durrington, Wiltshire. *Wiltshire Archaeological and Natural History Magazine* 54: 381-8.

Bradley, R. J. 1975. Maumbury Rings, Dorchester: the excavations of 1903-13. *Archaeologia* 105: 1-97.

Bradley, R. J. 1984. *The Social Foundations of Prehistoric Britain*. London: Longmans.

Bradley, R. J. 1997. *Rock Art and the Prehistory of Atlantic Europe: Signing the Land*. London: Routledge.

Bradley, R. J. 2000. *An Archaeology of Natural Places*. London: Routledge.

Bradley, R. J. and Chapman, R. C. 1984. Passage graves in the European Neolithic: a theory of convergent evolution. In Burrenhult, G. (ed.) *The Archaeology of Carrowmore*: 348-56. Stockholm: Institute of Archaeology.

Bradley, R. J. and Edmonds, M. R. 1993. *Interpreting the Axe Trade*. Cambridge: Cambridge University Press.

Brindley, A. 1999a. Sequence and dating in the Grooved Ware tradition. In Cleal, R. and MacSween, A. (eds) *Grooved Ware in Britain and Ireland*: 133-44. Oxford: Oxbow.

Brindley, A. 1999b. Irish Grooved Ware. In Cleal, R. and MacSween, A. (eds) *Grooved Ware in Britain and Ireland*: 23-35. Oxford: Oxbow.

Bronk Ramsey, C. 2009. Bayesian analysis of radiocarbon dates. *Radiocarbon* 51:1: 337-60.

Brück, J. 1999. Ritual and rationality: some problems of interpretation in European archaeology. *European Journal of Archaeology*, 2: 3: 313-44.

Care, V. 1979. The production and distribution of Mesolithic axes in southern England. *Proceedings of the Prehistoric Society* 45: 93-102.

Chapman, J. 2000. *Fragmentation in Archaeology: People Places and Broken Objects*. London: Routledge.

Childe, V. G. 1940. *Prehistoric Communities of the British Isles*. London: Chambers.

Clark, J. G. D. 1954. *Excavations at Star Carr*. Cambridge: Cambridge University Press.

Clark, J. G. D. and Piggott, S. 1933. The age of the British flint mines. *Antiquity* 7: 166-83.

Clarke, W. G. 1915. *Report of the Excavations at Grimes Graves, Weeting, Norfolk, March-May 1914*. London: Prehistoric Society of East Anglia.

Clutton-Brock, J. 1984. *Excavations at Grimes Graves: Norfolk, 1972-1976. a Biometric Analysis. Neolithic Antler Picks from Grimes Graves Norfolk and Durrington Walls, Wiltshire*. London: British Museum Press.

Coles, J. 1968. A God-Dolly from Somerset, England. *Antiquity* 42: 275-79.

Cooney, G. 2005. Stereo porphyry: quarrying and deposition on Lambay Island, Ireland. In Topping, P. and Lynott, M. (eds) *The Cultural Landscape of Prehistoric Mines*: 14-29. Oxford: Oxbow.

Craddock, P. T., Cowell, M. R., Leese, M. N. and Hughes, M. J. 1983. The trace element composition of polished flint axes as an indicator of source. *Archaeometry* 25: 135-63.

Cummings, V. and Whittle, A. W. R. 2004. *Places of Special Virtue: Megaliths in the Neolithic Landscapes of Wales*. Oxford: Oxbow.

Cunnington, M. 1929. *Woodhenge*. Devizes: Simpson.

Curwen, E. C. 1929. Excavations at The Trundle, Goodwood, 1928. *Sussex Archaeological Collections* 70: 32-85.

Curwen, E. C. 1931. Excavations at The Trundle, second season, 1930. *Sussex Archaeological Collections* 72: 100-50.

Curwen, E. C. 1934. Excavations at Whitehawk Camp, Brighton, 1932-33. *Antiquaries Journal* 56: 11-23.

Curwen, E. C. 1936. Excavations at Whitehawk Camp, Brighton, third season 1935. *Sussex Archaeological Collections* 77: 60-92.

Curwen, E. and Curwen, E. C. 1926. Harrow Hill flint-mine excavation 1924-5. *Sussex Archaeological Collections* 67: 103-38.

Darwin, C. 1859. *On the Origin of Species by Means of Natural Selection, or the Preservation of Favoured Races in the Struggle for Life*. London: John Murray.

DeMarrias E., Gosden, C. and Renfrew, C. 2004. *Rethinking Materiality: the Engagement of Mind with the Material World*. Oxford: McDonald Institute.

Drewett, P. L. 1978. Neolithic Sussex. In Drewett, P. L. (ed.) *The Archaeology of Sussex to AD 1500*: 23-9. London: Council British Archaeology.

Drewett, P. L. 1986. The excavation of a Neolithic oval barrow at North Marden, West Sussex, 1982. *Proceedings of the Prehistoric Society* 41: 201-41.

Edmonds, M. R. 1995. *Stone Tools and Society*. London: Batsford.

Edmonds, M. R. 1999. *Ancestral Geographies of the Neolithic*. London: Routledge.

Eliade, M. 1964 [1989]. *Shamanism: Archaic Techniques of Ecstasy*. London: Penguin.

Entwistle, R. and Grant, A. 1989. The evidence for cereal cultivation and animal husbandry in the southern British Neolithic and Bronze Age. In Miles, A., Williams, D. and Gardner N. (eds) *The Beginnings of Agriculture*: 203-15. Oxford: British Archaeological Reports S496.

Fowler, C. J. 2004. *The Archaeology of Personhood*. London: Routledge.

Gardiner, J. P. 1990. Flint procurement and Neolithic axe production on the South Downs: a re-assessment. *Oxford Journal of Archaeology* 9:2: 119-40.

Garrow, D. 2006. *Pits, Settlement and Deposition during the Neolithic and Early Bronze Age in East Anglia*. Oxford: John & Erica Hedges (British Archaeological Reports British Series 414).

Gell, A., 1996. Vogel's net: traps as art works and artworks as traps. *Journal of Material Culture* 1: 15-38.

Giørstad, H., Nakrem, H. A. and Tørhaug, V. 2004. Nature in society: reflections over a Mesolithic sculpture of a fossilised shell. *Norwegian Archaeological Review* 37: 95-110.

Goodman, C. H., Frost, M., Curwen, E. and Curwen, E. C., 1924. Blackpatch flint mine excavations, 1922: report prepared on behalf of the Worthing Archaeological Society. *Sussex Archaeological Collections* 65: 69-111.

Gordon-Williams, J. P. 1926. The Nab Head chipping floor. *Archaeologia Cambrensis* 81: 86-110.

Gosden, C. 1994. *Social Being and Time*. Oxford: Blackwell.

Gosden, C. 1999. *Archaeology and Anthropology: a Changing Relationship*. London: Routledge.

Gosden, C. 2005. Is science a foreign country? *Archaeometry* 47: 82-185

Green, M. 2000. *A Landscape Revealed: 10,000 Years on a Chalkland Farm*. Stroud: Tempus.

Greenwell, W. 1870. On the opening of Grimes Graves in Norfolk. *Journal of the Ethnological Society of London*, New Series 2: 419-39.

Grigson, C. 1966. The animal remains from Fussell's Lodge long barrow. *Archaeologia* 100: 63–73.

Grimes, W. F. 1979. The history of implement petrology in Britain. In Clough, T. H. Mc K. and Cummins, W. A. (eds) *Stone Axe Studies*: 5-12. London: Council for British Archaeology.

Grinsell, L. 1953. Early funerary superstitions in Britain. *Folklore* 64: 271-81.

Harcourt, R. A. 1971. The animal bones. In Wainwright, G. J. and Longworth, I. (eds) *Durrington Walls: Excavations 1966-68*: 338-50. London: Society of Antiquaries.

Harcourt, R. A. 1979. The animal bones. In Wainwright, G. J. (ed.) *Mount Pleasant, Dorset: Excavations 1970-71*: 214-23. London: Society of Antiquaries.

Harding, P. 1987. An experiment to produce a ground flint axe. In Sieveking, G. De G. and Newcomer M. H. (eds) *The Human Uses of Chert and Flint: Proceedings of the Fourth International Flint Symposium, held at Brighton Polytechnic 10-15 April 1983*: 37-42. Cambridge: Cambridge University Press.

Harding, P. 1988. The chalk plaque pit, Amesbury. *Proceedings of the Prehistoric Society* 54: 320-6

Harrison, J. P. 1877a. On marks found upon chalk at Cissbury. *Journal of the Anthropological Institute of Great Britain and Ireland* 6: 263-71.

Harrison, J. P. 1877b. Report on some further discoveries at Cissbury. *Journal of the Anthropological Institute of Great Britain and Ireland* 6: 430-42.

Harrison, J. P. 1878. Additional discoveries at Cissbury. *Journal of the Anthropological Institute of Great Britain and Ireland* 7: 412-33.

Hawkes, C. E. C. 1954. Archaeological theory and method: some suggestions from the Old World. *American Anthropologist* 56: 155-68.

Hawkes, J. 1951. *A Land*. London: Cresset.

Hayden, B. 1989. From chopper to celt: the evolution of resharpening techniques. In Torrence, R. (ed.). *Time Energy and Stone Tools*: 7-16. Cambridge: Cambridge University Press.

Healy, F. 1997. Site 3: Flagstones. In Smith, R. C., Healy, F., Allen, M. J., Morris, E. L., Barnes, I., and Woodward, P. J. (eds) *Excavations along the Route of the Dorchester By-pass, Dorset*: 27-48. Wessex Archaeological Reports 11.

Healy, F. 1998. The surface of the Breckland. In Ashton, N., Healy F. and Pettitt P. (eds) *Stone Age Archaeology: Essay in Honour of John Wymer*: 227-37. Oxford: Oxbow.

Healy, F. 2004. Hambledon Hill and its implications. In Pollard, J. and Cleal R. (eds) *Monuments and Material Culture. Papers in Honour of an Avebury Archaeologist: Isobel Smith*: 15-38. Salisbury: Hobnob.

Hill, J. D. 1995. *Ritual and Rubbish in the Iron Age of Wessex*. Oxford: British Archaeological Reports, British Series 242.

Hodder, I. 1999. *The Archaeological Process: An Introduction*. Oxford: Blackwell.

Holgate, R. 1991. *Prehistoric Flint Mines*. Princes Risborough: Shire Publications.

Holgate, R. 1995a. Neolithic flint mining in Britain. *Archaeologia Polona* 33: 133-61.

Holgate, R. 1995b. GB4, Harrow Hill near Findon, West Sussex. *Archaeologia Polona* 33: 347-50.

Holgate, R. 1995c. GB6 Long Down, near Chichester, West Sussex. *Archaeologia Polona* 33: 350-2.

Holleyman, G. 1937. Harrow Hill Excavations 1936. *Sussex Archaeological Collections* 78: 230-52.

Houlder, C. 1968. The henge monuments at Llandegai. *Antiquity* 42: 216-32.

Hutton, R. 1987. The Neolithic great goddess: a study in modern tradition. *Antiquity* 71: 91-99.

Ingold, T. 2000. *The Perception of the Environment: Essays in Livelihood, Dwelling and Skill*. London: Routledge.

Ingold, T. 2007. Materials against materiality. *Archaeological Dialogues* 14: 1-16.

Insoll, T. 2004. *An Archaeology of Religion*. London: Routledge.

Jessup, R. 1970. *South-east England*. London: Thames and Hudson.

Jones, A. 2002. *Archaeological Theory and Scientific Practice*. Cambridge: Cambridge University Press.

Jones, A. 2004. Archaeometry and material practice: materials-based analysis in theory and practice. *Archaeometry* 46: 327-338.

Kendall, H. G. O. 1920. Grimes Graves: Floors 47 to 59. *Proceedings of the Prehistoric Society of East Anglia* 3: 290-305.

Kennard, A. S. 1943. Report on the mollusca. In Wheeler, M. (ed.) *Maiden Castle, Dorset*: 372-3. London: Society of Antiquaries.

Kinnes, I. 1992. *Non Megalithic Long Barrows and Allied Structures in the British Neolithic*. London: British Museum.

Knappett, C. 2007. Materials *with* materiality? *Archaeological Dialogues* 14: 20-3.

Kopytoff, I. 1986. The cultural biography of things: commoditization as process. In Appadurai, A. (ed.) *The Social Life of Things: Commodities in Cultural Perspective*: 64-94. Cambridge: Cambridge University Press.

Lane Fox, A. H. 1876. Excavations in Cissbury Camp, Sussex; being a report of the Exploration Committee of the Anthropological Institute for the year 1875. *Journal of the Anthropological Institute of Great Britain and Ireland* 5: 357-90.

Layton, R. 1998. *An Introduction to Theory in Anthropology*. Cambridge: Cambridge University Press.

Legge, A. J. 1992. *Excavations at Grimes Graves Norfolk 1972-76: Animals, Environment and the Bronze Age Economy*. London: British Museum Press.

Lewis, H., French, C. and Green, M. 2000. A decorated megalith from Knowlton Henges, Dorset, England. *PAST* 35: 1.

Longworth, I. and Kinnes, I. A. 1985. *Catalogue of the Excavated Prehistoric and Romano-British Material in the Greenwell Collection*. London: British Museum Press.

Longworth, I., Ellison, A. and Rigby, V. 1988. *Excavations at Grimes Graves, Norfolk 1972-76: The Neolithic, Bronze Age and Later Pottery*. London: British Museum Press.

Longworth, I., Herne, A., Varndell, G. and Needham S. 1991. *Excavations at Grimes Graves, Norfolk 1972-76: Bronze Age Flint, Chalk and Metal Working*. London: British Museum Press.

Longworth, I. and Varndell, G. 1996. *Excavations at Grimes Graves, Norfolk 1972-76: Mining in the Deeper Mines*. London: British Museum Press.

Lubbock, J. 1865. *Pre-Historic Times*. London: Williams and Norgate.

McNabb, J., Felder, P. J., Kinnes, I. and Sieveking, G. De G. 1996. An archive report on recent excavations at Harrow Hill, Sussex. *Sussex Archaeological Collections* 135: 21-37.

Mellars, P. 1987. *Excavations on Oronsay. Prehistoric Human Ecology on a Small Island*. Edinburgh: Edinburgh University Press.

Mercer, R. J. 1980. *Hambledon Hill: A Neolithic Landscape*. Edinburgh: Edinburgh University Press.

Mercer, R. J. 1981a. *Grimes Graves Norfolk: Excavations 1971-2, Volume 1*. Department of the Environment Archaeological Report 11. London: HMSO.

Mercer, R. J. 1981b. *Grimes Graves Norfolk: Excavations 1971-2, Volume 2*. Department of the Environment Archaeological Report 11. London: HMSO.

Mercer, R. J. 1987. A flint quarry in the Hambledon Hill Neolithic enclosure complex. In Sieveking, G. De G. and Newcomer, M. H. (eds) *The Human Uses of Chert and Flint: Proceedings of the Fourth International Flint Symposium, held at Brighton Polytechnic 10-15 April 1983*: 159-64. Cambridge: Cambridge University Press.

Meskell, L. 2005. Introduction: object orientations. In Meskell, L. (ed.) *Archaeologies of Materiality*: 1-17. Oxford: Blackwell.

Momber, G. 2000. Drowned and deserted: a submerged prehistoric landscape in the Solent. *International Journal of Nautical Archaeology* 29:1: 86-99.

Needham, S. 2005. Rationalizing materiality. *Archaeometry* 47: 192-5.

O'Malley, M. 1978. Broom Hill, Braishfield: Mesolithic dwelling. *Current Archaeology* 60: 117-20.

O'Sullivan, M. 1986. Approaches to passage tomb art. *Journal of the Royal Society of Antiquaries of Ireland* 116: 68-83.

Parker Pearson, M. and Ramilisonina. 1998. Stonehenge for the ancestors: the stones pass on the message. *Antiquity* 72: 308-26.

Parker Pearson M., Richards, C., Allen, M. and Welham, K. 2006. A new avenue at Durrington Walls. *PAST* 52: 1.

Parker Pearson, M., Cleal, R,. Marshall, P., Needham, S., Pollard, J., Richards, C., Ruggles, C., Sheridan, A., Thomas, J., Tilley, C., Welham, K., Chamberlain, A., Chenery, C., Evans, J., Knüsel, C., Linford, N., Martin, L., Montgomery, J., Payne, A. and Richards, M. 2007. The age of Stonehenge. *Antiquity* 81: 617-39.

Peake, A. E. 1915. *Report on the Excavations at Grimes Graves, Weeting, Norfolk, March-May 1914*. London: Prehistoric Society of East Anglia.

Peake, A. E. 1917. Further excavations at Grimes Graves. *Proceedings of the Prehistoric Society of East Anglia* 2: 409-36.

Peake, A. E. 1919. Excavations at Grimes Graves during 1917. *Proceedings of the Prehistoric Society of East Anglia* 3: 33-93.

Piggott, S. 1954. *Neolithic Cultures of the British Isles*. Cambridge: Cambridge University Press.

Piggott, S. 1962. *The West Kennet Long Barrow*. London: HMSO.

Pitts, M. 1996. The stone axe in Neolithic Britain. *Proceedings of the Prehistoric Society* 62: 311-71.

Pollard, J. 1995. Inscribing space: formal deposition at the later Neolithic monument of Woodhenge, Wiltshire. *Proceedings of the Prehistoric Society* 61: 137-56.

Pollard, J. 2001. The aesthetics of depositional practice. *World Archaeology* 33.2: 315-33.

Pollard, J. 2004. The art of decay and the transformation of substance. In Renfrew, C., Gosden, C. and DeMarrais, E. (eds) *Substance, Memory, Display: Archaeology and Art*: 47-62. Cambridge: McDonald Institute.

Pollard, J. 2005. Memory, monuments and middens in the Neolithic landscape. In Brown, G., Field, D. and McOmish, D. (eds), *The Avebury Landscape: Aspects of the Field Archaeology of the Marlborough* Downs: 103-14. Oxford: Oxbow.

Pryor, F. 1998. *Etton: Excavations at a Neolithic Causewayed Enclosure near Maxey, Cambridgeshire, 1982-7*. London: English Heritage.

Pull, J. 1932. *The Flint Miners of Blackpatch*. London: Williams and Norgate.

Pye, E. 1968. *The Flint Mines at Blackpatch, Church Hill and Cissbury, Sussex. A Report on the late JH Pull's Excavations 1922-55*. Unpublished MA dissertation, University of Edinburgh.

Ray, K. and Thomas, J. S. 2003. In the kinship of cows: the social centrality of cattle in the earlier Neolithic of southern Britain. In Parker Pearson, M. (eds) *Food, Culture and Identity in the Neolithic and Early Bronze Age*: 37-44. British Archaeological Reports International Series 117. Oxford: Archaeopress.

Renfrew, C. 1976. Megaliths, territories and populations. In de Laet, S. (ed.) *Acculturation and Continuity in Atlantic Europe*: 98-220. Bruges: de Tempel.

Renfrew, C. 2001. Symbol before concept: material engagement and the early development of society. In Hodder, I. (ed.) *Archaeological Theory Today*: 98-121. Cambridge: Polity Press.

Renfrew, C. 2004. Towards a theory of material engagement. In DeMarrias, E., Gosden, C. and Renfrew, C. (eds), *Rethinking Materiality: the Engagement of Mind with the Material World*: 23-32. Oxford: McDonald Institute.

Richards, C. C. and Thomas, J. 1984. Ritual activity and structured deposition in later Neolithic Wessex. In Bradley R. and Gardiner, J. (eds) *Neolithic Studies*: 189-218. Oxford: British Archaeological Reports 133.

Richardson, D. 1920. A new celt making floor at Grimes Graves. *Proceedings of the Prehistoric Society of East Anglia* 3: 243-58.

Ride, D. 1998. Excavation of a linear earthwork and flint mines at Martin's Clump, Over Wallop, Hampshire, 1984. *Proceedings of the Hampshire Field Club Archaeological Society* 53:1-23.

Ride, D. 2006. *In Defence of Landscape: An Archaeology of Porton Down*. Stroud: Tempus.

Ride, D. and James, D. 1989. An account of the prehistoric flint mine at Martin's Clump, Over Wallop, Hampshire, 1954-5. *Proceedings of the Hampshire Field Club Archaeological Society* 45: 213-15.

Rolleston, G. 1877. Note on the animal remains found at Cissbury. *Journal of the Anthropological Institute* 7: 20-36.

Rolleston, G. 1879. Notes on a skeleton found at Cissbury, April 1878. *Journal of the Anthropological Institute* 8: 377-89.

Root, D. 1983. Information exchange and the spatial configuration of egalitarian societies. In Moore, J. and Keene, A. (eds) *Archaeological Hammers and Theories*: 193-219. New York: Academic Press.

Rudebeck, E. 1987. Flint mining in Sweden during the Neolithic period; new evidence from the Kvarnby-S. Sallerup area. In Sieveking, G. De G. and Newcomer, M. H. (eds) *The Human Uses of Chert and Flint: Proceedings of the Fourth International Flint Symposium, held at Brighton Polytechnic 10-15 April 1983*: 151-7. Cambridge: Cambridge University Press.

Russell, M. 2000. *Flint Mines in Neolithic Britain*. Stroud: Tempus.

Russell, M. 2001. *Rough Quarries, Rock and Hills: John Pull and the Neolithic Flint Mines of Sussex*. Oxford: Oxbow.

Russell. M. 2002. *Prehistoric Sussex*. Stroud: Tempus.

Russell-White, C. J., Lowe C. E. and McCullagh R. P. J. 1992. Excavations at three early Bronze Age burial monuments in Scotland. *Proceedings of the Prehistoric Society* 58: 285-324.

Salisbury, E. F. 1961. Prehistoric flint mines on Long Down. *Sussex Archaeological Collections* 99: 66-73.

Saville, A. 1981. The Flint Assemblage. In Mercer, R. (ed.) *Grimes Graves, Norfolk, Excavations 1971-2: Volume 2: The Flint Assemblage*: 1- 182. London: Department of the Environment Archaeological Reports 11.

Saville, A. 2005. Prehistoric quarrying of a secondary flint source. In Topping, P. and Lynott, M. (eds) *The Cultural Landscape of Prehistoric Mines*: 1-13. Oxford: Oxbow.

Schiffer, M. 1999. *The Material Life of Human Beings: Artifacts, Behaviour and Communication*. London: Routledge.

Schulting, R.J. and Richards, M. 2000. The use of stable isotopes in studies of subsistence and seasonality in the British Mesolithic. In Young, R. (ed.) *Mesolithic Lifeways: Current Research from Britain and Ireland*. Leicester Archaeological Monograph 7: 55-65. Leicester: University of Leicester.

Shee Twoig, E. 1981. *The Megalithic Art of Western Europe*. Oxford: Clarendon Press.

Shepherd, R. 1980. *Prehistoric Mining and Allied Industries*. London: Academic Press.

Sieveking, G. De G. 1979. Grimes Graves and prehistoric European flint mining. In Crawford, H. (ed.) *Subterranean Britain: Aspects of Underground Archaeology*: 1-43. London: Baker.

Sieveking, G. De G., Longworth, I. H., Hughes, M. S., Clark, A. J. and Millett, M. 1973. A new survey of Grimes Graves. *Proceedings of the Prehistoric Society* 39: 182-218.

Simpson, J. 1867. *Archaic Sculpturing of Cups Circles etc upon Stones and Rocks in Scotland, England etc and other Countries*. Edinburgh: Edmonston and Douglas.

Smith, I. 1965a. *Windmill Hill and Avebury*. Oxford: Clarendon Press.

Smith, I. 1965b. Excavation of a bell barrow, Avebury G.55. *Wiltshire Archaeological Magazine* 60: 24-46.

Smith, R. A. 1912. On the date of Grimes Graves and Cissbury flint mines. *Archaeologia* 63: 109-58.

Smolla, G. 1987. Prehistoric flint mining: the history of research - review. In Sieveking, G. De G. and Newcomer, M. H. (eds) *The Human Uses of Chert and Flint: Proceedings of the Fourth International Flint Symposium, held at Brighton Polytechnic 10-15 April 1983*: 127-31. Cambridge: Cambridge University Press.

Stone, J. F. S. 1932a. Easton Down, South Wiltshire, flint mine excavation 1930. *Wiltshire Archaeological and Natural History Magazine* 45: 350-65.

Stone, J. F. S. 1932b. A settlement site of the Beaker period on Easton Down, Winterslow, South Wiltshire. *Wiltshire Archaeological and Natural History Magazine* 45: 366-72.

Stone, J. F. S. 1933a. A middle Bronze Age urnfield on Easton Down, Winterslow. *Wiltshire Archaeological and Natural History Magazine* 46: 218-24.

Stone, J. F. S. 1933b. Excavations at Easton Down, Winterslow, 1931-2. *Wiltshire Archaeological and Natural History Magazine* 46: 225-42.

Stone, J. F. S. 1935. Excavations at Easton Down, Winterslow, 1933-4. *Wiltshire Archaeological and Natural History Magazine* 47: 68-80.

Stone, J. F. S., Piggott, S. and Booth, A. St J. 1954. Durrington Walls, Wiltshire: recent excavations at a ceremonial site of the early second millennium BC. *Antiquaries Journal* 34: 155-77.

Teather, A. M. 2007. Neolithic phallacies: a discussion of some southern British artefacts. In Larsson, M. and Parker Pearson, M. (eds) *From Stonehenge to the Baltic. Living with Cultural Diversity in the Third Millennium BC*: 205-11. BAR International Series 1692. Oxford: Archaeopress.

Thomas, J. S. 1984. A tale of two polities. In Bradley, R. J. and Gardiner, J. C. (eds) *Neolithic Studies*: 161-76. Oxford: British Archaeological Reports 133.

Thomas, J. S. 1990. Monuments from the inside: the case of the Irish Megalithic tombs. *World Archaeology* 22: 168-78.

Thomas, J. S. 1996. *Time, Culture and Identity: An Interpretive Archaeology.* London: Routledge.

Thomas, J. S. 1999a. *Understanding the Neolithic.* London: Routledge.

Thomas, J. S. 1999b. An economy of substances in earlier Neolithic Britain. In Robb, J. (ed.) *Material Symbols: Culture and Economy in Prehistory*: 70-89. Carbondale: Southern Illinois University Press.

Thomas, J. S. 2006. Phenomenology and Material Culture. In Tilley, C., Keene, W., Kuechler-Fogden, S., Rowlands, M. and Spyer, P. (eds) *Handbook of Material Culture*: 43-59. London: Sage.

Thomas, N. 1952. A Neolithic chalk cup from Wilsford in the Devizes Museum: and notes on others. *Wiltshire Archaeological and Natural History Magazine* 57: 452-62.

Thorpe, I. J. 1984. Ritual, power and ideology: a reconsideration of earlier Neolithic rituals in Wessex. In Bradley, R. J. and Gardiner, J. C. (eds) *Neolithic Studies*: 41-60. Oxford: British Archaeological Reports 133.

Thorpe, I. J. and Richards, C. C. 1984. The decline of ritual authority and the introduction of Beakers into Britain. In Bradley, R. J. and Gardiner, J. C. (eds) *Neolithic Studies*: 67-84. Oxford: British Archaeological Reports 133.

Tilley, C. 1991. *Material Culture and Text: the Art of Ambiguity.* London: Routledge.

Tilley, C. 1994. *A Phenomenology of Landscape.* Oxford: Berg.

Tilley, C. 1996. *An Ethnography of the Neolithic.* Cambridge: Cambridge University Press.

Tilley, C. 1999. *Metaphor and Material Culture.* Oxford: Blackwell.

Tilley, C. 2004. *The Materiality of Stone.* Oxford: Berg.

Tilley, C. 2007a. Materiality in materials. *Archaeological Dialogues* 14: 16-20.

Tilley, C. 2007b. The Neolithic sensory revolution: monumentality and the experience of landscape. In Whittle A. W. R. and Cummings V. (eds) *Going Over: The Mesolithic-Neolithic Transition in North-West Europe*: 329-46. Oxford: Oxford University Press for The British Academy.

Topping, P. 2005. Shaft 27 revisited: an ethnography. In Topping, P. and Lynott, M. (eds) *The Cultural Landscape of Prehistoric Mines*: 63-93. Oxford: Oxbow.

Torrence, R. 1989. Re-tooling: towards a behavioral theory of stone tools. In Torrence, R. (ed.) *Time Energy and Stone Tools* : 57-66. Cambridge: Cambridge University Press.

Trigger, B. G. 1989. *A History of Archaeological Thought.* Cambridge: Cambridge University Press.

Van Gennep, A. 1960. *The Rites of Passage.* London: Routledge and Kegan Paul.

Varndell, G. 1991. The worked chalk. In Longworth, I., Herne, A., Varndell, G. and Needham S. (eds) *Excavations at Grimes Graves, Norfolk 1972-76: Bronze Age Flint, Chalk and Metal Working*: 94-153. London: British Museum Press.

Varndell, G. 1999. An engraved chalk plaque from Hanging Cliff, Kilham. *Oxford Journal of Archaeology* 18: 351-55.

Varndell, G. 2005. Seeing things: A L Armstrong's flint crust engravings from Grimes Graves. In Topping, P. and Lynott, M. (eds) *The Cultural Landscape of Prehistoric Mines*: 51-62. Oxford: Oxbow.

Wade, A. G. 1922. Ancient flint mines at Stoke Down, Sussex. *Proceedings of the Prehistoric Society of East Anglia* 4: 82-91.

Wainwright, G. J. 1979. *Mount Pleasant, Dorset: Excavations 1970-71*. London: Society of Antiquaries of London.

Wainwright, G. J. and Longworth, I. 1971. *Durrington Walls: Excavations 1966-68*. London: Society of Antiquaries of London.

Waller, R. 2006. Neolithic to early Bronze Age resource assessment: The Isle of Wight. Oxford Archaeological Unit online publication.

Weisgerber G. 1987. The technological relationship between flint mining and early copper mining. In Sieveking, G. De G. and Newcomer, M. H. (eds) *The Human Uses of Chert and Flint: Proceedings of the Fourth International Flint Symposium, held at Brighton Polytechnic 10-15 April 1983*: 131-35. Cambridge: Cambridge University Press.

Wheeler, R. E. M. 1943. *Maiden Castle, Dorset*. London: Society of Antiquaries.

Whittle, A. W. R. 1996. *Europe in the Neolithic*. Cambridge: Cambridge University Press.

Whittle, A. W. R. 2003. *The Archaeology of People: Dimensions of Neolithic life*. London: Routledge.

Whittle, A. W. R., Pollard, J. and Grigson, C. 1999. *The Harmony of Symbols: the Windmill Hill Causewayed Enclosure, Wiltshire*. Oxford: Oxbow.

Willett, E. H. 1875. On flint workings at Cissbury, Sussex. *Archaeologia* 65: 337-48.

Woodward, P. J. 1988. Pictures from the Neolithic: discoveries from the Flagstones house excavations, Dorchester, Dorset. *Antiquity* 62: 266-74.

Wylie, A. 1985. The reaction against analogy. In Schiffer, M. (ed.) *Advances in Archaeological Method and Theory* 8: 63-111.

Wyse-Jackson, P. N. and Connolly, M. 2002. Fossils as Neolithic funereal adornments in County Kerry, south-west Ireland. *Geology Today* 18: 139-43.

Index

Antler: category of material culture 29, 33, 37, 38, 83, 90-2, 96, 102; dating 21; deposition of 3, 6, 16, 21, 90, 91, 94-5, 102; use in extraction 12, 85, 91

Artefact: excavated 85, 89; retrieved 85, 91; versus object 26-33, 36-7, 39, 83-5; transformed 85, 90-1, 93, 102

Axes: chalk 71, 77-8, 81, 102; flint 7-8, 10, 18, 21, 29, 33, 81, 102; stone 7, 8, 26, 28, 39

Blackpatch: dating 19, 20-3, 95; deposits 3, 20-3, 51-3, 65, 71-3, 75, 81, 88, 90, 95-6, 102; history of excavation 3, 5, 12

Black Patch 86

Bradley, R. 5, 8, 9, 10, 16, 19, 34, 36, 42-3, 60, 63, 66-7, 74, 80, 90, 98, 103

Categorisation 29-30, 37-8, 63, 65-9, 76, 78, 84, 93, 101

Cattle 5, 84-6, 90, 94-5, 98

Chalk art in situ 6, 38, 41-4, 49, 52, 54, 56-8, 61, 63, 66, 93, 95

Chalk blocks: decorated 24, 42, 44, 51, 54, 58-9, 63-4, 77; marked 6, 41-3, 46, 47, 51, 56-9; perforated 54, 66; unmarked 51, 54, 56

Chalk artefacts: axes 71, 77-8, 81, 102-3; balls 67, 72, 81; beads 69, 72, 75, 78; charms 21, 23, 65, 69, 71-8, 81, 86, 93, 95; cups 1, 65-8, 72-8, 81, 102; cylinders 39, 69, 73; discs/pendants 49, 69, 71-2, 77-8, 80; drums 69, 74-5, 78, 81; plaques 21, 51, 66, 75-6, 80-1; work(ing) surfaces 68-71, 75, 78, 81

Chesil Beach 17

Church Hill: dating 4, 12, 19-21; deposits 6, 21-2, 41, 46, 52-3, 60, 71-7, 80, 86, 88, 90, 93-6; history of excavation 5, 6, 14

Cissbury: Cave Pit 6, 42, 45-9, 53, 59, 61, 71, 75, 90, 95, 98; dating 4-6, 15, 18-20; deposits 10, 21-2, 35, 41, 43-9, 51-4, 58-61, 65, 71-2, 75, 77, 86-8, 90-3, 95-6, 98, 102; history of excavation 5-6, 14, 41, 65

Curation 85, 93, 94

Den of Boddam 4

Dogs 92, 95, 98

Durrington Walls: deposition 34, 66, 78, 80, 84, 88, 91, 95-7, 103; flint mining 16; henge 21, 22, 29, 58; recent excavations 22, 72, 87, 94

Dwelling pits 20, 22-3

Easton Down: dating 4, 18-20, 22-3; deposits 19, 22, 52, 87, 94, 96, 102; history of excavation 5-7, 11, 15

Edmonds, M. 5, 8-10, 19, 42, 97, 103

Etton 29, 75, 80, 81, 89, 96, 97

Excarnation 81, 84, 93, 94, 103

Flagstones 42, 56-7, 59, 60, 66, 77

Folkton Drums 74, 81

Fowler, C. 10, 32, 97

Grimes Graves: dating 7-8, 19-21; deposits 18, 21-3, 38, 46, 52-4, 56-7, 61, 64-9, 71-7, 80-1, 83, 86-7, 90-1, 93-8, 102-3; history of excavation 3-6, 14-5, 41

Harrow Hill: dating 3, 14, 19-20; deposits 6, 21, 38, 46, 49, 53-8, 60-1, 65, 71-3, 75, 77, 75-6; history of excavation 4-7, 11-6, 41

Hambledon Hill 16-7, 59, 84

Hodder, I. 28, 30, 33, 36, 39, 84-5, 97, 101

Horslip 77

Houses 19, 22-3, 89, 94, 102

Human remains 20, 29, 57-8, 61, 63-4, 83-4, 92-4, 98, 103

Isle of Wight 16-8, 72

Itford Hill 77-8

Knap Hill 77

Langdale 5, 8, 10

Lavant Drum 74, 81

Long Down: dating 4, 19; deposits 21-2, 52-3, 71-2, 94; history of excavation 6, 11, 14, 15

Maiden Castle 18, 54, 56-7, 59, 66, 77

Materiality 2, 25, 30-4, 39, 42, 65, 80, 84, 90, 94, 98, 101, 103

Martin's Clump 4, 6, 13-5, 18-20, 52-3, 56

Maumbury Rings 66, 74, 78, 80, 96

Middens 3, 17, 20-3, 56, 72, 84-6, 92, 94-5, 98

Monkton Up Wimborne 42, 54, 56, 57-60, 63, 77

Mount Pleasant 29, 34, 59, 75, 78, 95-6

North Marden 42, 54, 56-7, 59, 60, 66, 77, 101-2

Phenomenology 2, 25, 30-2, 39, 65, 84, 97, 101

Pollard, J. 22, 25, 31, 34-7, 65-6, 83-5, 94, 101, 103

Polissoir 7, 61-4, 75, 81, 103

Structured deposition 25, 30, 34-7, 39, 43, 65-6, 83-4, 91, 101, 103

Stoke Down 4-6, 13-5, 19, 52-3, 71, 73, 88

Stonehenge 66, 71, 78, 81, 103-4

Skulls: human 89, 92, 93, 94, 98; animal 20, 33, 84-6, 91, 93-5

Thomas, J. 1, 4, 20, 24-5, 29-36, 39, 48, 57-66, 74, 81, 83-5, 93, 95, 97-8, 101-3

Tilley, C. 9, 17-8, 25, 31-4, 37, 39, 97

Trundle 15, 18, 35, 48, 57-9, 66, 74, 77, 80, 96-7, 99; chalk ammonite 54-5, 59, 102

Typology 2, 27-8, 30, 32, 38-9, 42, 65-9, 71, 76, 78, 81, 102

Varndell, G. 3, 6-7, 12, 24, 39, 46, 66-73, 75-6, 86-7, 97

West Kennet 61-3, 84, 88, 94, 103

Whitehawk 18, 26, 35, 49, 54, 57-9, 66, 77

Whittle, A. 1, 4, 21, 84, 93, 95, 97

Winterbourne Stoke 96

Wilsford Barrow 78

Windmill Hill 17, 21, 35, 66, 72, 75, 77, 84, 96-7

Woodhenge 34-5, 72, 78, 81, 88

Working floors 7, 20-3, 94-5